Bernard Mulo Farenkia

Speech acts and politeness in French as a pluricentric language

Romanistische Linguistik

herausgegeben von

Klaus Hölker

Wissenschaftlicher Beirat:

Claudia Caffi (Università di Genova)
Colette Cortès (Université Paris 7)
Thomas Kotschi (Freie Universität Berlin)

Band 10

LIT

Bernard Mulo Farenkia

Speech acts and politeness in French as a pluricentric language

Illustrations from Cameroon and Canada

LIT

This book is printed on acid-free paper.

Bibliographic information published by the Deutsche Nationalbibliothek
The Deutsche Nationalbibliothek lists this publication in the Deutsche Nationalbibliografie; detailed bibliographic data are available in the Internet at http://dnb.d-nb.de.

ISBN 978-3-643-90456-0

A catalogue record for this book is available from the British Library

©LIT VERLAG GmbH & Co. KG Wien,　　LIT VERLAG Dr. W. Hopf
Zweigniederlassung Zürich 2014　　　　Berlin 2014
Klosbachstr. 107　　　　　　　　　　　　Fresnostr. 2
CH-8032 Zürich　　　　　　　　　　　　D-48159 Münster
Tel. +41 (0) 44-251 75 05　　　　　　　　Tel. +49 (0) 2 51-62 03 20
Fax +41 (0) 44-251 75 06　　　　　　　　Fax +49 (0) 2 51-23 19 72
E-Mail: zuerich@lit-verlag.ch　　　　　　E-Mail: lit@lit-verlag.de
http://www.lit-verlag.ch　　　　　　　　http://www.lit-verlag.de

Distribution:
In Germany: LIT Verlag Fresnostr. 2, D-48159 Münster
Tel. +49 (0) 2 51-620 32 22, Fax +49 (0) 2 51-922 60 99, E-mail: vertrieb@lit-verlag.de

In Austria: Medienlogistik Pichler-ÖBZ, e-mail: mlo@medien-logistik.at
In the UK: Global Book Marketing, e-mail: mo@centralbooks.com
In North America: International Specialized Book Services, e-mail: orders@isbs.com
e-books are available at www.litwebshop.de

Contents

Acknowledgments. 1
Introduction 3
1. Theoretical Framework 5
   1.1. Compliments, compliment responses, politeness and variation 5
   1.2. French as a pluricentric language 14
   1.3. Variational and postcolonial pragmatics. 15
      1.3.1. Variational pragmatics 15
      1.3.2. Postcolonial pragmatics 18
   1.4. Regional pragmatic variation in French 19
   1.5. Research questions 21
2. Methodology. 23
   2.1. Participants 23
   2.2. Instrument and procedure 24
   2.3. Data analysis 29
      2.3.1. The coding scheme for compliment strategies 29
      2.3.2. The coding scheme for compliment response strategies 35
3. Compliments On Appearance 39
   3.1. Move-structures in the realization of compliments 39
   3.2. Head acts 42
   3.3. Lexical and stylistic devices in head acts 45
      3.3.1. Lexical devices. 45
         3.3.1.1. Adjectives 45
            3.3.1.1.1. Types and frequency of adjectives . 45

    3.3.1.1.2. Situational distribution of
      adjectives 47
   3.3.1.2. Adverbs. 48
    3.3.1.2.1. Types and frequency of adverbs . . 48
    3.3.1.2.2. Situational distribution of adverbs . 50
   3.3.1.3. Verbs 52
    3.3.1.3.1. Types and frequency of verbs . . . 52
    3.3.1.3.2. Situational distribution of verbs . . 54
   3.3.1.4. Positively loaded nouns. 55
  3.3.2. Syntactic and stylistic devices 56
 3.4. External modification. 59
  3.4.1. Types and frequency of external modification 59
  3.4.2. Pre-compliments. 60
   3.4.2.1. Nominal address terms 61
   3.4.2.2. Interjections 62
   3.4.2.3. Greetings 62
   3.4.2.4. Questions and apology 63
  3.4.3. Post-compliments 63
   3.4.3.1. Advice 63
   3.4.3.2. Questions. 64
   3.4.3.3. Comments 64
   3.4.3.4. Other external modifications 65
  3.4.4. Situational distribution of external modification 65
 3.5. Summary of the findings 67
4. Compliments On Skills 69
 4.1. Move-structures in the realization of compliments 69
 4.2. Head acts 71
 4.3. Lexical and stylistic devices in head acts 73
  4.3.1. Lexical devices. 73
   4.3.1.1. Adjectives 73
    4.3.1.1.1. Types and frequency of adjectives . 73
    4.3.1.1.2. Situational distribution of
      adjectives 76

            4.3.1.2. Adverbs. 79
                4.3.1.2.1. Types and frequency of adverbs . . 79
                4.3.1.2.2. Situational distribution of adverbs . 80
            4.3.1.3. Verbs 82
                4.3.1.3.1. Types and frequency of verbs . . . 82
                4.3.1.3.2. Situational distribution of verbs . . 83
            4.3.1.4. Positively loaded nouns. 84
                4.3.1.4.1. Types and frequency of nouns . . . 84
                4.3.1.4.2. Situational distribution of nouns . . 84
        4.3.2. Syntactic and stylistic devices 85
    4.4. External modification. 90
        4.4.1. Types and frequency of external modification 90
        4.4.2. Pre-compliments 92
            4.4.2.1. Nominal address terms 92
            4.4.2.2. Interjections 93
            4.4.2.3. Greetings. 93
            4.4.2.4. Self-introduction 94
            4.4.2.5. Apologies. 95
        4.4.3. Post-compliments 96
            4.4.3.1. Thanks 96
            4.4.3.2. Wishes 97
            4.4.3.3. Comments 97
            4.4.3.4. Questions. 98
            4.4.3.5. Advice and encouragements 98
            4.4.3.6. Requests 99
            4.4.3.7. Promise. 99
            4.4.3.8. Other external modifications 100
        4.4.4. Situational distribution of external modification 100
    4.5. Summary of the findings 101
5. Compliments On Possessions. 103
    5.1. Move-structures in the realization of compliments 103
    5.2. Head acts 105

5.3. Lexical and stylistic devices in head acts 108
    5.3.1. Lexical devices. 108
        5.3.1.1. Adjectives 108
            5.3.1.1.1. Types and frequency of adjectives . 108
            5.3.1.1.2. Situational distribution of
                      adjectives 111
        5.3.1.2. Adverbs. 113
            5.3.1.2.1. Types and frequency of adverbs . . 113
            5.3.1.2.2. Situational distribution of adverbs . 114
        5.3.1.3. Verbs. 115
            5.3.1.3.1. Types and frequency of verbs . . . 115
            5.3.1.3.2. Situational distribution of verbs . . 117
        5.3.1.4. Positively loaded nouns. 118
            5.3.1.4.1. Types and frequency of nouns . . . 118
            5.3.1.4.2. Situational distribution of nouns . . 119
    5.3.2. Syntactic and stylistic devices 120
5.4. External modification. 123
    5.4.1. Types and frequency of external modification 123
    5.4.2. Pre-compliments 124
        5.4.2.1. Interjections 125
        5.4.2.2. Nominal address terms 126
        5.4.2.3. Greetings. 126
        5.4.2.4. Apologies. 127
        5.4.2.5. Self-introductions. 128
    5.4.3. Post-compliments 128
        5.4.3.1. Questions. 128
        5.4.3.2. Wishes 129
        5.4.3.3. Comments 130
        5.4.3.4. Requests 130
        5.4.3.5. Other external modifications 131
    5.4.4. Situational distribution of external modification 132
5.5. Summary of the findings 133

6. Compliment Responses. 135
    6.1. Overall frequency and compliment response types 135

6.2. Compliment response patterns 137
   6.2.1. Functions and realization patterns of simple responses . 137
      6.2.1.1. Thanks 139
      6.2.1.2. Advice 139
      6.2.1.3. Offer 140
      6.2.1.4. Credit shift 141
      6.2.1.5. Comment 142
      6.2.1.6. Downgrade 142
      6.2.1.7. Agreement 143
      6.2.1.8. Joy 143
      6.2.1.9. Praise upgrade 143
      6.2.1.10. Promise 144
      6.2.1.11. Asking for confirmation 144
      6.2.1.12. Request 145
      6.2.1.13. Encouragement 145
      6.2.1.14. Question 145
   6.2.2. Functions and realization patterns of complex
   responses 145
      6.2.2.1. Two-move responses 147
      6.2.2.2. Three-move responses 151
      6.2.2.3. Four-move responses 154
6.3. Linguistic features of compliment responses 155
   6.3.1. Expressions of thanks and/or joy 155
      6.3.1.1. Expressions of gratitude in Canadian French . 156
      6.3.1.2. Expressions of gratitude and joy in
                Cameroon French 158
   6.3.2. Expressions of credit shift 160
      6.3.2.1. Expressions of credit shifts in Cameroon
                French 161
      6.3.2.2. Expressions of credit shifts in Canadian
                French 163
   6.3.3. Expressions of advice 165
      6.3.3.1. Expressions of advice in Cameroon French . . 165
      6.3.3.2. Expressions of advice in Canadian French . . 166

6.3.4. Expressions of downgrading 168
    6.3.4.1. Expressions of downgrading in Cameroon
          French 168
    6.3.4.2. Expressions of downgrading in Canadian
          French 170
6.4. Situational distribution of compliment responses 172
    6.4.1. Most frequent compliment response strategies 172
    6.4.2. Description of the individual situations 174
        6.4.2.1. Situation 1: Academic award 174
        6.4.2.2. Situation 2: Oral presentation 176
        6.4.2.3. Situation 3: Exam Success 178
        6.4.2.4. Situation 4: Baking skills 180
        6.4.2.5. Situation 5: Sports skills 181
        6.4.2.6. Situation 6: New mobile phone 183
        6.4.2.7. Situation 7: New shoes 185
        6.4.2.8. Situation 8: Sports skills 187

Conclusion 189
References 203

Acknowledgments

Several people and institutions immensely contributed to the completion of this book. I would like to thank the Cape Breton University for the financial support, through numerous Research and Conference grants, which enabled me to collect data in Yaoundé (Cameroon) and Montreal (Canada), to present some of the findings at national and international conferences and to publish preliminary results of the study in journals. I am also grateful to the informants in Cameroon and Canada who participated in the study and many friends and colleagues who helped me in administering the questionnaires. Many thanks go to my research assistants for their help in transcribing the data collected. A very special thanks to the Alexander von Humboldt Foundation for the financial support of my three-month research stay at the University of Bayreuth in Germany (April–June 2013), which gave me an excellent opportunity to finalise this project. I am also grateful to Dr. Eric Anchimbe and his family for assisting me in various ways during my stay in Bayreuth. Finally, my love and special thanks go to my wife, Elise and our kids, Clover, Bethany, Melvin and Darryl, for being a blessing to me in various ways and for their constant love, prayers and support.

May God reward You All abundantly!

Bernard Mulo Farenkia

INTRODUCTION

The purpose of this work is to contribute to a growing body of research in *variational pragmatics* and *postcolonial pragmatics*, two emergent frameworks in cross-cultural pragmatics. Variational pragmatics studies pragmatic phenomena in regional varieties of the same language from a comparative perspective. Postcolonial pragmatics examines patterns of pragmatic phenomena in postcolonial spaces. The present study focuses on the realization patterns of compliments and compliment responses and the politeness strategies used in performing both speech acts in Cameroon French and in Canadian French.

The French-speaking world, commonly known as la *Francophonie*, is large and diverse. The ways in which people use, i.e. speak and write, and perceive the French language within this vast sociolinguistic context differ from one region to the other. Phonology, morphology, syntax, and semantics are well-established levels on which regional features of French have been documented. By contrast, there are very few studies that explore speech act realization patterns and politeness strategies across regional varieties of French. The present study is an attempt to provide such an analysis. It describes and compares the realization patterns of compliments and compliment responses and examines the politeness strategies employed in the two speech acts in both varieties of French.

Chapter 1 provides a theoretical background of the study. It provides a definition of compliments and compliment responses and highlights the complexity of both acts in terms of politeness and intercultural variation. This chapter also dwells on the concept of *French as a pluricentic language* and gives a brief presentation of variational pragmatics and postcolonial pragmatics, the theoretical and methodological framework of our analysis.

Chapter 2 presents the methodology, more precisely the instrument employed to collect the empirical data, the participants in the study and the scheme used to analyze the data collected.

Chapter 3 gives a very detailed account of the realization patterns of compliments on physical appearance, namely compliments on hairstyle and on outfit.

Chapter 4 present the strategies employed to compliment on the following skills: cooking /baking skills, sports skills / performance, and skills in oral presentation.

Chapter 5 provides a detailed description of the realization patterns of compliments on possessions such as a new mobile phone, a new house or apartment and new car.

Chapter 6 deals with patterns employed to respond to compliments, with the analysis also showing how the patterns found function as politeness strategies in the two varieties of French. Moreover, the chapter explores the linguistic realization forms of the attested compliment response patterns.

Finally, chapter 7 summarizes the findings and concludes the work with some suggestions and implications for future research.

CHAPTER 1

THEORETICAL FRAMEWORK

This chapter starts with a brief description of compliments and compliment responses within the framework of linguistic politeness (1.1), and explains the concept of French as a pluricentic language (1.2). A brief presentation of the two major frameworks of this study, postcolonial and variational pragmatics, is provided in 1.3. An overview of research on regional pragmatic variation in French is outlined in 1.4 and the research questions are introduced in 1.5.

1.1. COMPLIMENTS, COMPLIMENT RESPONSES, POLITENESS AND VARIATION

Research on speech act realization also takes into account the politeness system and practices of the speech communities where the speech act performance takes place. While politeness has been considered as one of the factors determining the use of specific realization patterns, reflections on the socio-affective values of speech acts and their impact on participants' faces have led to the conception and perception of speech acts as examples of face-threatening /impoliteness strategies or as examples of face-saving / politeness strategies (Leech 1983; Brown and Levinson 1987). Compliments and responses to compliments may be examined from the same perspective.

According to Kerbrat-Orecchioni (2005), compliments are "verbal gifts" that are employed to negotiate or affirm solidarity between speaker and addressee (Herbert 1989; Holmes 1988, etc.) in order to encourage desired behaviour in specific situations. They can serve as intensifiers of other speech acts or as indirect ways of apologizing, thanking, advising, asking for information, etc. and they may also be used as mitigating devices for face-threatening acts such as criticism, reprimanding, etc. Some speakers may also use compliments as conversation openers (Traverso 1996: 107). In general, compliments are presented as positive politeness strategies because they indicate that the compliment giver notices or attends to the recipient's face desires. The functions of compliments can also be traced in written discourse. In book reviews, for instance, "compliments contribute to establishing rapport and solidarity with the reviewee while redressing the face-threatening acts in the genre" (Gea Valor 2000: 24). The functions of compliments may be determined by cultural or situational factors. In a study on compliment behaviour in Cameroon (Mulo Farenkia 2006), it was found that compliments in asymmetric situations, in professional settings, are generally used by speakers of lower status as "face flattering acts" to obtain favours from addressees in higher positions.

Although compliments can generally be seen as markers of positive politeness, they may, more specifically, be considered as examples of some of the positive politeness strategies in Brown and Levinson's model (1987: 102–128). As a matter of fact, compliments function as "prime examples of the first positive politeness strategy, that is, 'Notice, attend to H (his interests, wants, needs, goods' [...] since complimenters indicate that they have noticed and attend to the recipients' needs and interests and attempt to make the addressee feel good" (Sifianou 2001: 396). Compliments could also be seen as "the output of [the] second positive politeness strategy, that is, 'Exaggerate (interest, approval, sympathy with H)'" (ibid.) and this aspect is usually reflected in the use of intensifiers in the compliment utterances. A compliment can also function as an example of strategy 7, that is, "Presuppose / raise / assert common ground", in the sense that the compliment indicates a kind of commonality with regard to taste, values, etc. Compliments may also function as examples of the last positive politeness strategy, that is, "Give gifts to H", which consists in offering goods, sympathy, understanding, cooperation, etc. In other words by giving a compliment, the speaker indicates that s/he knows "the addressee's 'human relation wants' to be liked and admired and tries to satisfy them" (ibid.). It is safe to say that "irrespective of the particular strategy they are outputs of, compliments are clearly positive politeness devices" (Sifianou 2001: 398). As mentioned earlier, compliments may function as devices of negative politeness, when they

1.1. COMPLIMENTS, COMPLIMENT RESPONSES, POLITENESS 7

are employed to mitigate face-threatening acts such as requests, criticism, etc. An analysis of the devices employed in offering compliments may also highlight the use of positive or negative politeness markers. For instance, the use of positively loaded lexical items, namely adjectives, adverbs, verbs, and nouns, and the use of rhetorical devices such as metaphors, comparisons, code-switching, etc., could be seen as the speaker's attempt to exaggerate interest, approval, or sympathy with regard to the compliment recipient. Also, the combination of core compliments with some positively loaded supportive moves could be seen as a strategy to reinforce the positive politeness of compliments.

However, the positive interpretation of compliments depends on how successful the speaker weighs specific situational, linguistic and sociocultural factors like gender, social distance, power distance, setting, linguistic forms, topic, etc. Otherwise, compliments may also threaten the face of people involved in the verbal exchange. For example, if the addressee believes that the compliments are not sincere, exaggerated, that they represent an intrusion into his or her private sphere, or compel him or her to share complimented objects with the speaker, the compliments may then provoke negative reactions. Compliments can endanger interpersonal communication when they are perceived as intrusive, not sincere, or blatant manifestations of flattery, mockery, or envy. In other words: "whether a compliment is a positive or negative speech act depends upon a number of factors, including context, cultural protocols, and individual interpretation" (Tang and Zhang 2009: 327). In intercultural encounters, compliments could lead to misunderstandings, since the speech acts produced are based on different cultural norms. For instance, compliments to an unknown addressee or to an addressee of the opposite sex in a public context and on sensitive topics like appearance etc. could be considered as face-threatening, depending on the cultural practices / background of the speaker and the addressee. The way a compliment is articulated and perceived may have an impact on the type of compliment response.

A compliment response is the second part of an adjacency pair, i.e. the reaction to a compliment, the initiative act. With regard to the concept of politeness, it is difficult to classify the types of compliment responses as positive or negative per se, because of situational, individual and cultural differences in terms of preferred and non-preferred response types. In other words, some compliment responses may be regarded as primarily face-threatening or face-boosting in some situational or cultural contexts in that they flout or concur with prevailing discourse practices or politeness maxims.

Pomerantz' (1978) pioneer research on compliment responses was based on the principle that people generally face the dilemma of accepting the compliment and respecting the modesty principle. This problematic has given rise to a huge number of studies in which the researchers attempt to examine if and how speakers of different languages react to this dilemma. Most of the work on compliment responses has been carried out on Western (European and North American) and Asian cultures and on more than 15 languages or regional varieties of languages. Golato (2005: 213) identified 12 languages, to which the following languages should be added: Arabic (Nelson, El-Bakary and Al-Batal 1993; Al Falasi 2007), Greek (Sifianou 2001), Turkish (Ruhi and Doğan 2001; Ruhi 2006), Thaï (Gajaseni 1994; Cedar 2006), Persian (Sharifian 2008), and Cameroon French (Mulo Farenkia 2004, 2005, 2006), Canadian / Quebec French (Mulo Farenkia 2012), Italian (Ravetto 2012), Russian (Mironovschi 2009).

Overall, these studies point at linguistic and cultural specificities in terms of choice, frequency, realization forms, and interpretations of compliment response strategies. While some of these analyses indicate that recipients generally react to compliments as supportive or assessment actions (Downes 1998), some researchers, like Ruhi (2006), consider compliment responses as manifestations of politeness strategies (Brown and Levinson)[1].

According to Pomerantz (1978), Wolfson (1989), R. Chen (1993), etc., although most Americans attempt to comply with the double-binding principle 1987) or politeness maxims (Leech 1983). For instance, it is argued that the agreement maxim plays a key role in responding to compliments in English-speaking countries (Holmes 1988; Herbert 1989) and that the modesty maxim is most relevant in Chinese (R. Chen 1993; PU 2003). In other

---

[1] See PU (2003: 180) for Chinese responses; Daikuhara (1986) and Barlund and Araki (1985) for Japanese responses; Gajaseni (1994) and Cedar (2006) for Thai responses.

1.1. COMPLIMENTS, COMPLIMENT RESPONSES, POLITENESS

words, compliment acceptances dominate in English whereas rejections are the most common responses in Chinese.

According to R. Chen (1993), S. E. Chen (2003), PU (2003), Daikuhara (1986), Gajaseni (1994), Cedar (2006), etc., responses to compliments in Asian cultures, i.e. China, Japan, Thailand, etc., are generally influenced by the concept of "modesty". As a matter of fact, verbal interactions in these cultural settings are governed by the principle that accepting compliments directly is an infringement against the modesty principle and a threat to individual and/or collective face. This explains the use of different strategies destined to avoid any attempt of boosting the face of the recipient (e.g. compliment rejection, self-mockery, silence, smile, ignoring the compliment, etc.) (acceptance and modesty), they most frequently respond to compliments with appreciation tokens (such as "thank you"). Although most research on compliment responses in France seems to indicate the growing preference for appreciation tokens such as *merci* (Weil 1983; Wieland 1995; Kerbrat-Orecchioni 2005), there is still, according to Weil (1983: 230), a strong trend according to which it is better to reject a compliment[2]: "En France, [...] il est de bon ton de paraître refuser un compliment, comme si on ne le méritait pas vraiment". In her study on compliment and compliment responses in French and American culture, Wieland (1995) establishes that "agreements with a compliment" are rarely used by the French speakers because this strategy violates the law of modesty in the French culture. By contrast, negative as well as mitigated responses involving a minimization or diminishing of the compliment are commonly used by the French speakers. When the participants in the study were asked to reflect on their own culture's ways of handling complimenting,

all 32 of them commented that receiving compliments makes them feel uncomfortable, to varying degrees. This uneasiness is reflected in the comment of one informant who said, "Je ne dis pas 'merci' parce que je ne veux pas encourager ce genre de choses."Another said, "Les Français, si tu les complimentes par exemple sur un vêtement qu'ils portent, leur reflexe sera de dire, 'oh, c'est vieux,' 'oh, je l'ai eu d'occasion,"oh, tiens, c'est ma mère qui me l'a offert.' On ne sait pas quoi

---

[2] Traverso (1996) however points out that the possibility to accept compliments in close relationships is higher than in other situations.

en faire."This informant goes on to explain why he thinks the French have such a hard time accepting compliments: "C'est peut-être qu'il y a toujours un minimum de scepticisme chez les Français. On se demande, 'est-ce que ce ne serait pas ironique?' L'ironie est si importante en français que si quelqu'un te dit, 'tiens, j'adore ton pull,' ça peut très bien être que c'est horrible. On s'en méfie."Another French informant proposed that this difficulty in accepting compliments may stem from the influence of Catholic ideology (or in many cases, simply vestiges thereof) on French culture; in Catholicism, pride is considered a sin. Accepting a compliment would imply that you were proud of something. In French, *orgueil*, which is viewed negatively, and *fierté*, which is viewed positively, are carefully distinguished. In English, pride usually carries a positive connotation. Whatever the motivations might be, compliments are viewed in French culture as a stronger threat to the receiver's negative face than as an enhancement of their positive face (Wieland 1995: 809).

A study of compliment and compliment responses in Cameroon French (Mulo Farenkia 2006) reveals that the majority of the Cameroonian participants in the study consider the following patterns as the most preferred positive responses to compliments.

- Expression of gratitude or agreement:
1) *Merci pour le compliment.*
   'Thanks for the compliment'
2) *Je le trouve aussi.*
   'Me too / I like it too'
- Returning the compliment:
3) *Comme toi d'ailleurs / Toi aussi tu es frais.*
   'You too, by the way / You also look elegant'
- Downgrading / Expression of self-denigration:
4) *Oh, c'est rien d'extraordinaire!*
   'Oh, it's nothing extraordinary.'
- Making positive comments:
5) *Merci, je me suis énormément investi pour arriver à ce résultat.*
   'Thanks, I invested a lot in order to obtain this result.'
- Responding with a smile

The same respondents perceive the following types as negative responses to compliments:

- Rejection:
6) *C'est ça qu'on mange?*
   'Is that what I am going to eat?'[3]
- Upgrading the compliment of expression of self-praise:
7) *C'est dans le sang!*
   'It's in the blood.'
8) *Tu sais, je ne suis pas n'importe qui.*
   'You know, I am not anybody.'
- Showing indifference (e.g. keeping silent)

Commenting on the aforementioned positive responses, some of the informants had this to say:

9) *Selon moi le compliment constitue un bienfait, dans la mesure où il peut amener l'interlocuteur à changer et surtout positivement, ou à maintenir quelque chose qu'il a déjà. Donc l'interlocuteur doit se montrer reconnaissant par rapport à ce bienfait dont il profite.*
   'I think that a compliment is something good because it can encourage the recipient to change positively or it can encourage them to keep up something they already have. For this reason, the recipient should show appreciation for the gift they benefit from.'
10) *J'attends en principe une réaction positive, parce qu'on veut établir une bonne relation. C'est difficile de faire des compliments à son ennemi. Le compliment c'est une marque d'amitié ou de sympathie.*
    'I generally expect a positive response because my intent is to establish a good relationship with the other person. It is difficult to compliment your enemies. Compliment is a mark of friendship or sympathy / affection.'
11) *En faisant des compliments, j'ai une bonne intention. Je veux faire comprendre à mon interlocuteur qu'il a fait quelque chose de bien. Donc en retour il doit tout simplement me remercier.*
    'By offering compliments I have a good intention. I want the recipient to understand that they did something good. They should, in return, simply thank me.'
12) *La personne doit dire 'merci', 'cela me va droit au cœur' (...) montrer un sourire ou elle tend la main.*

---

[3] The compliment is rejected because it is not as important as food.

'The recipient should say "thanks", "I am really happy to hear that"'smile or shake hands with me.'

With regard to "comments" and "compliments in return" other participants made the following comments:

13) *Si l'interlocuteur me fait un commentaire par rapport à tout ce qu'il a entrepris pour arriver à ce résultat, je prendrais cela comme une sorte d'exemple à suivre. Cette réaction est donc positive.*
'If the recipient of the compliment makes a comment on what they did to obtain the complimented object, I would see it as an example to follow. So, this type of response is positive.'

14) *Lorsqu'on me renvoie le compliment, cela me permet de me revoir, de me découvrir aussi. Cela me permet de savoir que je suis aussi considéré.*
'When the other person returns the compliment to me it helps me to take another look at myself and to discover myself. This type of response will make me feel that I am also being acknowledged.'

15) *Généralement j'aime qu'on m'en fasse aussi, parce que rester indifférent au compliment de quelqu'un, c'est comme si on se moque de son compliment.*
'I generally like to receive compliments in return because indifference to somebody's compliment, it's like mockery of that person's compliment.'

With regard to negative responses, all the participants stress the fact that responses such as "upgrading the compliment received" and "expressions of self-praise" are by far the strongest face-threatening responses. One of them said:

16) *Si celui que je complimente dit 'c'est dans le sang', 'c'est ma nature, je suis toujours comme ça' etc., je crois que je n'aurais pas envie de lui faire des compliments. Ces réactions veulent tout simplement dire que mon jugement n'a pas sa place. C'est une façon de dire qu'on n'a pas besoin de mon appréciation. C'est une insulte indirecte.*
'If the person I compliment says "it's in the blood", "it's my nature, I am always like that", etc. I think I would no more be motivated to offer them compliments. These types of responses simply mean that my evaluation

is worthless. It is a way to say that they do not need my compliment. The response is an indirect insult.'

Another informant underlined the impact of social distance in the production and interpretation of self-praises as responses to compliments. According to this participant, self-praises are not deemed face threatening when both interlocutors know each other very well:

17) *Il y a des réactions comme 'c'est dans le sang'. Si elle vient de quelqu'un qu'on connaît bien, un camarade par exemple, elle ne blesse pas. Mais si un étranger répond ainsi au compliment que je lui ai fait, je serai vexée. [...] Certains peuvent plutôt insulter celui qui dit 'c'est dans le sang'.*
'There are responses such as "it's in the blood". If this response is given by somebody I know well, a friend for instance, it does not hurt. But, if a stranger responds this way to compliment I offer to them, I would be annoyed. [...] Others may insult those who respond by saying "it's in the blood".'

While commenting on responses such as "rejecting compliments" and "keeping silent", many participants thought that these types of responses may be interpreted as a threat to the face of the compliment giver:

18) *Rester indifférent au compliment de quelqu'un, c'est comme si la personne n'avait pas mon temps, c'est comme si je n'existais pas, c'est comme si la personne voudrait me minimiser, me mettre en bas.*
'To be indifferent to somebody's compliment would mean that the recipient does not care, that the person offering the compliment does not exist. This type of response could be interpreted as way to minimize the speaker or to look down on them.'

The brief discussion above shows that the interpretation of compliment responses as polite or impolite may vary across languages and cultures. Although the present study focuses on similarities and differences in the realization patterns and situational distribution of compliment and compliment responses in two regional varieties of French, it is important to note that variation may also be observed in terms of perceptions of compliment response types by speakers of different regional varieties of French.

1.2. FRENCH AS A PLURICENTRIC LANGUAGE

The present study is based on the conception of French as a pluricentric language, i.e. a language "with several interacting centers, each providing a national variety with at least some of its own (codified) norms"(Clyne 1992: 1).[4] The analysis focuses on non-hexagonal varieties of French, i.e. varieties employed outside of France. In other words, the present study is situated within the framework of *Francophonies Périphériques* (cf. Pöll 2001). Studies of non-hexagonal varieties French have focused on regional variation at the phonological, morphological, syntactic, lexical and semantic levels. Researchers such as Dumont, 1983; Manessy, 1994; Pöll, 2001, 2005; Thibault, 2008, etc., have dealt with features and status of French outside France. There are numerous works on Canadian French, more precisely on French spoken in Québec, Ontario, Acadia, etc. (cf. Mougeon and Beniak 1989; Martineau et. al. 2009; Wiesmuth 2006) and many scholars have also examined features of Cameroon French (e.g. Feussi 2008; Biloa 2003; Mendo Ze 1999; Zang Zang 1998). Overall, these studies have exclusively focused on regional variation with regard to lexical, semantic, syntactic and phraseological items. While research on regional pragmatic variation of other pluricentric languages such as English, Spanish, German, etc., has increased in the recent years (cf. Schneider and Barron 2008), regional pragmatic variation in French has not received great attention. With regard to the types of speech acts examined, much research has been undertaken on requests, apologies, thanks, etc.[5] As far as the speech acts of complimenting and responding to compliments are concerned, there are several studies on different languages and cultures[6]. However, very little has been done within the framework of variational pragmatics (see section 3.1). Also, as far as French as a pluricentric language is concerned, there

---

[4] Also see Pöll (2005:19), who defines a pluricentric language as " une langue qui n'a pas qu'un seul centre dont émanent les normes " [a language which does not have only one center from which norms emerge].

[5] See the edited volume by Schneider/Barron (2008), comprising studies on speech acts (requests, expression of gratitude, apologies, invitations, etc.) and other pragmatic phenomena (the use of address forms, response tokens, small talk, etc.) in the following pluricentric languages: Dutch, English, French, German, and Spanish.

[6] For details see Golato (2005)

are very few accounts of regional pragmatic variation. The present study, which focuses on regional pragmatic variation in French, is based on the assumptions that

in any language each illocution can be performed in different ways. The different structural patterns and lexico-semantic devices conventionally available for performing a given illocution [...] represent different strategic option for the speaker. [...] The strategies and forms conventionally employed to realize a given speech act differ across varieties of the same language (Schneider 2005: 101–102).

As a matter of fact, the francophone world is characterized by a multitude of regional or indigenized varieties, which result from a combination of factors such as history, sociolinguistic environment, cultural norms, language policies, etc. While several studies have highlighted the impact of such factors on various aspects of the French language, very few have examined how regional factors impact the functions and realization forms of speech acts within the framework of variational pragmatics.

1.3. VARIATIONAL AND POSTCOLONIAL PRAGMATICS

1.3.1. VARIATIONAL PRAGMATICS

The scope of most of the cross-cultural pragmatic studies on speech acts has been to pinpoint interlingual and/or intercultural variation, i.e. variation between different languages and/or cultures (Wierzbicka 2003). In intercultural pragmatic studies "languages are seen as homogenous wholes from a pragmatic point of view" (Barron 2005: 520). It is very often ignored that

speakers who share the same native language do not necessarily share the same culture. For instance, native speakers of English in Ireland and the United States use language in different ways [...]. Neither do Americans in the US all use English in the same way [...]. On the other hand, cultures may be shared by speakers with different native languages. Thus, as language use in interaction is shaped by cultural values, pragmatic similarities may occur across languages, while pragmatic differences may occur across varieties of the same language (Barron and Schneider 2009: 425).

Differences between varieties of the same language have been either neglected or treated as peripheral phenomena. In most cross-culturally oriented studies, the impact of region has not been addressed. For instance, the seminal work of Blum-Kulka et al. (1989) in their *Cross-Cultural Speech Act Realization Project* dealt with many languages and language varieties. However, there was no explicit attempt to compare the data across varieties of the same languages. On the other hand, dialectology, a study of language variation, has long been concerned with how macro-social factors correlate with linguistic choices, but has focused on "the central levels of the language system, i.e. on pronunciation, vocabulary and grammar, whereas language use in terms of communicative functions, linguistic action and interactive behaviour has been almost completely ignored" (Schneider and Barron 2008: 3). In other words, while cross-cultural pragmatics has ignored the pragmatic variation across varieties of the same language[7], dialectology has ignored pragmatic aspects in the study of language variation[8]. Although the focus on regional pragmatic variation within the same language had been demonstrated in a number of previous studies, the research paradigm was officially introduced in 2005 by Barron and Schneider and further developed (Schneider 2010) into a framework known as 'variational pragmatics'. This new trend was conceptualized as a discipline at the interface of pragmatics and sociolinguistics, aimed at "introducing the examination of regional and social variation in pragmatics research [and] adding the pragmatic level to the other language levels overwhelmingly analyzed in dialectology" (Schneider 2010: 238). As the "'dialectologisation' of pragmatics" and the "'pragmaticisation' of dialectology" (Schneider 2010: 238), variational pragmatics studies intra-lingual pragmatic variation, i.e. pragmatic variation across varieties of the same language.

Research in variational pragmatics is based on the *principle of empiricity*, which stipulates that research should be data driven and not based on a researcher's intuition, the *contrastivity principle*, which states that "linguistic features can be considered variety-specific only if the variety under study is contrasted with at least one other variety of the same kind and of

---

[7] Barron (2005: 521) calls this "pragmatics without macro-social variation".
[8] In Barron's (2005: 522) terms, "macro-social variation without pragmatics".

1.3. VARIATIONAL AND POSTCOLONIAL PRAGMATICS

the same language" (Barron and Schneider 2009: 429), and the *principle of comparability*, according to which the data sets used for comparison must be produced by speakers of the same sex, group, social class, etc. (Barron and Schneider 2009: 429). Also, research in variational pragmatics dwells on differences across varieties of the same language (intralingual pragmatic variation) at all levels of pragmatic analysis[9], and the majorities of studies carried out within this framework mostly compare speech act performance across two regional or national varieties of a pluricentric language, a trend which has witnessed a rapid growth.[10]

It is worth mentioning that the term *regional* is generally used with reference to two levels of analysis. "Regional variation" can be observed at the level of national varieties of pluricentric languages such as French (e.g. Cameroon French, Belgian French, Canadian French), English (e.g. British English, Cameroon English, American English), Spanish (e.g. Peruvian Spanish, Uruguayan Spanish), German (e.g. Austrian German, German German), etc. "Regional variation" can also be analysed at the level of internal varieties of a language "geographically distributed within a given country" (Schneider and Barron 2008: 17) such as Acadian French and Québec French in Canada. Placencia (2012: 80) is absolutely right to underline that "the majority of studies currently available focus on the national level; however, in practice, most of these studies offer a contrast of language use of a subvariety within the national variety in question." With respect to the present study, it has to be noted that the analysis contrasts speech act realization in Yaoundé, Cameroon and Montréal, Canada, two locations that may represent a particular subvariety of Cameroon and Canadian French, respectively.

---

[9] For details see Schneider and Barron (2008: 19–21) and Schneider (2010: 244–246).
[10] See Schneider and Barron (2008), a volume comprising studies on pluricentric languages such as Dutch, English, French, German, Spanish, and on speech acts such as requests, thanking, apologies, invitations, etc., and other pragmatic phenomena like the use of address forms, response tokens, and small talk. See Félix-Brasdefer (2009) for an overview on intralingual pragmatic variation across varieties of Spanish.

1.3.2. POSTCOLONIAL PRAGMATICS

Since the present study examines speech acts in Cameroon and Canadian French, the framework of postcolonial pragmatics, introduced by Janney (2009), Anchimbe and Janney (2011), could be helpful in analyzing speech act performance and politeness strategies in these postcolonial societies, each characterized 'by its own distinctive mixture of ethnic, cultural, lingual, and historical influences on its members' social experiences and pragmatic strategies in everyday discourse.' (Janney 2009: 107). According to Anchimbe (2011: 421–422), postcolonial pragmatics is based on 'experiences, interactions, challenges, and communicative strategies of members of postcolonial communities using ex-colonial languages, non-colonial languages, pidgin and creoles in their activities.' For Anchimbe and Janney (2011: 1451), postcolonial pragmatics has the following aims and goals:

> Postcolonial pragmatics takes intermixed languages and communicative practices as its point of departure, investigating different forms, functions, and effects of hybridic discourse in postcolonial speech contexts. Rooted in the lives of postcolonial users of language whose identities, relationships, living conditions, communicative needs, and social perceptions and expectations have been shaped historically by the complex social environments into which they were born, it seeks to explain hybridic postcolonial pragmatic practices in terms that are understandable within the societies in which they occur. Its goal is neither comparative nor contrastive strictly speaking, but rather constitutive: that is, postcolonial pragmatics does not attempt to eliminate differences between multilingual non-Western pragmatic practices and monolingual Western ones in search of underlying pragmatic universals; rather, it seeks to focus precisely on these variant features and explain their social and cultural significance. It attempts to describe postcolonial interaction in its own right, on its own terms, free of the conceptual constraints of monolingual, monocultural pragmatic analytical frameworks.

A few scholars have dealt with the pragmatics of discourse in postcolonial communities. For a brief survey of studies in postcolonial pragmatics, see Anchimbe and Janney (2011), Anchimbe (2011). The present study focuses on compliments and responses to compliments in two postcolonial communities, Cameroon and Canada, with the aim to analyze and compare the patterns used by members of both societies to offer compliments and to respond to them. An attempt will be made to show the impact of social distance, social hierarchy and topics on compliment utterances, the use of lexical, stylistic and external modification devices and the politeness strategies involved in offering and responding to compliments.

1.4. REGIONAL PRAGMATIC VARIATION IN FRENCH

Clyne et. al (2003: 96)[11] are right in their claim that "there has been relatively little research so far on pragmatic variation among national varieties of pluricentric languages". This assertion seems to apply to French. As a matter of fact, among the pluricentric languages examined within the framework of variational pragmatics,

English, with about a dozen national native speaker varieties around the world, and Spanish, with more than twenty national varieties spoken natively in Europe and the Americas, are the two pluricentric languages which have been examined extensively in variational pragmatics (Schneider 2010: 256).

Although regional pragmatic variation in French has been examined by several scholars, the existing studies seem to focus on Canadian / Quebec French and French used in France. The most recent work in this category is the monograph of Rohrbacher (2010), in which the author examines request strategies. With regard to the realization of head act strategies, it was found that there are no major statistically significant differences, although the Quebec data shows more variation. At the level of internal modification of requests, no major cultural differences were identified. However, the Quebec respondents tend to use more lexical modification devices than their French counterparts. The analysis of external modification reveals a dominance of supportive moves appearing after the core requests in the French corpus. With regard to strategies employed to introduce requests, namely address forms, apologies and other attention getters, the French participants appear to prefer apologies or negative politeness strategies while the respondents in Quebec make use of address forms intended to express deference and/or positive politeness such as in-group identity. Drescher (2009) analyzed swearwords/expressions in Québec French and French in France. With regard to forms, the author found that contrary to the French swear-

---

[11] Cited by Warga (2008: 246).

words, the swearwords in Quebec French have a very rich repertoire of linguistic realization forms. Drescher also showed that the swearwords are employed in the two varieties of French for communicative purposes such as intensifying utterance with affective, evaluative or subjective connotations, reacting to sudden topic change in discourse, expressing backchannel, indicating a change in communication perspective. In a study on apologies, Schölmberger (2008) found many parallels in the overall realization strategies of apologies in French spoken in France and French in Quebec. However, the examination of the individual situations reveals some differences with regard to the following aspects: a) introducing an apology, i.e. the use of alerters and preparators; b) the strategies used in the head acts (implicit and explicit strategies), the use of expressions of regret, offers of apologies, requests for forgiveness, justification, etc.; c) Post-sequence to an apology (e.g. offers of repair). In her book *Conversations francophones*, Berrier (2004) examined and compared conversational styles of female participants from three French-speaking regions: Haiti, France and Quebec. This is the first attempt to compare language use in French spoken in three different regions. In her Master thesis, Dubois (2000) proposed a comparative description of exclamation and/or exclamatory structures in Quebec French and French spoken in France from a morphological, syntactical and semantic perspective. The major chapters of this work (namely chapters 3 and 4) are devoted to the analysis of a) typical exclamatory structures using exclamation markers such as "que", "quell", "si", "tant", "comment", "comme", "combine", "ce que", etc., and b) interrogative structures ('questclamatives') employed to realize expressive speech acts. She found some similarities between the two varieties of French with regard to the use of interrogative structures of typical exclamatory sentences. In an investigation of interactions between mothers and their daughters in French spoken in France and Quebec, Bernicot et. al. (1994), found significant differences between the Quebec and French mothers: the mothers in Quebec speak more than the French mothers, and the Quebec mothers produce a greater number of assertive and expressive speech acts than did the French mothers. Differences were also found with regard to the types of speech used in both varieties and according to the mother's child-caring style. A few studies have compared compliments and compliment responses in Canadian /

Quebec French and Cameroon French. While our three recent articles focus on realization patterns of compliments on skills (Mulo Farenkia 2012a), appearance (Mulo Farenkia 2012b), and possessions (Mulo Farenkia 2012c), only one study deals with compliment responses (Mulo Farenkia 2012d) in both varieties of French. The aim of the present monograph is to offer a more detailed account of compliment and compliment response patterns in Cameroon French and Canadian French by highlighting intra-corpora and inter-corpora comparisons on various levels.

1.5. RESEARCH QUESTIONS

The previous sections have established that compliments are examples of positive politeness, that compliments may generate many types of responses and that the realization patterns and the functions of compliments and compliment responses may differ across languages and cultures. From the viewpoint of variational pragmatic research it has been established that speech act and politeness patterns also differ across regional varieties of languages such as English, German, Spanish, French, Dutch, etc. Focusing on the French language and the speech acts of complimenting and responding to compliments, the present study attempts to shed light on the patterns employed by Cameroonian and Canadian French speakers. The following research questions will be dealt with:

- Question 1: compliment patterns

    - Does the compliment behaviour of Cameroonian and Canadian French speakers differ with regard to the use of direct and indirect compliments, simple compliments (i.e. compliments realized using one utterance) and complex compliments (i.e. compliments appearing in the form of multiple utterances)?
    - Are there any differences concerning the frequency and types of lexical devices (e.g. adjectives, adverbs, verbs, nouns) appearing in the compliment utterances?
    - Are there differences in the way Cameroonian and Canadian French speakers use external modification devices / supportive moves in compliment utterances?

- Are there differences with regard to the situational distribution of the above mentioned compliment strategies in both varieties of French?

• Question 2: Compliment response patterns

- Are there differences in terms of the types and frequencies of compliment responses by Canadian and Cameroonian French speakers?
- Are there differences concerning the realization patterns and situational distribution of compliment responses in Cameroon and Canadian French?

CHAPTER 2

METHODOLOGY

This chapter presents the participants of the study (2.1), the instrument and procedure of data collection (2.2) and outlines the coding scheme used to analyze the collected data (2.3).

2.1. PARTICIPANTS

Two groups of students took part in the present study: one group of 39 Canadian French speakers (10 females and 29 males), aged from 14 to 17, and one group of 55 Cameroonian French speakers (39 females and 16 males). The majority of the Cameroonian participants (50 out of 55) were aged from 15 to 19. Three of the respondents were aged 20 and two were aged 22. The Canadian population was predominantly male (74.36%), while the Cameroonian group was predominantly female (70.91%). With regard to age, the Cameroonians were slightly older than the Canadians. Also, the Cameroonian respondents were speakers of French in a multilingual context where two official languages (French and English) are permanently in contact with more than 250 native languages[12]. The Canadian respondents were students at a secondary school within the Montréal School Board (Québec), and the Cameroonian participants were students in three high schools (Lycées) in Yaoundé. Although the present study is based on a small population of respondents in Canada (Quebec) and in Cameroon, we are conscious of the fact that examples from different groups and from other cities in Canada and Cameroon may reveal instances of sub-regional variation in complimenting and responding to compliments.

---

[12] All of the respondents indicated that they spoke a native Cameroonian language (e.g. *ewondo, douala, medumba, yemba*, etc.).

2.2. INSTRUMENT AND PROCEDURE

The data were collected by means of a DCT (Discourse Completion Task) questionnaire consisting of sixteen situations (eight situations to elicit compliments and eight situations in which the participants were asked to produce compliment responses). All 94 participants had to complete a questionnaire in which each situation was briefly described, setting "the general circumstances [...] and the relevant situational parameters concerning social dominance, social distance and degree of imposition" (Barron 2008: 43), and the participants were asked to write what they would say in the given situations. The situations included a variety of day-to-day life situations such as compliments on appearance (haircut, clothes, shoes), skills, talents, performance (sports, cooking, presentation in class), and possessions (mobile phone, car). The compliments were given to friends, teachers, friend's parents, classmates, strangers, etc. The scenarios used were the following:

For compliments

1) **Hairstyle**:
   Votre petit(e) ami(e) vient de se faire une nouvelle coiffure qui lui va très bien. Vous aimez la coiffure et vous voulez le lui faire savoir. Vous lui dites:
   Votre petit(e) ami(e) répond: Oh! Merci pour le compliment.
   'Your boyfriend or girlfriend has just got a new hairstyle, which suits them well. You like the hairstyle and you would like him or her to know. You say to her/him:
   Your boyfriend or girlfriend responds: "Oh! Thanks for the compliment!"'

2) **Outfit**
   Votre professeur(e), âgé(e) d'environ 35 ans, est particulièrement gentil(e) envers vous. Vous avez souvent l'occasion de bavarder après le cours. Un jour, vous le/la rencontrez sur le campus et vous vous rendez compte qu'il / elle a porté une belle chemise/robe. Vous lui dites:
   Votre enseignant(e): Oh. C'est gentil de ta part. Merci!
   'Your teacher, about 30 years of age, is particularly nice to you. You often have the opportunity to chat with her/him after class. One day you

meet her/him around the school or university campus and you notice that s/he is wearing a lovely shirt or dress. You say to him/her:
Your teacher: "Oh. That's nice of you to say.'"

3) **Meal**
Vous êtes invité(e) chez l'un(e) de vos ami(e)s. Ses parents vous offrent à manger. Après le repas que vous as particulièrement apprécié. Vous dites aux parents de votre ami:
Les parents de votre ami(e): Merci. C'est gentil!
'You are invited to your friend's place. His/Her parents ask you to stay for supper. After the meal, which you particularly appreciated, what do you say to your friend's parents? You say to your friend's parents:
Your friend's parents respond: "Thank you. That's so nice!"'

4) **Sports skills**
Vous assistez à un match de football/basketball/hockey et vous êtes particulièrement impressionné(e) par la prestation d'un(e) joueur/joueuse. A la fin du match, vous allez voir le joueur / la joueuse en question pour lui dire votre admiration. Vous lui dites:
Le/la joueur/joueuse répond: C'est vrai? Merci d'avoir assisté au match
'You attend a soccer/hockey/basketball game and you are particularly impressed by the performance of one of the players. At the end of the game, you go to see the player in question to let him know your admiration. You say to him/her:
The player: "Really? Thanks for coming to the game!"'

5) **Oral presentation**
Un(e) camarade a fait une excellente présentation en classe. Vous ne le/la connaissez pas très bien mais vous voudriez lui dire qu'il/elle a fait un excellent travail. Vous lui dites:
Il/elle répond: Merci. Ça vraiment plaisir d'entendre cela! J'ai mis des heures pour préparer cet exposé.
'A classmate of the opposite sex made an excellent presentation in class. You don't know him/her very well but you would like to tell them that they did an excellent job. You say to him/her:
Your classmate responds: "Thank you. It makes me really happy to hear that!"'

6) **New mobile phone**
    Vous rencontrez un(e) élève/étudiant(e) que vous ne connaissez pas dans la cours de votre lycée / université. Celui-ci / celle-ci a une nouvelle marque de téléphone portable qui vous plait beaucoup. Vous vous approchez de lui / d'elle pour lui dire votre admiration. Vous lui dites:
    L'élève / l'étudiant(e) répond: Merci. Ma mère me l'a offerte pour mon anniversaire.
    'You meet a student you do not know in one of your classes at school or university. This student has a new cell phone brand that you really like. You approach the student in question to let him/her know that you like it. You say to him/her:
    The student responds: "Thanks. My mother gave to me as a birthday present."'
7) **New house / Apartment**
    Pendant les vacances, votre meilleur(e) ami(e) et ses parents ont déménagé. A la rentrée, vous leur rendez visite et vous êtes particulièrement impressionné(e) par leur nouvelle maison. Vous lui dites:
    Votre ami(e): Elle n'est pas plus belle que la vôtre.
    'Your best friend and his/her parents moved during the summer vacation. At the start of the school year you pay them a visit and are particularly impressed by their new house. You say to him/her:
    Your friend: "It is not more beautiful than yours."'
8) **New car**
    Vous constatez que votre professeur vient de s'acheter une nouvelle voiture, qui vous plait beaucoup. Vous lui dites:
    Votre professeur(e): Oh merci.
    'You notice that your teacher has just bought a new car that you like a lot. You say to him/her:
    Your teacher responds: "Oh Thanks."'

For compliment responses

1) **Academic award**
    Vous venez de recevoir un prix d'excellence pour votre travail

2.2. INSTRUMENT AND PROCEDURE

académique et votre mère/père vous dit 'Bravo, mon fils / ma fille! Tu as fait du bon travail!' Vous répondez:
'You just received an award or scholarship for your academic work and your mother or father says: "Bravo, my son/daughter! You did a good job!"
You reply:'

2) **Class presentation**
Vous venez de faire un exposé en classe. A la fin du cours, l'un(e) de vos camarades vient vous voir et vous dit 'Wow, Tu as fait un excellent travail. J'ai vraiment aimé ta présentation. J'aimerais vraiment faire comme toi'.
Vous répondez:
'You have just made a presentation or a talk to your class. At the end of the lesson, one of your friends comes up to you and says "Wow, you did an excellent job. I really liked your presentation. I would like to do as well as you." You reply:'

3) **Exam**
Vous avez réussi à votre examen de fin d'année. Vous rencontrez votre ancien(ne) professeur(e) qui est content(e) d'apprendre la bonne nouvelle. Celui-ci / celle-ci vous dit 'Félicitations. Tu as fait du bon travail. Tu as toujours été un(e) élève / étudiant(e) travailleur / travailleuse et discipliné(e).' Vous répondez:
'You passed your final exam. You meet your former professor who is happy to learn of the good news. He or she says "Congratulations. You did a good job. You were always a hardworking and disciplined student." You reply:'

4) **Baking skills**
Pour fêter votre anniversaire vous avez apporté un gros gâteau en classe que vous avez fait vous-même. Vos amis vous dissent.
Vos amis: Ummm, ton gâteau est vraiment délicieux! Vous répondez:
'To celebrate your birthday you brought a big cake to class that you made yourself. Your friends like your cake and say: "Yum, your cake is really delicious!" You reply:'

5) **Sports skills**
Vous avez très bien joué au cours d'un match de foot-

ball/basketball/hockey opposant votre faculté/université à une autre faculté/université. Après le match, votre professeur vient vous voir et vous dit 'tu as très bien joué. En fait, tu étais le meilleur joueur! Bravo! Vous répondez:
'You played well during a soccer/hockey game where your school was competing against another school. After the game your teacher comes to see you and says "You played very well. In fact, you were the best player." You respond:'

6) **New mobile phone**
Vous venez d'acheter une nouvelle marque de téléphone portable. Votre professeur en est vraiment impressionné(e) et vous dit 'ton téléphone est vraiment beau! La forme me plait vraiment.' Vous répondez:'
'You just bought a new cell phone model. Your professor is really impressed by it and tells you: "Your phone is really nice! I really like the style." You reply:'

7) **New shoes**
Vous portez une nouvelle paire de chaussures et un(e) de vos camarades de classe vous regarde longuement et vous dit 'Gars, tes nouvelles chaussures te vont très bien. J'aime la couleur. Elle va très bien avec ton pantalon!'
Vous répondez:'
'You are wearing a new pair of shoes; one of your classmates looks at them for a long time and says "Your new shoes really suit you. I like the colour. They look really good with your jeans!" You respond:'

8) **Sports skills**
Après votre match de football/basketball/hockey, un(e) spectateur/spectatrice que vous ne connaissez pas vient vous voir et vous dit 'Excusez-moi. Je voulais seulement vous dire que vous avez très bien joué! Tout le monde a apprécié vos dribbles et vos passes!' Vous répondez:
'After your soccer/hockey/basketball game, a spectator that you do not know comes up to you and says: "I wanted to tell you that you played very well! Bravo!" You answer:'

As can be seen from the description above, the situations to elicit compliments and compliment responses were controlled for situational variables such as social distance (friends, acquaintances, parents, strangers), power distance (equals or superiors, e.g. teacher) and topic (appearance, skills and possessions).

2.3. DATA ANALYSIS

2.3.1. THE CODING SCHEME FOR COMPLIMENT STRATEGIES

The compliments provided by the informants were analyzed in the following aspects: the move structure of the compliment utterances, the compliment strategies (direct vs. indirect compliments), the internal modification or the use of lexical and stylistic devices, the external modification and the situational distribution of compliment strategies. The first step was to classify compliments into subcategories based on whether they occur as *head acts only* or core compliments, as *head acts + external modification* or core compliments accompanied by supportive moves, as *supportive moves only* or indirect compliments, i.e. by using forms which are generally employed to realize supportive moves. Secondly, we focused on the head acts or core compliments, i.e. the minimal units used to express admiration. The strategies used to realize head acts were analyzed to find out if they are direct or indirect. In direct compliment realizations (direct/explicit compliments), the illocutionary force of the utterance (the positive evaluation) is overtly verbalized. Direct head acts appear in structures containing positive evaluation markers (e.g. adjectives, adverbs, verbs, verbal constructions, etc.) as in (1) or explicit performative constructions as in (2).

1) *Tu as une jolie coiffure.*[13] [C, CF]
   'You have a nice haircut.'
2) *Je te félicite pour le travail bien fait.* [P, CMF]
   'I congratulate you for a job well done.'

Indirect head acts, on the other hand, express the positive assessment (the illocutionary act of complementing) by using the forms of different types of speech acts, thus needing "more inferences on the part of the addressee to

---
[13] Examples are written as found in the data, i.e. grammatical and spelling errors remained uncorrected.

reconstruct the intended meaning conveyed in the message by the speaker" (Yu 2005: 98) as in (3).

3) *Du courage dans ton travail*[14]. [P, CMF]
'Hang in there (with respect to work).'

The head acts were also examined to find out whether they consist of either one single move, i.e. one utterance (single head acts), or a combination of at least two moves (multiple head acts). Single head acts occur in the data as complete syntactic structures as in (4) – (6) or as elliptical expressions as in (7).

4) *Ma chérie, ton travail était vraiment excellent.* [P, CMF]
'My dear, your work was really excellent.'
5) *J'aime beaucoup votre nouvelle coiffure.* [H, CF]
'I really love your new haircut.'
6) *C'est beau!* [CF]
'It is beautiful!'
7) *Bon travail*! [P, CF] 'Good job!'; *Très bien* ! [CF] 'Very good!'; *Génial!* [CF] 'Genius!'

Multiple head acts consist of at least two single head acts and may be realized in many different ways: e.g. by repeating the first direct compliment as in (8) or by reformulating the first compliment or focusing on a new aspect of the complimented object as in (9) – (12).

8) *C'est bon! C'est (vraiment) bon!* [M, CMF]
'It is good/nice. It is (really) good/nice!'
9) *Bravo! Mon pote, tu as été excellent tout à l'heure. J'ai beaucoup apprécié.* [P, CMF]
'Bravo! My friend, you were excellent a while ago. I really loved it.'
10) *Hey bravo, tu as vraiment fait une superbe présentation*! [P, CF]
'Hey, bravo, you really gave a superb presentation.'
11) *Ta nouvelle coupe de cheveux est très belle, cela te va merveilleusement bien.* [H, CF]
'Your new hairstyle is very beautiful, it fits you very well.'

---

[14] This example can be understood as a compliment, since it implies that the interlocutor is performing an activity that is positively evaluated.

12) *Tu es beau aujourd'hui. Ta coiffure te va bien. Quelle belle apparence!*
[H, CMF]
'You are beautiful today. Your hairstyle fits you well. What a beautiful appearance!'

The third step was to explore the lexical devices (adjectives, adverbs, verbs, and positive loaded nouns) and stylistic devices used in the head acts. We predominantly considered the frequency and kinds/types of adverbs used to intensify or mitigate the compliments, as shown in the examples below.

13) *Cette marque est **vraiment** la meilleure sur le marché pour le moment.*
[C, CMF]
'This car brand is **really** the best on the market at the moment.'
14) *Merci pour le spectacle, vous avez **merveilleusement** joué et j'étais **vraiment** heureux d'avoir assisté à ce match.* [S, CMF]
'Thanks for the performance, you played **marvellously** (well) and I was **really** happy I watched the game.'

Adjectives are positive evaluation markers and they are an integral part of direct compliments. Thus, they are not considered as internal modification devices. However, some of these elements are intrinsically stronger than others in terms of their positive connotation. For instance, by using a hyperbolic adjective, e.g. *excellent*, instead of a weaker adjective such as *bon* 'good', the speaker shows more positive politeness to the addressee. Thus, adjectives in compliments could be examined with regard to their types, frequency and situational distribution. This remark is also applicable to verbs of liking such as *aimer* 'to like', *adorer* 'to adore', admirer 'to admire', *déguster/ savourer* 'to enjoy', *envier* 'to envy', etc. and positively loaded constructions as in (15) and (16).

15) *Vous avez été éblouissant(e) et **j'ai pris du plaisir à** vous observer.* [S, CMF]
'You were amazing and **I had pleasure** watching you.'
16) *Bravo pour ton oral, tu as **capté mon attention** du début à la fin.* [P, CF]
'Congrats on your presentation, you **caught my attention** from the beginning to the end.'

Positively loaded nouns were also considered as an important feature of the lexical content of compliments as in (17) and (18).

17) *Merci c'était un* **délice**. [M, CMF]
'Thanks. It was a delicacy.'
18) *Wow, on dirait que c'est un* **prof** *qui parle*. [P, CF]
'Wow, one could say you sound like a **professor**.'

Stylistic devices employed to mitigate or intensify the compliments as in (19) and (20) were also explored. These devices mainly function as markers of negative or positive politeness. Stylistic devices can be used to intensify compliments as in (19) and (20).

19) *Salut, j'ai regardé le match et* ***je dois t'avouer que*** *ton jeu m'a impressionné*. [S, CMF]
'Hi, I watched the match and **I must admit that** your play style impressed me.'
20) *Salut toi, on se connait pas, mais* ***je veux te dire que*** *ta présentation était vraiment bonne*. [P, CF]
'Hi there, we don't know each other, but **I want to tell you that** your presentation was really good.'

Some respondents make use of devices to mitigate their compliments, namely cajolers (e.g. *tu sais* 'you know.') the conditional mode (e.g. *j'aimerais te dire que ...* 'I would like to tell you that), downtoners such as *juste* 'just' used to minimize any threat to the addressee's face (time, privacy, etc.). In most cases, the downtoner was combined with a verb in the past tense (e.g. *je voulais juste vous dire que* 'I just wanted to tell you that') or in the conditional (e.g. *je voudrais juste vous dire que* 'I just wanted to tell you that.) as in (21) and (22)

21) *Salut!* ***je voudrais juste vous dire que*** *votre travail était bien et m'a beaucoup plu*. [P, CMF]
'Hi, **I just wanted to tell you that** your work was good and really pleased me.'
22) *Yo,* ***j'voulais juste te dire que*** *j'ai VRAIMENT aimé ton exposé*. [P, CF]
'Yo,**I just wanted to tell you that** I REALLY loved your presentation.

2.3. DATA ANALYSIS

The next step of the data analysis was to consider external modification devices in the compliments. As already mentioned, compliment utterances can be complex in that they consist of core compliments and external modifications or *supportive moves* (Blum-Kulka et al. 1989) or other types of speech acts. Some supportive moves are used to mitigate the head acts (negative politeness) while others are employed to intensify the head acts (positive politeness). External modification devices found in the data belong to two subcategories: pre-posed supportive moves or pre-compliments, i.e. those supportive moves appearing before the head acts and post-posed supportive moves or post-compliments, i.e. external modifications that occurred after the head acts. This subcategory of *pre-compliments* includes all pragmatic strategies employed to introduce the head acts. Although many speech acts occur as pre-compliments, we will apply this terminology exclusively to those supportive moves in the data that essentially appear before compliments. The pre-compliments include nominal address forms as in (23), interjections as in (24), greetings as in (25), self-introductions as in (26) and apologies as in (27).

23) **Mon amour**, *j'aime ta nouvelle coiffure, elle te va très bien.* [H, CF]
'**My love**, I like your new hairstyle, it fits you very well.'
24) *Oh la la! Tu sais j'ai bien aimé ta façon de jouer et tu as un grand talent.* [S, CMF]
'Oh la la! You know I really like your play style and you have a great talent.'
25) *Salut! Comment tu vas? C'est pas possible ton téléphone est mortel.* [T, CMF]
'Hi! How are you doing? It's not possible your phone is wonderful.'
26) *Bonjour toi! je m'appelle Muriel au fait je voulais juste te dire que j'ai beaucoup aimé ta prestation en classe.* [P, CMF]
'Good morning you! **my name is Muriel**, in fact I just wanted to tell you that I liked your performance very much.'
27) *Excuse-moi , je tiens à te dire que ta présentation a été excellente, j'ai aimé.* [P, CMF]
'**Excuse me**, I want to tell you that your presentation was excellent. I loved it.'

To the subcategory of post-compliments belong all other types of speech acts that appear after the head acts, such as thanks as in (28), advice as in (29), and many other speech acts. It is worth mentioning that post-compliments play an important role in the manifestation of negative or positive politeness when offering compliments. The frequency, function and type of these supportive moves depend, to a great extent, on the situation (i.e. complimented object, social / power distance).

28) **Merci beaucoup madame** *c'était délicieux, ce plat en particulier: vous êtes un chef*.[M, CMF]
 '**Thank you very much ma'am**, it was delicious, this dish in particular. You are a chef.'
29) *T'as vraiment bien joué ce soir,* **continue comme ça**. [S, CF]
 'You really played well this evening, **keep up the good work**!'

The following examples from the data may help us to illustrate the various aspects under investigation in the next chapters.

30) *Oh my god! T'étais* **vraiment** *bonne, c'tait fou*. [S, CF]
 '**Oh my god**! You were **really** good. That was crazy.'
31) *Ce gars , ta présentation était excellente*. [P, CMF]
 '**Man**, your presentation was excellent.'
32) *Bonjour compagnon. Pardon de te perturber mais j'aimerais te dire que tu as été parfait tout au long de ton exposé et je conte m'intégrer dans ton groupe la prochaine fois qu'il y aura encore exposé*. [CMF]
 '**Good morning, buddy. Excuse me for bothering you** but I would like to tell you that you were perfect during your presentation and **I look forward to joining your group the next time there is another presentation**.'

In (30) the compliment giver uses an interjection (attention getter) *oh my god* to introduce the head act *T'étais vraiment bonne*. 'You were really good.' This direct compliment is intensified by the adverb *vraiment* 'really'. A second core compliment is used to intensify the first head act *c'tait fou* 'That was crazy'. In (31), the head act is preceded by the address form *Ce gars* 'Man', which serves as an attention getter as well as a solidarity marker, employed to reinforce the core compliment. As the discussion below will show, the address form belongs to a heterogeneous category

2.3. DATA ANALYSIS

of external modification devices comprising pre-compliments such as interjections, greetings, apologies, etc., used by the compliment giver to get the attention of the addressee or to establish a positive atmosphere prior to the core compliment. In (32), the speaker uses different types of pre-compliments, namely a combination of greeting and address forms *Bonjour compagnon* 'Good morning, buddy', and an apology *Pardon de te perturber mais* 'Excuse me for bothering you but' prior to the head act *J'aimerais te dire que tu as été parfait tout au long de ton exposé* 'I would like to tell you that you were perfect during your presentation'. Also, this head act contains the syntactic device *j'aimerais te dire que* 'I would like to tell you that', which serves as an internal introduction to the direct compliment. The core compliment is followed by another type of external modification: the expression of a wish *et je conte m'intégrer dans ton groupe la prochaine fois qu'il y aura encore exposé* 'and I look forward to joining your group the next time there is another presentation'.

The following three chapters will focus on the a) frequency of the move structures used in the compliments, b) types, frequency and realization patterns of head acts, c) types, frequency and situational distribution of lexical and syntactic devices in the head acts, and d) types, frequency, realization patterns and situational distribution of external modifications.

2.3.2. THE CODING SCHEME FOR COMPLIMENT RESPONSE STRATEGIES

A total of 309[15] compliment responses were elicited from the Canadian informants while 434[16] compliment responses emerged from the data in Cameroon French. Overall, 743 compliment responses were collected and coded. The first step was to identify two major strategies based on the difference between nonverbal responses, i.e. responses in the form of nodding, smiling, laughing, silence, etc., and verbal responses, i.e. responses produced by using utterances constructed involving features of a given lan-

---

[15] This number "309", instead of "312", is due to the fact that three examples were not further considered because they were not appropriate.
[16] Instead of 440 responses, we retained 434 because six appeared to be inappropriate for this study.

guage, i.e. single words, groups of words, grammatically complete structures, sets of sentences, etc.

Then followed the classification of verbal responses, taking into account the number of moves involved in a response. A distinction was made between simple or one-move responses, i.e. responses that employ one speech act / illocution (e.g. thanks as in (33), advice as in (34), credit shift as in (35), and complex or multi-move-responses, i.e. responses that combine at least two (e.g. thanks + credit shift as in (36) or thanks + comment as in (37).

33) *Merci pour le compliment.*
'Thanks for the compliment.'
34) *Tu n'as qu'a t'y mettre et tout sera très facile pour toi aussi.*
'You just have to devote yourself and everything will be easy for you too.'
35) *C'est grâce à vos conseils*
'It's thanks to your advice.'
36) *Merci madame c'est aussi grâce à votre bon travail que j'ai réussi à mon examen de fin d'année*
'Thanks mam, it's also due to your good work that I passed my end of year exam.'
37) *Merci! Je me suis donné à fond.*
'Thanks. I gave my best shot.'

The third stage of the analysis was to examine the kinds of speech acts and the realization forms / patterns used in the simple and the complex responses and to see how these patterns relate to the politeness strategies in Brown and Levinson's framework. In other words, the simple and complex responses were considered as either face-saving (positive or negative politeness) or face-threatening (impoliteness) strategies. With respect to complex responses a distinction was made between intensified complex responses and ambiguous complex responses. Intensified complex responses consist in duplicating of the same simple response types (e.g. thanking + thanking; downgrading + downgrading) or combinations of two or more simple responses that could have the same effect on the addressee in terms of positive or negative politeness (e.g. thanking + expressing joy; thanking +

returning compliment). Responses of this group are generally used to reinforce the communicative intention of the compliment recipient. Ambiguous complex responses, by contrast, involve two or more contradictory simple responses. An example of this group would be thanks + praise upgrade. The analysis also dealt with the linguistic realization of the major compliment responses. Finally, the situational distribution of simple and complex responses was examined. The analysis also focused on the individual situations in order to highlight the impact of social distance and / power distance on the types of responses.

The next four chapters present the results on each of the aforementioned aspects in Cameroon French and in Canadian French.

CHAPTER 3

COMPLIMENTS ON APPEARANCE

This chapter presents the realization patterns of compliments on physical appearance by the Cameroonian and Canadian participants. Two situations of the DCT questionnaire were used to elicit examples from the informants. The participants of both groups were asked to produce compliments on the new hairstyle/haircut of their girl-/boyfriend and compliments on the outfit of their teacher/professor. In the hairstyle situation, the compliment giver and the addressee have equal power position, and they know each other very well [= P, - D]. In the outfit situation, the addressee has a higher power position, while the speaker and the recipient know each other as acquaintances [+ P, = D]. Overall, the 94 informants provided 185 responses (instead of 188) for the two questionnaire situations (hairstyle and outfit): 107 answers by the Cameroonians and 78 examples by the Canadian participants. Three Cameroonians did not provide compliments on hairstyle.

The chapter presents move structures (3.1) and head act strategies employed in the realization of compliments (3.2). Lexical and stylistic devices are discussed in 3.3, while external modification patterns are outlined in 3.4. The summary of the findings is provided in 3.5.

3.1. MOVE-STRUCTURES IN THE REALIZATION OF COMPLIMENTS

In the examples obtained, expressions of admiration occur either as core compliments (*head only*), or as combinations of core compliments and other types of speech acts (*head + supportive(s)*). Table 1 and Figure 1 present the frequency of the attested move structures in the two corpora.

3. COMPLIMENTS ON APPEARANCE

Table 1: Distribution of move structures in Cameroonian and Canadian compliments on appearance

	Cameroon	Canada
Head only	43 (40.19%)	42 (53.85%)
Head + supportive(s)	64 (59.81%)	36 (46.15%)
Total	107 (100%)	78 (100%)

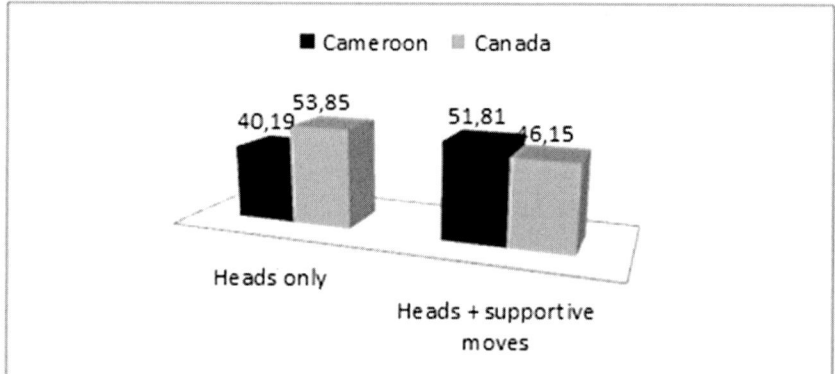

Figure 1: Distribution of move structures in Cameroonian and Canadian compliments on appearance

As can be seen in Table 1 and Figure 1, the Canadians adopt more 'head act only' patterns (42 of 78 or 53.85%)) than the 'head act(s) + supportive moves' patterns (36 of 78 or 46.15%)), while the Cameroonians mostly prefer combinations of 'head act(s) + supportive moves' (64 of 107 or 59.81%). There are also differences in the situational distribution of the main compliment patterns, as can be seen in Table 2 and Figures 2 and 3.

Figure 2 below indicates that the participants of both groups have different choices when offering compliments on hairstyle. The two patterns are equally distributed in the Cameroonian data. The Canadian speakers of French, by contrast, mostly prefer combinations of heads and supportive moves when giving compliments on their friends' hairdo.

Figure 3 reveals that the Cameroonian participants mostly use combinations of head acts and supportive moves when complimenting the outfit of their superior. The supportive moves consist mostly of greetings and ad-

3.1. MOVE-STRUCTURES IN THE REALIZATION OF COMPLIMENTS

Table 2: Situational distribution of move structures

	Hairstyle		Outfit	
	Cameroon	Canada	Cameroon	Canada
Head acts only	26 (50%)	19 (48.72%)	17 (30.90%)	23 (58.97%)
Head acts + supportive moves	26 (50%)	20 (51.28%)	38 (69.10%)	16 (41.83%)
Total	52 (100%)	39 (100%)	55 (100%)	39 (100%)

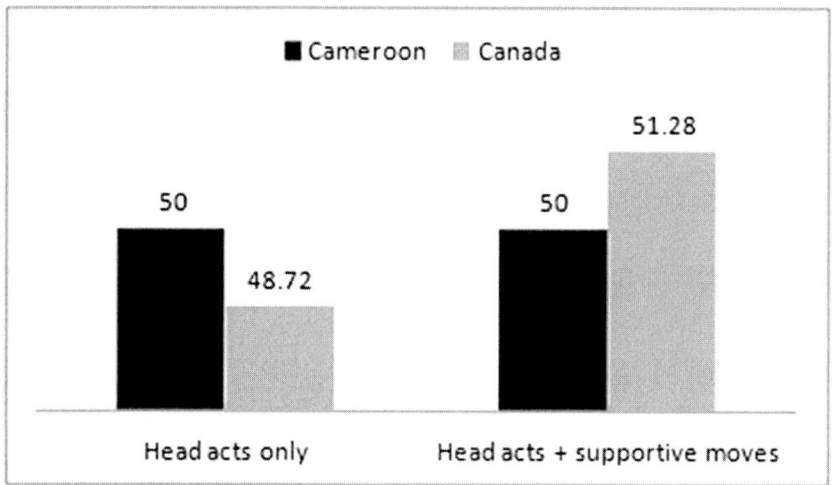

Figure 2: Distribution of move structures in compliments on hairstyle

dress terms. The Cameroonian speakers of French seem to feel that it is against socio-cultural norms to praise a person of higher status (a teacher in this context) without any introductory formulas. So, they use greetings and address terms, etc., to create contact with the superior and to show them respect prior to the compliments proper. The Canadian respondents, by contrast, mostly prefer the head acts only patterns, which means they do not deem it necessary to use as much preparatory and other types of supportive moves as the Cameroonians do.

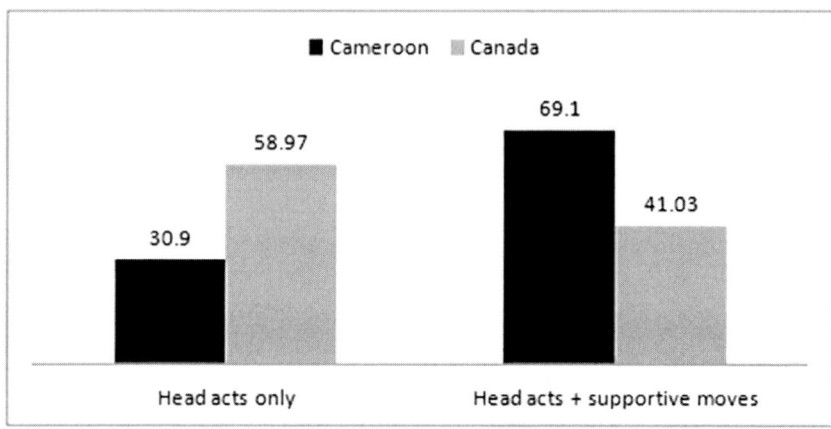

Figure 3: Distribution of move structures in compliments on outfit

3.2. HEAD ACTS

All the 43 examples of 'head act only' found in the Cameroonian corpus are direct head acts consisting of 13 (30.23%) single heads as in (1) and (2), and 30 (69.77%) multiple heads.

1) *Ta coiffure est jolie.* [H[17], CMF]
   'Your hairstyle is beautiful.'
2) *Vous êtes élégant aujourd'hui avec cette belle chemise.* [O, CMF]
   'You look smart today in that nice shirt.'

The multiple head acts comprise 29 (96.67%) double head acts as in (3) and (4), and 1 (3.33%) triple head act as in (5)

3) *Ta coiffure te va à merveille. Tu parais plus beau qu'auparavant.* [H, CMF]
   'Your hairstyle fits you well. You look more beautiful than before.'
4) *Cette chemise vous va à merveille, elle est vraiment faite pour vous.*
   'That shirt fits you well, it's really made for you.'
5) *Tu es beau aujourd'hui. Ta coiffure te va bien. Quelle belle apparence!* [H, CMF]

---

[17] In this chapter, H is used to indicate examples of compliments from the 'Hairstyle\situation, O indicates examples from the 'Outfit' situation.

3.2. HEAD ACTS

'You are beautiful today. Your hairstyle fits you well. What a nice appearance!'

Of the 42 head acts in the Canadian data set 24 (57.14%) are single head acts as in (6) and (7) and 18 (42.86%) are multiple head acts.

6) *Ta nouvelle coupe de cheveux est chil.* [H, CF]
   'Your new haircut is nice.'
7) *Qu'est-ce que vous êtes ravissante ce matin.* [O, CF]
   'How charming you are this morning.'

The multiple head acts comprise 17 (94.44%) double head acts as in (80 and (9) and 1 (5.56%) triple head act as in (10).

8) *Ta nouvelle coupe de cheveux est très belle, cela te va merveilleusement bien.* [H, CF]
   'Your new hairstyle is very beautiful, it fits you very well.'
9) *C'est vraiment beau c'que vous portez, j'aime vraiment ça.* [O, CF]
   'What you are wearing is really beautiful, I really love it.'
10) *J'aime ta nouvelle coupe, ça te va vraiment bien. Tu as l'air encore plus belle!* [H, CF]
    'I love your new hairstyle, it fits you really well. You look much more beautiful.'

The Cameroonians use more multiple heads than single heads while the Canadian respondents choose more single heads than multiple heads. With regard to the use of compound compliments, the double heads are by far more frequent than triple heads in both varieties of French. Some differences appear in terms of the distribution of single and multiple head acts across the two situations, as can be seen in Table 3 and in Figures 4 and 5.

Table 3: Situational distribution of head act strategies

	Hairstyle		Outfit	
	Cameroon	Canada	Cameroon	Canada
Single heads	6 (23.87%)	8 (42.11%)	7 (41.18%)	16 (69.57%)
Double heads	19 (73.08%)	10 (52.63%)	10 (58.82%)	7 (30.43%)
Triple heads	1 (3.85%)	1 (5.26%)	0	0
Total	26 (100%)	19 (100%)	17 (100%)	23 (100%)

3. COMPLIMENTS ON APPEARANCE

Figure 4 shows that the respondents of both groups mostly prefer double heads in compliments on hairstyle, with the Cameroonian choosing the double heads in a much higher frequency than the Canadians. Triple heads are the least used by both groups.

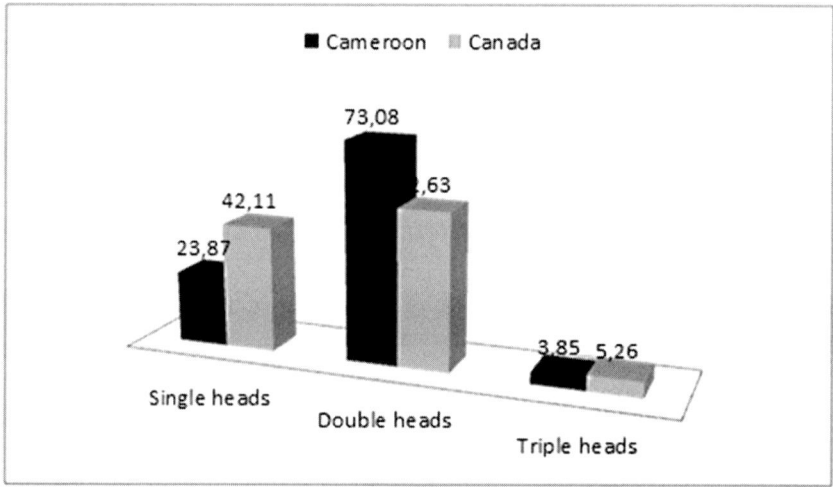

Figure 4: Distribution of head strategies in compliments on hairstyle

Figure 5 indicates that, while the Canadians most frequently adopt single heads in compliments on outfit, the Cameroonians mostly choose double heads. The respondents of both groups do not use triple heads when giving compliments on the addressee's outfit.

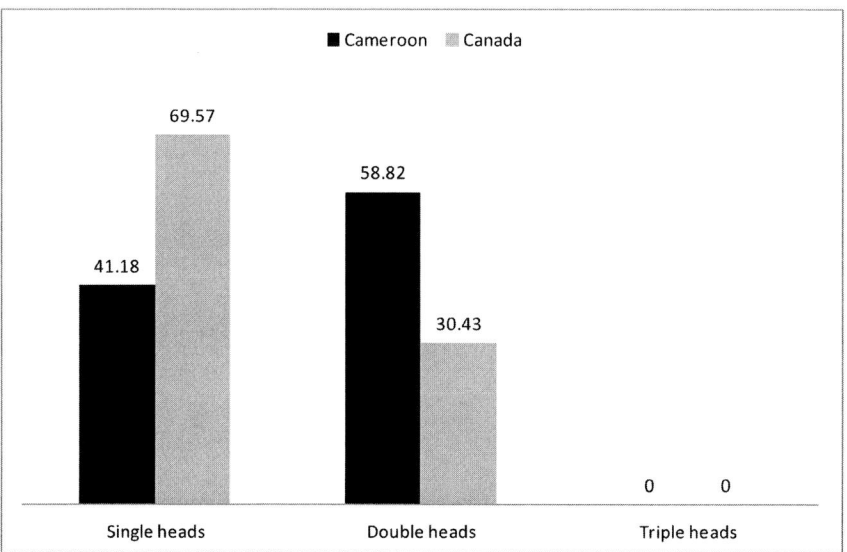

Figure 5: Distribution of head strategies in compliments on outfit

3.3. LEXICAL AND STYLISTIC DEVICES IN HEAD ACTS

3.3.1. LEXICAL DEVICES

In order to express and/or intensify their compliments, the Canadians use 55 adjectives, 73 adverbs, 51 verbs / verb phrases and three nouns, while the Cameroonians employ 99 adjectives, 124 adverbs, 58 verbs / verb phrases and four nouns.

3.3.1.1. ADJECTIVES

3.3.1.1.1. TYPES AND FREQUENCY OF ADJECTIVES

Table 4, below, presents a breakdown of the adjectives in compliments on physical appearance by the informants of both groups.

Table 4: Distribution of adjectives in compliments on appearance

Adjectives	Cameroon	Canada
Beau/belle 'beautiful'	51	36
Joli(e) 'pretty'	13	5

46   3. COMPLIMENTS ON APPEARANCE

Raviassant 'pretty'	6	1
Migon(ne) 'cute'	5	0
Resplendisaant 'radiant'	3	0
Séduisant 'charming'	1	0
Approprié 'appropriate'	1	0
Professionel 'professional'	1	0
Rayonnant 'radiant'	1	0
Bien coiffée 'great/well styled (haircut)	1	0
Bien 'well/great'	1	0
Élégant 'elegant'	9	0
Inoui 'fabulous'	1	0
Sexy/sexi 'sexy'	2	1
Chaud 'elegant'	1	0
Bien vêtu 'well dressed'	1	0
Magnifique 'magnificent'	1	6
Chil/chill	0	2
Nouveau 'new'	0	1
Nice	0	1
Remarquable 'remarkable'	0	1
Splendide 'splendid'	0	1
Total	99	55

As can be seen in Table 4, above, 12 different adjectives occur in the Cameroonian corpus, while the Canadian participants employ eight different adjectives. The results show a higher frequency of adjectives in the Cameroonian data: 99 adjectives appear in the 107 compliments of the Cameroonian corpus (92.52%) and 55 are employed in the 78 compliments of the Canadian data set (70.51%).

Adjectives are the second most used lexical devices by the informants of both groups. As Table 4 shows, the three most common adjectives in the Cameroonian compliments are *beau/belle* (51 instances or 51.52%]), *joli(e)* (13 tokens or 13.13%]) and *élégant* (9 examples or 9.09%]). While the three most favored adjectives with the Canadian informants are *beau/belle*

(36 tokens or 65.45%]), *magnifique* (6 occurrences or 10.91%]), and *joli(e)* (5 examples or 9.09%]). Although *beau/belle* is by far the most preferred adjective in both data sets, the Canadian informants use it more than their Cameroonian counterparts to give compliments on appearance. There is also a difference regarding the kinds of adjectives attested in the corpus. The Cameroonian repertoire is larger and more varied than the Canadian and many adjectives in the Cameroonian compliments do not occur in the Canadian compliments. Two adjectives in the Canadian corpus, namely *chil*, and *nice*, are borrowed from English. There is also one adjective in the Cameroonian data set, namely *chaud* 'elegant': this is an example of a semantic shift by which an adjective that indicates temperature in standard French is used with a quite different connotation to acknowledge the elegance of the hearer's outfit. Finally, two adjectives in the Cameroonian data, namely *bien coiffée* and *bien vêtu*, are compound devices consisting of *bien* and the past participles of the verbs *coiffer* and *vêtir*.

3.3.1.1.2. SITUATIONAL DISTRIBUTION OF ADJECTIVES

The distribution of adjectives in the two situations also reveals some differences. As can be seen in Table 5, the Cameroonians most frequently employ *beau/belle* in both situations. Also, there are seven tokens of *joli(e)* in compliments on hairstyle and six examples of the same adjective in compliments on outfit. The third adjective *ravissant* is much more frequently used in compliments on hairstyle. Only one token of *ravissant* is found in the other situation. In the Canadian corpus *beau/belle* is the most preferred adjective in both situations. The second most chosen adjective *magnifique* is much more employed in compliments on hairstyle. There third adjective *joli(e)* appears almost equally in both situations. The majority of the adjectives in both corpora are exclusively employed either in compliments on hairstyle or in compliments on outfit.

Table 5: Situational distribution of adjectives in compliments on appearance

	Hairstyle		Outfit	
	Cameroon	Canada	Cameroon	Canada
Beau / belle	24	16	27	20
Joli(e)	7	2	6	3

3. COMPLIMENTS ON APPEARANCE

Raviassant	5	0	1	1
Migon(ne)	4	0	1	0
Resplendisaant	2	0	1	0
Séduisant	1	0	0	0
Approprié	1	0	0	0
Professionel	1	0	0	0
Rayonnant	1	0	0	0
Bien coiffée	1	0	0	0
Bien	0	0	1	0
Élégant	0	0	9	0
Inoui	0	0	1	0
Sexy/sexi	0	1	2	0
Chaud	0	0	1	0
Bien vêtu	0	0	1	0
Magnifique	0	4	1	2
Chil/chill	0	2	0	0
Nouveau	0	1	0	0
Nice	0	1	0	0
Remarquable	0	1	0	0
Splendide	0	0	0	1
Total	47	28	52	27

3.3.1.2. ADVERBS

3.3.1.2.1. TYPES AND FREQUENCY OF ADVERBS

Adverbs are the most frequently used devices in the two varieties of French. As can be seen in Table 6, below, the Cameroonian informants use 21 different adverbs, while the Canadians employ 12 different adverbs. The frequency of adverbs in the Cameroonian compliments is higher than that of adverbs in Canadian compliments. The three most favoured adverbs in the Cameroonian data set are in decreasing order *très* 'very' (40 instances, i.e. 32.26% of all adverbs); *bien* 'very/well' (22 occurrences, i.e. 17.74% of adverbs in the corpus) and *à merveille* 'very well' (18 examples, i.e. 14.51% of adverbs in the data). The Canadians mostly used *bien* (21 examples, i.e. 28.77% of adverbs in the corpus) *très* and *vraiment* 'really/very' (17 tokens,

3.3. LEXICAL AND STYLISTIC DEVICES IN HEAD ACTS

respectively, i.e. 23.29% of the data). Many adverbs in the Cameroonian compliments do not appear in the Canadian corpus. There is a statistical difference in the use of *à merveille*, which is found only three times in the Canadian corpus, while the Cameroonians employ this adverb eighteen times. With regard to the form or structure of the attested adverbs, it is interesting to notice that some informants of both groups make use of complex devices that generally consist of two adverbs: e.g. *très bien, encore plus, surtout très*. The Canadian repertoire also reveals the use of the swear word *fucking*, borrowed from the English language, as an adverb of intensity in a compliment on appearance. The results also show that the participants of both groups use adverbs ending with *–ment* less frequently than other types of adverbs and the Cameroonians employ four different types of adverbs with *–ment*, while the Canadian only make use of *vraiment*.

Table 6: Distribution of adverbs in compliments on appearance

Adverbs	Cameroon	Canada
Très 'very'	40	17
Bien 'well'	22	21
À merveille 'well'	18	3
Vraiment 'really'	8	17
Plus 'more'	3	0
Encore plus 'even more'	4	4
Beaucoup 'much'	2	2
Spécialement 'specially'	1	0
Si 'so'	2	0
En vrai 'really'	1	0
Plus que d'habitude 'more than usually'	1	0
Particulièrement 'particularly'	9	0
Très bien 'very well'	4	0
Parfaitement 'perfectly'	2	0
Trop 'very'	1	2
Plus que 'more than'	1	0
Toujours 'always'	1	0

Comme d'habitude 'as usual'	1	0
Comme un gant 'like a glove / perfectly'	1	0
Super	0	3
À ravir 'well'	0	1
Fucking	0	1
Encore plus que jamais 'like never before'	0	1
Ben 'well'	0	1
Surtout très 'notably very'	1	0
De plus 'in addition'	1	0
Total	124	73

3.3.1.2.2. SITUATIONAL DISTRIBUTION OF ADVERBS

The distribution of the adverbs across the two situations in both data sets is summarized in Table 7, below.

Table 7: Situational distribution of adverbs in compliments on appearance

	Hairstyle		Outfit	
	Cameroon	Canada	Cameroon	Canada
Très	24	6	16	11
Bien	18	10	4	11
À merveille	10	2	8	1
Vraiment	5	10	3	7
Plus	3	0	0	0
Encore plus	2	4	2	0
Beaucoup	2	1	0	1
Spécialement	1	0	0	0
Si	1	0	1	0
En vrai	1	0	0	0
Plus que d'habitude	1	0	0	0
Particulièrement	0	0	9	0
Très bien	0	0	4	0

3.3. LEXICAL AND STYLISTIC DEVICES IN HEAD ACTS 51

Parfaitement	0	0	2	0
Trop	0	2	1	0
Plus que	0	0	1	0
Toujours	0	0	1	0
Comme d'habitude	0	0	1	0
Comme un gant	0	0	1	0
Super	0	3	0	0
À ravir	0	1	0	0
Fucking	0	1	0	0
Encore plus que jamais	0	1	0	0
Ben	0	0	0	1
Surtout très	0	0	1	0
De plus	0	0	1	0
Total	68	41	56	32

The Canadian informants use much more types of adverbs in compliments on hairstyle. While the three most favoured adverbs by the participants of both groups, namely *très, bien, à merveille* for Cameroonians, and *très, bien, vraiment* for Canadians, are used in the two questionnaire situations, the other less common adverbs mostly appear in one situation. While *très* is much more frequently used in compliments on hairstyle than in compliments on outfit by the Cameroonians, the Canadians do the opposite with regard to the use of this adverb in both situations. The second most employed adverb by the Cameroonians, *bien*, is much more frequent in compliments on hairstyle, whereas this adverb is equally distributed in both situations in the Canadian data set. Table 7 also indicates that *particulièrement*, which occur only in the Cameroonian corpus, appears exclusively in compliments on outfit. Although the Cameroonians employ more adverbs in compliments on hairstyle, Table 7 shows that they use many more types of adverbs in compliments on outfit. The picture is quite different in the Canadian data set: compliments on hairstyle contain a higher number of adverbs and the participants employ many more types of adverbs in compliments on hairstyle than in the outfit situation. In general, the Cameroonians and the Canadians tend to intensify compliments on hairstyle much more than compliments on outfit. This choice may be explained by the fact that, when complimenting the appearance of friends, the speaker may feel the need to be as expressive or sincere as possible, as a sign of friendship. Social distance and power distance seem to have an impact on the choice of lexical devices in compliments on appearance.

3.3.1.3. VERBS

3.3.1.3.1. TYPES AND FREQUENCY OF VERBS

The frequency and types of verbs and verb phrases employed by the participants of both groups are summarized in Table 8, below.

Table 8: Distribution of verbs and verb phrases in compliments on appearance

Verbs and verbal phrases	Cameroon	Canada
Aller à 'to suit/fit'	42	20
Aimer 'to like'	5	19
Apprécier 'to like'	1	0
Briller 'to shine'	1	0
Plaire 'to like'	1	0
Convenir à 'to suit/fit'	1	0
Aller avec 'to match (with)'	1	0
Adorer 'to adore/love'	1	0
Féliciter 'to congratulate'	1	0
Faire le bon choix 'to make the wright choice'	1	0
Se mettre sur son trente (et) un	1	0
Être fait pour 'to be made for'	1	0
Être la taille de 'to be the size of'	1	0
Embellir 'to beautify'	0	2
Éblouir 'to amaze'	0	2
Faire bien 'to make someone look good'	0	5

3.3. LEXICAL AND STYLISTIC DEVICES IN HEAD ACTS

Faire changement 'to make a change'	0	1
Mettre en valeur 'to bring out / draw attention to'	0	1
Avoir du goût 'to have good taste'	0	2
Total	58	52

As can be seen in Table 8 above, the Cameroonian informants use 13 different verbs or verbal phrases. Of the 58 tokens of attested verbs, *aller à* 'to suit/fit' is by far the most frequent (42 examples out of 58). The other verbs show low percentages and some of them appear in complex or idiomatic structures as in the following examples:

- *faire le bon choix* 'to make the right choice';
11) *Bonjour monsieur votre chemise est très belle.* **Vous avez fait le bon choix.** [O, CMF]
   'Good morning sir, your shirt is very beautiful. **You have made the right choice.**'
- *se mettre sur son trente (et) un* 'to get all dressed up / to be wearing your best.'
12) *Mais monsieur, vous vous êtes mis sur votre trente un.* [O, CMF]
   'But sir, you've got all dressed up.'
- *Être fait pour quelqu'un* 'to be made for somebody (with regard to clothing)'
13) *Cette chemise vous va à merveille,* **elle est vraiment faite pour vous.** [O, CMF]
   'That shirt fits you well, **it's really made for you.**'
- *Être la taille de* 'to be somebody's size'
14) *Madame votre robe est très belle sur vous* **c'est votre taille.** [O, CMF]
   'Madam your dress is very nice on you, **it's your size.**'

Also noteworthy is the fact that the verb *féliciter* is not used in the sense of 'to congratulate' but should be understood as 'to admire' as in

15) *Salut monsieur je félicite votre chemise que vous avez eu à porter aujourd'hui.* [O, CMF]
   'Hi sir, **I admire the shirt** you have put on today.'

Verbs are the second most frequent devices in the Canadian corpus. The participants use eight different verbs or verbal constructions in their compliments. Of the attested 52 tokens in the two questionnaire situations, *aller à* 'to fit/suit' (n = 20; [38.46%]) and *aimer* 'to like' (n = 19; [36.54%]) are by far the two most preferred verbs by the respondents. It is also found that some Canadian informants make use of complex positively loaded verbal clauses. Those who do use complex expressions mostly employ the combinations *faire bien* 'to make someone look good', *faire changement* 'to make a change' and *avoir du gout* 'to have (good) taste' as in the following examples:

16) *Oh! Vous avez une belle robe,* **elle vous fait très bien.** [O, CF]
  'Oh! You have a beautiful dress. **It makes you look good.**' [O, CF]
17) *Hey, j'aime ta nouvelle coupe,* **ça fait changement.** [H, CF]
  'Hey, I like your new hairstyle, **it makes a change.**'

Other examples with complex positively loaded verb phrases are as follows:

- *Avoir du gout* 'to have taste'
18) *J'aime bien votre chemise,* **vous avez vraiment du goût.** [O, CF]
  'I really like your shirt, **you really have taste.**'
- *Mettre en valeur* 'to bring out / draw attention to'
19) *Cette robe-ci* **met vraiment en valeur** *vos yeux splendides.* [O, CF]
  'This dress really **brings out** your splendid eyes.'

With regard to the types of verbs and verb phrases found in the compliments, it is important to note that the Canadians and the Cameroonians employ more verbs than verb phrases. When using verb phrases, many Canadian participants choose constructions that contained the verb *faire*. While the expression *faire bien* is employed as a synonym *aller bien* 'to suit/fit', the structure *faire changement* is used to indicate that the outfit 'makes / brings a (positive) change'.

3.3.1.3.2. SITUATIONAL DISTRIBUTION OF VERBS

The analysis of the distribution of the verbs and verb phrases used by Cameroonians and Canadians in the two situations also reveal some interesting features. As Table 9, below, indicates, the Cameroonians use 30 tokens of six different verbs in compliments on hairstyle and 28 examples of nine different verbs in the outfit situation. In the Canadian corpus there

3.3. LEXICAL AND STYLISTIC DEVICES IN HEAD ACTS 55

are 29 instances of six different kinds of verbs in the hairstyle situation and 22 occurrences of five different verbs in compliments on outfit. The most favoured verb, *aller à,* is equally distributed in the two situations in both data sets. And the second most common verb, *aimer,* is used by the participants of both groups in both situations.

Table 9: Situational distribution of verbs in compliments on appearance

Verbs and verbal phrases	Hairstyle		Outfit	
	CMF	CF	CMF	CF
Aller à	23	11	19	9
Aimer	3	11	2	8
Apprécier	1	0	0	0
Briller	1	0	0	0
Plaire	1	0	0	0
Convenir à	1	0	0	0
Aller avec	0	0	1	0
Adorer	0	0	1	0
Féliciter	0	0	1	0
Faire le bon choix	0	0	1	0
Se mettre sur son trente (et) un	0	0	1	0
Être fait pour	0	0	1	0
Être la taille de	0	0	1	0
Embellir	0	2	0	0
Éblouir	0	2	0	0
Faire bien	0	2	0	0
Faire changement	0	1	0	0
Mettre en valeur	0	0	0	1
Avoir du goût	0	0	0	1
Total	30	29	28	22

3.3.1.4. POSITIVELY LOADED NOUNS

The four nouns identified in the Cameroonian data, namely *élégance* 'elegance' (3 examples) and *fraicheur 'freshness/elegance'* (1 occurrence) occur only in compliments on outfit. Generally, the notion of *freshness* is expressed in compliments on appearance either by the noun *fraicheur* as in (20) or by the form of the adjective *frais/fraiche* as in (21)

20) *Quelle fraicheur! / Tu respires la fraicheur.* [O. CMF]
'What an elegance! / You look good.'
21) *Tu es frais/fraiche (dans ton habillement.* [O, CMF]
'You look elegant in your outfit.'

The three nouns attested in the Canadian data, namely *beauté* 'beauty' (1), *splendeur* 'spendor' (1), and *ange* 'angel' (1) are used to reinforce compliments on hairstyle.

3.3.2. SYNTACTIC AND STYLISTIC DEVICES

The frequency of syntactic devices attested in both data sets is shown in Table 10 and Figure 6, below.

Table 10: Distribution of syntactic/stylistic devices in compliments on appearance

	Cameroon	Canada
Intensifying devices	8 (50%)	1 (33.33%)
Mitigating devices	8 (50%)	2 (66.67%)
Total	16 (100%)	3 (100%)

Table 10 and Figure 6 show that while the two types of syntactic and stylistic devices are equally distributed in the Cameroonian corpus, the Canadians mostly employ mitigating devices in compliments on appearance.

The Cameroonians employ 16 instances of stylistic modification devices. These modifiers are equally employed in the two questionnaire situations. Some of these devices are used to soften the compliments (negative politeness) while others serve to reinforce expressions of admiration (positive politeness)

The Cameroonians employ the following devices with the purpose of mitigating their compliments.

- *Devices used to express the subjective nature of the compliments*, such

3.3. LEXICAL AND STYLISTIC DEVICES IN HEAD ACTS 57

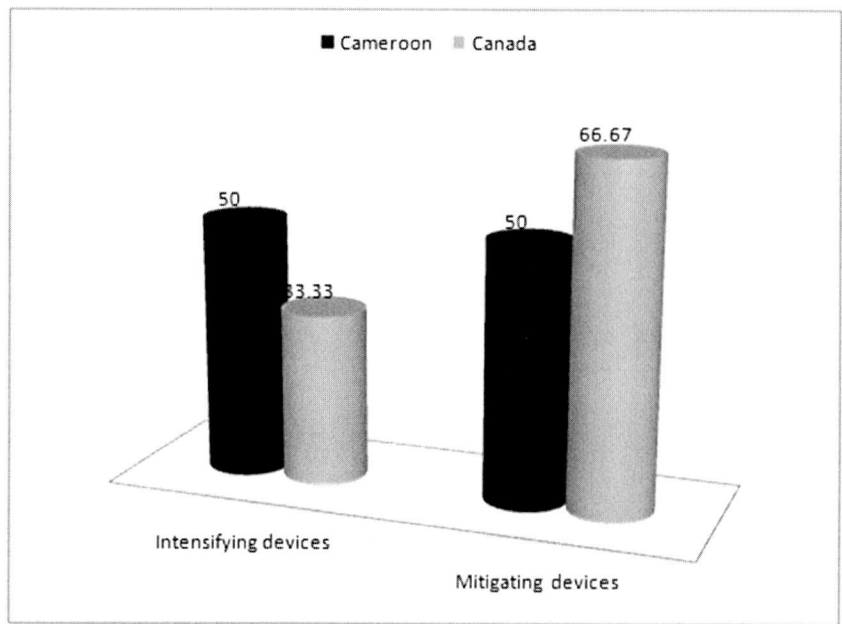

Figure 6: Distribution of syntactic/stylistic devices in compliments on appearance

as *on croirait* 'one would say / think'; *on dirait* and *on aurait dit* 'one would have said'

22) *Messieurs, votre chemise vous va parfaitement.* **On aurait dit** *un enseignant âgé d'environ 25 ans.* [O, CMF]
    'Sir your shirt fits you perfectly. **One would think** of 25-year-old teacher.'

- *Consultative devices and preparators*

There is one consultative device or attention getter *tu sais / vous savez* 'you know'. In the first example, the device is combined with a term of endearment and both appear before the compliments proper. In the second example the device is used after the compliment.

23) *Chéri* **tu sais,** *ta coiffure est belle et te va très bien.* [H, CMF]
    'Darling you know, your hairstyle is beautiful and it fits you very well.'
24) *Oh madame! quelle belle robe vous avez là et ça vous va bien* **vous savez.** [O, CMF]

'Oh madame! What a beautiful dress you have on and it fits you well **you know.**

The devices *je vois que* 'I can see' and *je constate que* 'I notice that' are used as preparatory acts to announce the compliment.

25) ***Je vois que*** *tu étais chez le coiffeur, il est très fort, elle te va bien.* [H, CMF]
 '**I can see** you were at the hairdresser, he is very good, it [the hairstyle] fits you well.'
- Combination of a subjectiviser and the a downtowner *juste*

26) *[...] je vous trouve **juste** trop élégant avec votre belle chemise.* [O, CMF]
 '[...] **I think you are just** too elegant in your nice shirt.'
- Asking tor for permission to offer a compliment

27) ***Permettez-moi de vous dire*** *combien votre robe/chemise est ravissante.* [O, CMF]
 '**Let me tell you how** beautiful your dress/shirt looks.'

In order to intensify their compliments the participants employ the devices listed below.

- Devices used to express the strong desire to offer a compliment

28) ***Je ne peux m'empêcher de*** *vous faire part de mon admiration envers votre belle coiffure.* [H, CMF]
 '**I can't help expressing** my admiration for your beautiful hairstyle.'
- Devices to establish positive comparisons

29) ***Tu ressembles à*** *une star américaine.* [H, CMF]
 '**You look like** an American star.'

30) *Votre habillement d'aujourd'hui est bien,* ***comparé aux autres jours.*** [O, CMF]
 'Your outfit today looks good, **compared to other days.**'

According to Kerbrat-Orecchioni (1998; 208), example (31) is a "deceptive compliment" because it is formulated with a temporal restriction (today), which in this case would lead to the interpretation "you are not always like that / it's not always the case."

- Devices to announce the eagerness to compliment

31) *Monsieur, je tiens à vous dire que vous êtes particulièrement élégant ce jour.* [O, CMF]
'Sir **I really want to tell you that** you are particularly elegant today.'

The Canadians make use of stylistic devices in a very low percentage. The three features attested are found in the hairstyle situation. These devices consist of the subjectivity marker *je te trouve* 'I find it' the appealer *tu sais que* 'you know that' and a comparative structure including the verb *ressembler à,* which are used to intensify the compliment:

3.4. EXTERNAL MODIFICATION

3.4.1. TYPES AND FREQUENCY OF EXTERNAL MODIFICATION

Overall, the Cameroonians employ ten and the Canadians four different types of external modification devices. These strategies occur either before (pre-compliments) or after (post-compliments) the head acts. Apart from interjections, address forms, greetings and apologies that are exclusively used to realize pre-compliments (mostly in the Cameroonian data), some respondents make use of comments and questions as pre-sequences. Table 11 presents the types and frequency of external modifications found in both varieties of French.

Table 11: Distribution of external modifications in compliments on appearance

	External modification devices	Cameroon	Canada
	Pre-compliments	81 (82.65%)	41 (83.67%)
Post-compliments	Suggestions/ advice/ encouragements	9 (9.18%)	3 (6.12%)
	Questions	4 (4.08%)	2 (4.08%)
	Comments	1 (1.02%)	3 (6.12%)
	Requests	1 (1.02%)	0
	Wish	1 (1.02%)	0
	Joke	1 (1.02%)	0
	Total	98 (100%)	49 (100%)

With regard to the overall frequency of pre-compliments and post-compliments, Figure 7 shows that the pre-posed supportive moves, i.e.

preparatory acts, are by far the most preferred devices to externally modify compliments in both data sets.

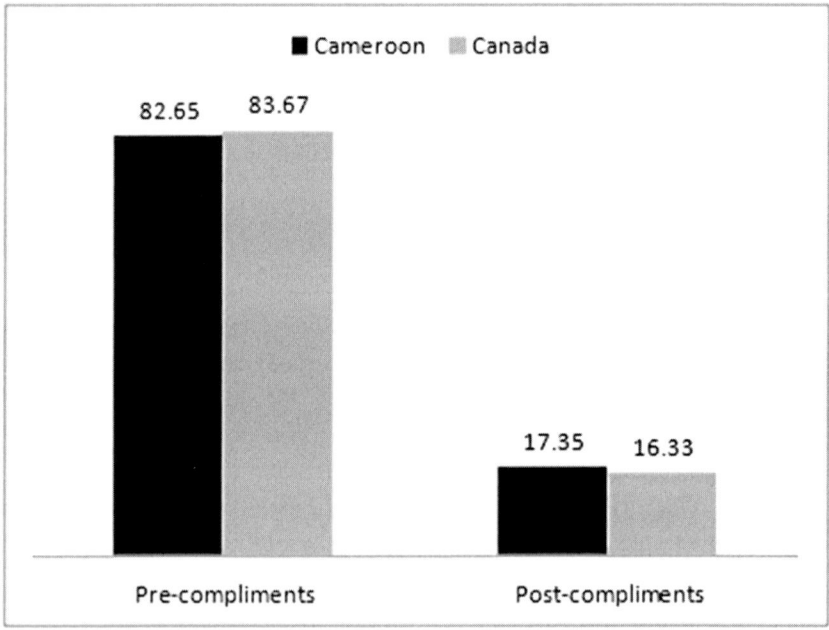

Figure 7: Distribution of pre-compliments and post-compliments

The types and frequencies of post-compliments show differences between both varieties of French, as can be seen in Figure 8 below.

Both Cameroonians and Canadians mostly use advice or suggestions to boost their compliments and the positive face of their interlocutors.

3.4.2. PRE-COMPLIMENTS

The 81 examples of pre-compliments in the Cameroonian corpus consist of 10 interjections, 52 address terms, 14 instances of greetings, 2 comments, 2 questions and one apology. The 41 occurrences of pre-compliments in the Canadian data sets comprise 16 interjections, 21 examples of nominal address forms and 4 instances of comments.

3.4. EXTERNAL MODIFICATION

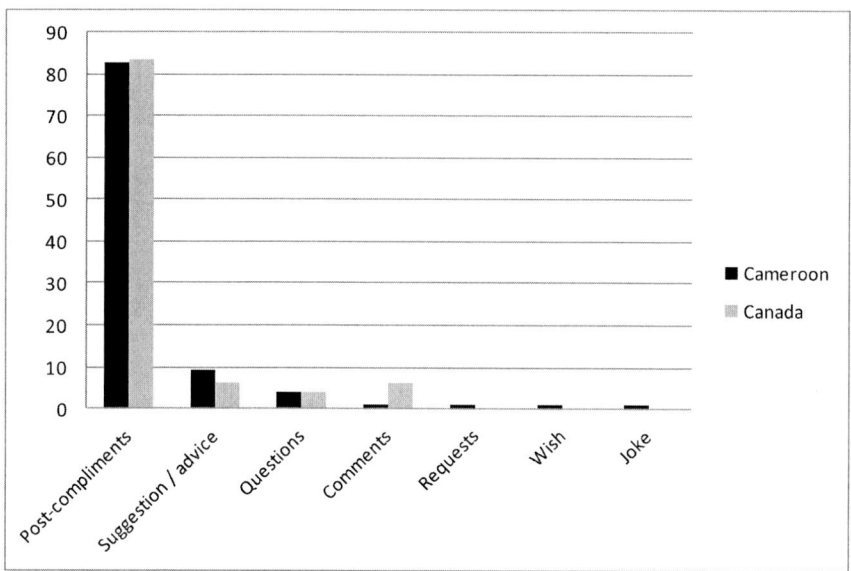

Figure 8: Distribution of supportive moves in compliments on appearance

3.4.2.1. NOMINAL ADDRESS TERMS

The address terms are mostly employed as attention getters prior to the compliments proper. Overall, the Cameroonians choose terms of endearment such as *ma bien aimée / ma chérie / mon chéri* 'my darling' *bébé* 'baby', *mon amour* 'my love' and terms of respects such as *monsieur* 'sir' / *madame* 'madam'. In some examples, the address terms are combined with other external modification devices (e.g. greetings, interjections, apologies, etc.)

32) ***Bonjour monsieur!*** *excusez-moi je vous trouve juste trop élégant avec votre belle chemise.* [O, CMF]
   '**Good morning sir, excuse me**, I just think you are very smart in your new shirt.'

The Canadians make use of terms of endearment such as *mon amour* 'my love', *chérie* 'darling' and terms of respect such as *monsieur* 'sir' and *madame* 'madam.'

33) ***Mon amour***, *j'aime ta nouvelle coiffure, elle te va très bien.* [H, CF]
   '**My love**, I like your new hairstyle, it suits you very well.'

3.4.2.2. INTERJECTIONS

The Cameroonian respondents use interjections such as *wow, oh, eh, waouh, mais, ça alors*, to express positive surprise prior to compliments as in (34). Some of the interjections are combined with address terms as in (35).

34) **Waouh!** *que tu est resplendissant.* [H, CMF]
  '**Wow!** How splendid you look!'
35) **Oh madame !** *quelle belle robe vous avez là et ça vous va bien vous savez!* [O, CMF]
  '**Oh madame!** what a beautiful dress you have and it fits you well, you know.'

The Canadian participants employ interjections such as *wow, oh, oh waow, hm*, were used to express positive surprise as in (36).

36) **Oh!** *Vous avez une belle robe, elle vous fait très bien.* [O, CF] '
  '**Oh!** You have a beautiful dress. It fits you very well.'

3.4.2.3. GREETINGS

The Cameroonian respondents use the following linguistic forms to greet their communicative partners: *bonjour* 'good morning', *salut* 'hi' , *ça va?* 'how are you?' The greetings formulas are mostly combined with terms of respects as in (37), apologies as in (38) or other greeting forms as in (39). These acts serve to initiate the interaction with the hearer, to soften any treat on the interlocutor's face or to enhance the face of both compliment giver and recipient.

37) **Bonjour monsieur.** *Vous êtes élégant dans votre nouvelle chemise et de plus elle va avec votre pantalon.* [O, CMF]
  '**Good morning sir**. You look smart in your new shirt and moreover it matches with your pants.'
38) **Bonjour monsieur!** *excusez-moi je vous trouve juste trop élégant avec votre belle chemise.* [O, CMF]
  '**Good morning sir! excuse-me** I think you are just too elegant in your nice shirt.'
39) **Bonjour, ça va** , *elle est jolie votre chemise, elle vous va bien.* [O, CMF]
  '**Good morning, how are you**, your shirt is beautiful, it fits you well.'

3.4.2.4. QUESTIONS AND APOLOGY

Two questions are used as preparatory acts in the Cameroonian data to seek for information about the person who did the hairstyle. In one of the examples, the question *Qui est le coiffeur qui a su modifier radicalement ton physique?* 'Who is the hairdresser who knew how to radically change your appearance?' is combined with two other supportive moves, namely *Ça alors mon chéri* 'wow darling'. In the other example, the preparatory act is an attempt to unveil the motivation for the hairstyle. The apology attested in the Cameroonian data set is intensified by a preceding greeting formula as in (40).

40) *Bonjour monsieur!* **excusez-moi** *je vous trouve juste trop élégant avec votre belle chemise.* [O, CMF]
'Good morning sir, **excuse me**, I think you look very smart in your beautiful shirt.'

3.4.3. POST-COMPLIMENTS

3.4.3.1. ADVICE

The Cameroonians mostly employ the following strategies to give advice to or encourage the compliment recipient:

- Modal expressions: *(Il) faudra que '(you) should'* ; *vous devriez* 'you should'; *c'est elle qu'il faudra faire* 'that's what you should do'
41) *Quelle belle coiffure tu as là!* ***Tu sais quoi faudra que tu la fasses souvent (...).*** [H, CMF]
'What a beautiful hairstyle you have. You know **what, you should have it done often.**' [Note: An informed guess at the translation... it did not make sense before.]
42) *Chéri que tu es beau, cette coiffure te va à merveille,* ***dorénavant c'est elle qu'il faudra faire sur ta tête.*** [H, CMF]
'Darling how handsome you look, that hairstyle fits you well, **that's the hairstyle you should have henceforth.**'
- Perfomative expressions: *je te conseille* 'I advise you to'
43) *Que ta coiffure est jolie, ma bien aimée tu ressembles à une star Américaine.* ***Je te conseille de la faire pour nos sorties.*** [H, CMF]

64   3. COMPLIMENTS ON APPEARANCE

'How beautiful is your hairstyle, my love, you look like an American star. **I advise you to have it done when we go out.**'
- Expressions of desire with regard to an action concerning the complimented object: *j'aimerais que tu* 'I would like you to'.

44) *Ta nouvelle coiffure te convient très bien, **j'aimerais que tu continues à te coiffer ainsi**.* [H, CMF]
   'Your new hairstyle fits you very well, **I would like you to continue to style your hair the same way.**'

The Canadians also use modal expressions like *tu devrais* 'you should' and an expression of desire as in (45).

45) *Chérie, tu as été chez le coiffeur à ce que je vois! C'est vraiment très beau, **j'aimerais que tu gardes cette coiffure**.* [H, CF]
   'Darling, I can see you went to the hairdresser! It is really beautiful, **I would like you to keep up that hairstyle.**'

As earlier said, the respondents of both groups use advice and suggestions to reinforce their compliments and to encourage their interlocutors to maintain the admired haircut. By so doing, the recipient feels closer to the compliment giver and any suspicion of jealousy is cleared.

3.4.3.2. QUESTIONS

The questions attested in both data sets are used to seek information about the origin of the hairstyle, i.e. who did it and/or where the compliment recipient had it done, or the purpose of the outfit. Questions functioning as supportive moves to compliments on appearance demonstrate the speaker's interest in what is happening to the hearer. The respondents make use of interrogative structures such as *Qui t'a coiffé?* 'Who did your hair?' ; *C'est qui ton coiffeur?* 'Who is your hair-dresser?' , *Où vous l'avez acheté?* 'Where did you buy it?'

3.4.3.3. COMMENTS

In general, the comments occurring after the head acts in the two data sets are employed to reinforce the illocutionary force of the complimentary utterance as in (46) and (47).

46) (...) *Ta coiffure te va très bien! Dorénavant je t'appellerai l'ange de l'amour.* [H, CMF]
'Your hairstyle fits you very well! **Henceforth, I'll call you 'angel of love'.**

47) *J'aime bien ta nouvelle coiffure, elle fait ressortir tes yeux.* [H, CF]
'I really like your new hairstyle **it brings out your eyes.**'

3.4.3.4. OTHER EXTERNAL MODIFICATIONS

Request, wish and joke are the least preferred strategies by the participants. The only example of request found in the data appears in the hairstyle situation of the Cameroonian corpus. The expression of wish is used once in the Cameroonian data set. One Cameroonian compliment giver makes a joke to tease the recipient. The use of humour in this context is due to close relationship between speaker and hearer.

48) *Elle te va bien, mais c'est pas toi détrompe-toi.* [H, CMF]
'It fits you well, **but, it's not you, don't deceive yourself.**'

3.4.4. SITUATIONAL DISTRIBUTION OF EXTERNAL MODIFICATION

The analysis of the frequency and situational distribution of the external modification devices also revealed some interesting patterns, as can be seen in Table 12, below.

Table 12: Situational distribution of external modification in compliments on appearance

	External modification	Hairstyle		Outfit	
		CMF	CF	CMF	CF
Pre-compliments	Interjections	7	9	3	7
	Address terms	11	8	41	13
	Greetings	1	0	13	0
	Comments	1	3	1	1
	Questions	2	0	0	0
	Apology	0	0	1	0

Post-compliments	Suggestions/Advice/Encouragement	8	2	1	1
	Questions	3	1	1	1
	Comments	1	5	1	2
	Requests	1	0	0	0
	Wish	0	0	1	0
	Joke	1	0	0	0
	Total	36	25	62	24

While the number of supportive moves in the outfit scenario is significantly higher than the frequency of external modification devices in the hairstyle situation in the Cameroonian data, supportive moves are equally distributed across the two situations in the Canadian data. With regard to the type of external modifications, Table 12 shows, for instance, that greetings are exclusively used by the Cameroonian participants, and these preparatory acts mostly accompany (13 of 14 examples or 92.85%) compliments on outfit. Also, 41 of 52 instances (78.84%) of the address terms used by the Cameroonians appear in the outfit situation, where they are generally combined with greetings. This pattern, i.e. the combination of greetings and address forms in the outfit scenario, is a means to establish a link with the superior before praising him/her. The Cameroonians seem to perceive compliments on superior's outfit as potentially face-threatening. The combination of greetings and address forms is thus intended to mitigate the face-threat. The Canadian informants also use more address forms in the outfit situation. However, the difference here is not as clear as in the Cameroonian corpus. With regards to interjections, Table 12 indicates that the Canadians choose more interjections with compliments on outfit than their Cameroonian counterparts. Suggesting and giving advice, two directive speech acts, are clearly favoured in the less formal hairstyle situation by the participants of both groups (Cameroonians: 7 out of 8 cases or 87.5%; Canadians: 2 out 3 examples or 66.66%).

In all, it was found that the Cameroonians use more interjections with compliments on friend's hairstyle than with compliments on a superior's outfit. The choice may be due to the fact that the Cameroonian speakers of French feel being very expressive when talking to a superior may threaten his/her face, while the close relationship with a friend allows for unrestrained verbalization of emotions. The distribution of interjections in the Canadian corpus seems to suggest that sociocultural constraints regarding emotions when talking to superior are not as strict as in the Cameroonian context. Also, while address terms have a very high frequency in compliments on superior's outfit, they are used with a much lower number in the Canadian data. This result shows two different approaches with interlocutors of higher status in both societies. In Cameroon, it is expected to show respect and enhance the face of the superior explicitly, even if the latter is being complimented. In Canada, by contrast, it seems that the speaker puts more emphasis on the positive politeness of the compliment, irrespective of who is being complimented.

3.5. Summary of the findings

This chapter has focused on strategies employed by speakers of Cameroon French and speakers of Canadian French to offer compliments on physical appearance (hairstyle and outfit). The findings show some similarities and differences with regard to the strategies, their realization forms and distribution across the two situations. Two main strategies emerged from the data: 'head act' strategies and 'head act(s) + external modification'.

Move structure and Head acts

It was found that the respondents of both groups use single heads and multiple heads. The Canadian participants appear to employ more single head acts, while the speakers of Cameroon French use more multiple head acts. Also, the informants of both groups generate double and triple head acts, whereby the double compliments are by far more frequent than combinations of three single heads in both sub-corpora.

Lexical and stylistic devices

The results show that, although the speakers of both varieties of French make more use of lexical tokens, the Cameroonians employ more lexical and stylistic devices than the Canadians. Overall, adverbs are the most frequent lexical devices in both data sets.

External modification
The analysis reveals that the Cameroonian participants provide many more examples than the Canadians. Overall, the Cameroonians employ ten different kinds of supportive moves, mostly used in pre-sequences. The Canadian participants use five different types of supportive moves in their compliments and most commonly make use of pre-compliments as well. In contrast to the Canadian data set, in which the supportive moves occur more equally in both situations, the Cameroonians mostly employ external modifiers in the outfit situation.

Chapter 4

Compliments on Skills

This chapter deals with the realization patterns of compliments on skills by Cameroonian and Canadian speakers of French. The scenarios used to elicit the compliment utterances focus on the following aspects: a) meal offered by the parents of the speaker's friend, b) sports skills / performance of a stranger and c) oral presentation by a classmate of the speaker. The meal situation is a case where the addressee has a higher social status and the compliment giver and recipient know each other [+P, - D]. In the sports situation the compliment giver and recipient have equal social status and do not know each other [=P, +D], while the presentation situation is a context where the interlocutors have equal social status and know each other as acquaintances [=P, =D].

The description outlines the move structures (4.1) and head act strategies used in the realization of compliments (4.2). Lexical and stylistic devices are discussed in 4.3, while external modification patterns are treated in 4.4. The summary of the findings is provided in 4.5.

4.1. Move-structures in the realization of compliments

Overall, the 94 participants provided 277 answers to the three questionnaire tasks. The Cameroonian respondents produced 161 responses: 54 in the sports, 54 in the presentation and 53 examples in the meal situation. In each of these situations, one informant did not offer a compliment. Moreover, one answer in the meal situation did not contain a compliment, but consisted of two supportive moves, namely an expression of gratitude and parting (e.g. *Merci on se verra prochainement.* 'Thanks we will see each other next time.'). The Canadian participants provided 116 examples. One respondent did not provide an answer in the sports situation. Of the 277 examples in which compliments were offered, 109 occur as head acts only (39.35%), 163 appeared as combinations of head acts and supportive moves (58.84%) and 5 (1.80%) as supportive moves only. Table 13 and Figure 9 show the distribution of these patterns, as found in the two varieties of French.

Table 13: Distribution of move structures used in Cameroonian and Canadian compliments on skills

	Cameroon	Canada
Head acts only	57 (35.40%)	52 (44.83%)
Head acts + supportive moves	99 (61.49%)	64 (55.17%)
Supportive moves only	5 (3.10%)	0
Total	161 (100%)	116 (100%)

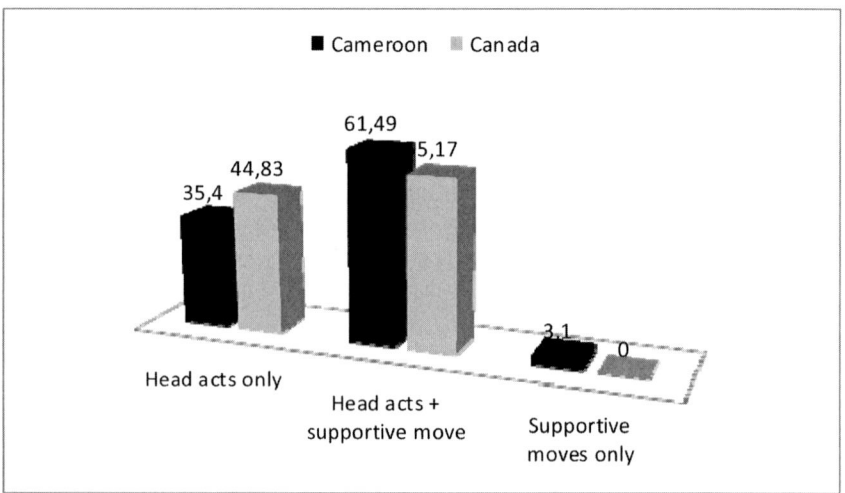

Figure 9: Distribution of move structures used in Cameroonian and Canadian compliments on skills

As can be seen in Table 13 and Figure 9, while the Canadians choose the 'head act only' pattern much more frequently than their Cameroonian counterparts, the 'head act(s) + supportive move(s)' pattern occurs more frequently in the Cameroonian than in the Canadian data. The supportive only pattern is attested only in the Cameroonian data set.

4.2. HEAD ACTS

In the Cameroonian corpus, the direct head acts consist of 17 (29.82%) single head acts as in (1) and 40 (70.18%) multiple head acts or compound compliments. The multiple head acts comprise 34 (85%) double head acts as in (2), four (10%) triple head acts as in (3) and two (5%) quadruple head acts as in (4).

1) *Impressionnant ce que vous venez de faire là.* [P[18], CMF]
   'Impressive what you have just done.'
2) *Ton exposé, super, excellent. Je l'ai vraiment trouvé intéressant.* [P, CMF]
   'Your presentation [was] super, excellent. I really found it interesting.'
3) *Bravo, tu as joué de façon extraordinaire, j'en suis restée scotchée!* [S, CMF]
   'Bravo, you played in an extraordinary way, I was really amazed!'
4) *Vous avez très bien joué. Vous étiez le/la meilleur(e) joueur(euse)! Bravo. Le match était excellent.* [S, CMF]
   'You played very well. You were the best player. Bravo! The match was excellent.'

All the 52 head acts in the Canadian data set are direct head acts, consisting of 25 (48.08%) single head acts as in (5), and 27 (51.92%) multiple head acts. The combinations of head acts consist of 19 (70.37%) double head acts as in (6) and 8 (29.63%) triple head acts as in (7). There is no occurrence of quadruple head acts in the Canadian responses.

5) *Bonne présentation!* [P, CF]
   'Good presentation!'
6) *J'ai vraiment aimé ce que vous avez cuisiné. C'était délicieux.* [M, CF]
   'I really liked what you cooked. It was delicious.'

---

[18] In this chapter, P is used to indicate examples of compliments from the 'Presentation' situation, S indicates examples of compliments on 'Sports' and M is used for examples of compliments on a 'Meal'.

7) *Bravo, t'as vraiment bien joué, t'étais le meilleur sur le jeu.* [S, CF]
   'Bravo, you played well. You were the best on the pitch.'

While the Cameroonians show a higher preference for double head acts, the Canadian participants much more prefer single head acts.

There is no occurrence of indirect compliments in the Canadian data. The Cameroonian informants, by contrast, produce five indirect compliments, of which four occur in the meal and one in the presentation situation. Indirect compliments on meals are mostly (3 out of 4) realized as expressions of gratitude containing adjectives with positive connotation such as *bon* ('good/nice'), *délicieux* ('delicious'), as in (8).

8) *Merci cher parent pour ce repas très délicieux.* [M, CMF]
   'Dear parent, thank you for this very delicious meal.'

The fourth example of an indirect compliment in the meal scenario is the speech act of promising as in (9). The promise to come back for a culinary lesson can obviously be interpreted as a positive assessment of the addressee's talents, from which the speaker would like to benefit.

9) *Chers parents je reviendrai prendre le cours de cuisine chez vous un de ces quatre.* [M, CMF]
   'Dear parents, I'll come back one of these days for a cooking lesson.'

In the presentation situation, the indirect head act appears as an expression of encouragement as in (10).

10) *Du courage dans ton travail.* [P, CMF]
    'Hang in there (with respect to work.)'

As can be seen in Table 14, there are differences in the situational distribution of single head acts and multiple head acts in the two varieties of French.

Table 14: Situational distribution of head acts in Cameroonian and Canadian compliments on skills

Head acts	Meal		Sports		Presentation	
	CMF	CF	CMF	CF	CMF	CF
Single head acts	5	2	7	7	5	16
Double head acts	2	4	18	7	14	8
Triple head acts	0	1	2	6	2	1

4.3. LEXICAL AND STYLISTIC DEVICES IN HEAD ACTS   73

Quadruple head acts	0	0	2	0	0	0
Indirect head acts	4	0	0	0	1	0
Total	11	7	29	20	22	25

Table 14 indicates that the Canadian respondents mostly use single head acts to express admiration in the oral presentation situation, while this strategy is used with the lowest frequency in the meal situation. The Cameroonians, by contrast, mostly adopt combinations of two head acts in the sports situation. The two examples of quadruple head acts by the Cameroonians appear in the sports situation, in which the Canadians much more prefer triple heads than their Cameroonian counterparts.

4.3. LEXICAL AND STYLISTIC DEVICES IN HEAD ACTS

4.3.1. LEXICAL DEVICES

4.3.1.1. ADJECTIVES

4.3.1.1.1. TYPES AND FREQUENCY OF ADJECTIVES

The vast majority of compliments in both data sets are adjectival. There are 150 adjectives in the 161 Cameroonian compliments (93.16%) and 109 adjectives in the 116 Canadian compliments (93.96%). In all, 64 different adjectives occur in the Cameroonian data, while 28 different adjectives are attested in the Canadian corpus, as shown in Table 15, below.

Table 15: Types and frequency of adjectives in Cameroonian and Canadian compliment on skills

	Cameroon	Canada
Délicieux 'delicious'	33	8
Bon 'good/nice'	20	58
Excellent	24	4
Appétissant 'appetizing'	2	0
Préféré[19] 'favorite (with respect to meal/dish'	1	0

---
[19] Occurred in the expression "un de mes plats préférés " [one of my favorite dishes].

Ravi[20] 'delighted/happy'	3	0
Bien préparé 'well cooked'	1	1
Agréable 'good/nice'	2	0
Circulent[21] 'tasty'	1	0
Merveilleux 'marvellous'	1	0
Bien 'good/nice'	4	0
Exquis 'exquisite'	1	0
Fabuleux 'fabulous'	1	0
Précieux 'precious'	1	0
Chaleureux[22] 'warm (with respect to invitation/reception)'	1	0
Vrai 'real'	1	0
Capable	1	1
Impressionnant 'impressive'	4	0
Magnifique 'magnificent'	5	0
Grand 'big/great'	2	0
Génial 'genius'	1	0
Fantastique 'fantastic'	1	1
Formidable 'formidable'	1	1
Remarquable 'remarkable'	1	1
Pas mal 'not bad'	1	0
Bien joué 'well done (with respect to sports)	1	0
Compétent 'competent'	1	0
Admirable 'admirable'	2	0
Talentueux 'talented'	1	0
Éblouissant 'amazing'	1	1
Superbe 'superb'	2	3
Magique 'magic'	1	0
Plein d'admiration 'full of admiration'	1	0

---

[20] In "je suis ravi" [I am happy/delighted].
[21] This adjective seems to be an incorrect use of *succulent* 'delicious'
[22] In " *accueil chaleureux*" [warm reception].

4.3. LEXICAL AND STYLISTIC DEVICES IN HEAD ACTS

Fair-play	1	0
Marquée 'impressed'	1	0
Fort 'strong/good'	1	6
Satisfait 'satisfied'	1	0
Heureux 'happy'	1	0
Impressionné 'impressesd'	1	0
Beau/belle 'nice/good'	6	1
Doué 'gifted'	1	0
Bien fait 'well done'	1	1
Parfait 'perfect'	2	0
Extraordinaire 'extraordinary'	1	0
Performant 'efficient'	1	0
Joli 'beautiful'	1	0
Sans reproche 'without reproach'	1	0
Intelligent	1	0
Super 'super'	1	0
Intéressant 'interesting'	1	5
Sérieux 'serious'	1	1
International	1	0
Savoureux 'delicious'	0	1
Joyeux 'happy'	0	1
Spectaculaire 'spectacular'	0	1
Énorme 'immense'	0	1
Malade 'sick'	0	1
Sale 'dirty'	0	1
Impeccable	1	1
Incroyable 'incredible'	0	1
Fou 'crazy'	0	3
Nice	0	2
Fier 'proud'	0	1
Good	0	1
Beautiful	0	1
Total	150	109

4. COMPLIMENTS ON SKILLS

As Table 15 above shows, the three most frequent adjectives in the Cameroonian compliments are *délicieux* 'delicious' (33 tokens, i.e. 22% of all adjectives), *excellent* (24 examples, i.e. 16% of the data) and *bon* 'good/nice' (20 instances, i.e. 13.33% of the adjectives), while the three most favoured adjectives with the Canadian participants are *bon* (58 tokens, i.e. 53.21% of the corpus), *délicieux* (8 examples, i.e. 7.34% of all adjectives) and *fort* 'strong' (6 occurrences, i.e. 5.50% of all adjectives). In some of the examples *bon* appears in the comparative or superlative form (e.g. (*le/la*) *meilleur(e)* 'better / the best'). Although the most frequent adjectives in both data sets make up to half (or more) of the total number of adjectives used, the adjective *bon* alone represents 50% of the adjectives used in the Canadian compliments. The most striking difference between both varieties of French is the fact that the repertoire of adjectives in the Cameroonian responses is larger than that produced by the Canadian informants. Consequently, there are many adjectives in the Cameroonian compliments that do not appear in the Canadian compliments. In addition to that, some adjectives in the Canadian data are examples of a semantic shift by which negatively coloured adjectives such as *malade* 'sick' and *sale* 'dirty' are used with a positive connotation to reinforce compliments. This phenomenon may be the result of the exposure of young Canadian speakers of French to English as this trend also occurs in the language of young English speaking Canadians. Another language contact phenomenon is the use of English adjectives such as *nice, beautiful,* and *good* in the Canadian compliments, a phenomenon that is not observed in the Cameroonian data.

4.3.1.1.2. SITUATIONAL DISTRIBUTION OF ADJECTIVES

Table 16 summarizes the situational distribution of the adjectives, as found in both data sets.

Table 16: Situational distribution of adjectives in Cameroonian and Canadian compliments on skills

Adjectives	Meal		Sports		Presentation	
	CMF	CF	CMF	CF	CMF	CF
Délicieux	33	8	0	0	0	0
Bon	9	24	3	19	8	15

4.3. LEXICAL AND STYLISTIC DEVICES IN HEAD ACTS

Excellent	3	1	4	1	17	2
Appétissant	2	0	0	0	0	0
Préféré[23]	1	0	0	0	0	0
Ravi[24]	2	0	0	0	1	0
Bien préparé	1	0	0	0	0	0
Agréable	1	0	1	0	0	0
Circulent[25]	1	0	0	0	0	0
Merveilleux	1	0	0	0	0	0
Bien	1	0	0	0	3	0
Exquis	1	0	0	0	0	0
Fabuleux	1	0	0	0	0	0
Précieux	1	0	0	0	0	0
Chaleureux[26]	1	0	0	0	0	0
Vrai	1	0	0	0	0	0
Capable	0	0	1	1	0	0
Impressionnant	0	0	3	0	1	0
Magnifique	0	0	3	0	2	0
Grand	0	0	2	0	0	0
Génial	0	0	1	0	0	0
Fantastique	0	0	1	0	1	0
Formidable	0	1	1	0	0	0
Remarquable	0	0	1	0	0	1
Pas mal	0	0	1	0	0	0
Bien joué	0	0	1	0	0	0
Compétent	0	0	1	0	0	0
Admirable	0	0	1	0	1	0
Talentueux	0	0	1	0	0	0
Éblouissant	0	0	1	1	0	0
Superbe	0	0	1	1	1	2

---

[23] Occurred in the expression "un de mes plats préférés " [one of my favorite dishes].
[24] In "je suis ravi" [I am happy/delighted].
[25] This adjective seems to be an incorrect use of *succulent* 'delicious'.
[26] In " *accueil chaleureux"* [warm reception].

4. Compliments On Skills

Magique	0	0	1	0	0	0
Plein d'admiration	0	0	1	0	0	0
Fair-play	0	0	1	0	0	0
Marquée	0	0	1	0	0	0
Fort	0	2	1	3	0	0
Satisfait	0	0	1	0	0	0
Heureux	0	0	1	0	0	0
Impressionné	0	0	1	0	0	0
Beau/belle	0	0	0	0	3	0
Doué	0	0	0	0	1	0
Bien fait	0	0	0	0	1	1
Parfait	0	0	0	0	2	0
Extraordinaire	0	0	0	1	1	0
Performant	0	0	0	0	1	0
Joli	0	0	0	0	1	0
Sans reproche	0	0	0	0	1	0
Intelligent	0	0	0	0	1	0
Super	0	0	0	0	1	0
Intéressant	0	0	0	0	1	5
Sérieux	0	0	0	0	1	1
International	0	0	1	0	0	0
Savoureux	0	1	0	0	0	0
Joyeux	0	1	0	0	0	0
Spectaculaire	0	0	0	1	0	0
Énorme	0	0	0	1	0	0
Malade	0	0	0	1	0	0
Sale	0	0	0	1	0	0
Impeccable	0	0	1	1	0	0
Incroyable	0	0	0	1	0	0
Fou	0	0	0	3	0	0
Nice	0	0	0	1	0	0
Fier	0	0	0	1	0	0
Good	0	0	0	0	0	1

| Beautiful | 0 | 0 | 0 | 0 | 0 | 1 |
| Total | 60 | 38 | 38 | 38 | 50 | 30 |

4.3.1.2. ADVERBS

4.3.1.2.1. TYPES AND FREQUENCY OF ADVERBS

The Canadian participants use a higher number of compliments modified by adverbs (95 adverbs in 116 compliments, or 81.89%) than the Cameroonian informants (98 adverbs in 162 compliments, i.e. 60.49%). Table 17 presents the frequency of the attested adverbs in both data sets.

Table 17: Frequency of adverbs used in Cameroonian and Canadian compliments on skills

Adverbs	Cameroon	Canada
Vraiment 'really'	31	36
Très 'very/really'	24	21
Bien 'very/well'	17	18
Beaucoup 'very (much)'	14	2
Énormément 'enormously'	1	0
Merveilleusement 'marvellously'	1	0
Encore plus 'much/more'	1	0
Si 'very/so'	1	0
Tellement 'really/so'	1	3
Trop 'very (much)'	1	2
De façon extraordinaire 'in an extraordinary way'	1	0
En plus 'moreover/besides'	1	0
Super	0	6
Maudit 'damned'	0	1
En tout cas 'all the same'	1	0
Honnêtement 'honestly'	0	1
Sincèrement 'sincerely'	0	1
Fucking	0	1
Sérieusement 'seriously'	0	2
Full	0	1

En particulier 'in particular'	1	0
A fond 'deeply/really'	1	0
Total	97	95

The Cameroonian respondents use 14 different adverbs, while their Canadian counterparts choose 13 different types. The participants of both groups demonstrate a preference for specific adverbs. As a matter of fact, the most favoured adverbs in both varieties are *vraiment* 'really, very' (31 instances in the Cameroonian corpus vs. 36 in the Canadian data), *très* 'very' (24 examples in the Cameroonian data vs. 21 tokens in the Canadian compliments) and *bien* 'good' (17 tokens in the Cameroonian corpus vs. 18 examples in the Canadian data). There is a statistically significant difference in the use of *beaucoup* 'a lot / very much', which is found only twice in the Canadian data, while the Cameroonians use this adverb fourteen times. The Canadians employ much more adverbs ending with – *ment* than the Cameroonians. While the Canadians exclusively use single adverbs, some Cameroonians prefer adverbial phrases such as *de façon extraordinaire* 'in an extraordinary way', *en particulier* 'in particular', etc. Also, some Canadian participants borrow adjectives/adverbs from the English language, namely *fucking* and *full,* to intensify their compliments, a phenomenon which does not occur in the Cameroonian responses. Another interesting aspect is the use of *maudit* 'damned', an adjective used as an intensifying adverb and which appears before a positively loaded adjective (cf. Bilodeau 2001: 128). Generally, the adverbs in both data sets appear before adjectives or verbs, while some of the intensifying adverbials occur in combinations such as *vraiment très bien* 'really very well' , *trop bien* 'too well', etc.

4.3.1.2.2. SITUATIONAL DISTRIBUTION OF ADVERBS

Table 18 below indicates that both the Cameroonians and the Canadians use adverbs much more in the sports situation, and the two most preferred adverbs by the informants of both groups (*vraiment* and *très*) are employed in the three situations. Although *vraiment* is equally distributed across the three situations in the Canadian data set, the results shows that the Canadians employ the other adverbs with – *ment* mostly in compliments on sports skills. In the Cameroonian corpus, *bien* does not occur in the meal situation and mostly appear in compliments on sports skills.

Table 18: Situational distribution of adverbs used in Cameroonian and Canadian compliments on skills

Adverbs	Meal		Sports		Presentation	
	CMF	CF	CMF	CF	CMF	CF
Vraiment	12	11	11	11	8	14
Très	12	12	9	5	3	4
Bien	0	4	15	11	2	3
Beaucoup	1	0	5	2	8	0
Énormément	1	0	0	0	0	0
Merveilleusement	0	0	1	0	0	0
Encore plus	0	0	1	0	0	0
Si	0	0	1	0	0	0
Tellement	0	0	1	3	0	0
Trop	0	0	1	2	0	0
De façon extraordinaire	0	0	1	0	0	0
En plus	0	0	0	0	1	0
Super	0	3	0	3	0	0
Maudit	0	1	0	0	0	0
En tout cas	1	0	0	0	0	0
Honnêtement	0	1	0	0	0	0
Sincèrement	0	0	0	2	0	0
Fucking	0	0	0	1	0	0
Sérieusement	0	0	0	2	0	0
Full	0	0	0	0	0	1
En particulier	1	0	0	0	0	0
A fond	0	0	1	0	0	0
Total	28	32	47	42	22	22

4.3.1.3. VERBS
4.3.1.3.1. TYPES AND FREQUENCY OF VERBS

The repertoire found in the data includes verbs with complimentary connotation such as verbs of liking (*aimer*), admiration (*admirer*), know-how (*savoir cuisine / jouer*), etc. Of the 74 verbs found in the data, 57 (77.07%) occur in the Cameroonian responses, and 17 (22.97%) are chosen by the Canadian respondents, as shown in Table 19.

Table 19: Types and frequency of positively loaded verbs in Cameroonian and Canadian compliments on skills

Verbs and verbal phrases	Cameroon	Canada
Aimer 'to love/like'	11	8
Admirer 'to admire'	9	1
Apprécier 'to like'	23	1
Se régaler 'to relish/enjoy'	2	0
Déguster 'to relish/enjoy'	1	0
Savoir cuisiner 'to know how to cook'	1	0
Adorer 'to adore/love'	2	1
Impressionner 'to impress'	3	4
Plaire 'to please'	1	0
Féliciter 'to congratulate'	1	0
Savourer 'to enjoy'	1	0
Remarquer 'to notice'	1	0
Subjuguer 'to charm'	1	0
Se démarquer 'to distinguish oneself'	0	1
Marquer 'to impress'	0	1
Capter 'to captivate'	0	1
Total	57	18

Table 19 indicates that the most favoured verb in the Cameroonian data is *apprécier* 'to love/like' (23 tokens), which shows a percentage twice as high as that of the second most preferred verb *aimer* 'to love' (11 occurrences). The most preferred verb by the Canadian respondents is *aimer* (8 instances), with a percentage twice as high as that of *impressionner* 'to impress', the second most preferred verb in the Canadian responses. A striking difference between both data sets is the fact that the verb *apprécier*, which is frequently used by the Cameroonian informants, appears only once in the Canadian responses. Moreover, the Cameroonians display a larger repertoire of verbs to express admiration, although most of the verbs show a very low percentage as compared to the most frequent ones.

4.3.1.3.2. SITUATIONAL DISTRIBUTION OF VERBS

There are differences in the situational distribution of verbs, as can be seen in Table 20.

Table 20: Situational distribution of complimentary verbs in Cameroonian and Canadian compliments on skills

Verbs and verbal phrases	Meal		Sports		Presentation	
	CMF	CF	CMF	CF	CMF	CF
Aimer	4	3	3	0	4	5
Admirer	0	0	8	1	1	0
Apprécier	2	1	12	0	9	0
Se régaler	2	0	0	0	0	0
Déguster	1	0	0	0	0	0
Savoir cuisiner	1	0	0	0	0	0
Adorer	0	1	2	0	0	0
Impressionner	0	0	1	4	2	0
Plaire	0	0	0	0	1	0
Féliciter	0	0	0	0	1	0
Savourer	0	0	0	0	1	0
Remarquer	0	0	0	0	1	0
Subjuguer	0	0	0	0	1	0
Se démarquer	0	0	0	1	0	0
Marquer	0	0	0	1	0	0
Capter	0	0	0	0	0	1
Total	10	5	26	7	21	6

4.3.1.4. POSITIVELY LOADED NOUNS

4.3.1.4.1. TYPES AND FREQUENCY OF NOUNS

Finally, the results show that 31 positively loaded nouns appear in compliments on skills. These devices are used by the participants of both groups to reinforce some of the other types of devices mentioned above. Some of the nouns thus occur in metaphorical structures. Although these devices appear with a very low percentage, their combination with other positive evaluation markers contributes to the face flattering aspect of the compliment. The nouns identified in the Cameroonian data include *festin* 'feast' (2 examples), *délice* 'delicacy' (1 token) as in (11), *merveilles* 'marvel' (1 instance), *chef* 'master chef' (1 occurrence), *cordon bleu* 'cordon bleu chef[27]' (2 examples) as in (12), *gentillesse* 'kindness' (1 token), *plaisir* 'pleasure' (1 instance), *talent* (6 occurrences), *homme du match* 'man of the match' (1 example), *spectacle* (1 instance), *champion* (1 token), *star* (1 example), *courage* (3 occurrences), *inspiration* (1 instance), *intelligence* (1 example), *sagesse* 'wisdom' (1 instance), *modèle* 'example / role model' (1 token).

11) Merci c'était un **délice**. [M, CMF]
    'Thanks. It was a **delicacy**.'

12) Vous êtes **un cordon bleu** ! Le repas était bon et très délicieux. [M, CMF]
    'You are **a cordon bleu chef**. The food was really delicious.'

The repertoire of positive nouns used by the Canadian respondents include: *talent* (1 example), *MVP* 'Most Valuable Player' (1 token), *idole* 'idol' (2 occurrences) and *prof* 'teacher' (1 instance). The Cameroonian participants obviously use more positively loaded nouns to reinforce their compliments than the Canadians do.

4.3.1.4.2. SITUATIONAL DISTRIBUTION OF NOUNS

The repertoire of the positively loaded nouns presented above gives a hint about their distribution across the three situations, as can be seen in Table 21.

---

[27] 'Cordon bleu' is used to describe cooking of very high quality. A 'cordon bleu chef' is a skilled cook or the main cook in a restaurant.

4.3. LEXICAL AND STYLISTIC DEVICES IN HEAD ACTS

Table 21: Situational distribution of positively loaded nouns in Cameroonian and Canadian compliments on skills

Positively loaded nouns	Meal		Sports		Presentation	
	CMF	CF	CMF	CF	CMF	CF
Festin	2	0	0	0	0	0
Délice	1	0	0	0	0	0
Merveilles	1	0	0	0	0	0
Chef	1	0	0	0	0	0
Cordon bleu	2	0	0	0	0	0
Gentillesse	1	0	0	0	0	0
Plaisir	1	0	0	0	0	0
Talent	0	0	6	1	0	0
L'homme du match	0	0	1	0	0	0
Spectacle	0	0	1	0	0	0
Champion	0	0	1	0	0	0
Star	0	0	1	0	0	0
Courage	0	0	0	0	3	0
Inspiration	0	0	0	0	1	0
Intelligence	0	0	0	0	1	0
MVP du match	0	0	0	1	0	0
Idole	0	0	0	2	0	0
Prof	0	0	0	0	0	1
Total	9	0	10	4	7	1

4.3.2. SYNTACTIC AND STYLISTIC DEVICES

The devices found in both data sets have either mitigating or intensifying functions. Table 22 and Figure 10 present a breakdown of the types and frequency of syntactic modifiers in both data sets.

Table 22: Distribution of syntactic devices in Cameroonian and Canadian compliments on skills

	Cameroon	Canada
Intensifying devices	16 (47.06%)	10 (71.43%)
Mitigating devices	18 (52.94%)	4 (28.57%)
Total	34 (100%)	14 (100%)

4. Compliments On Skills

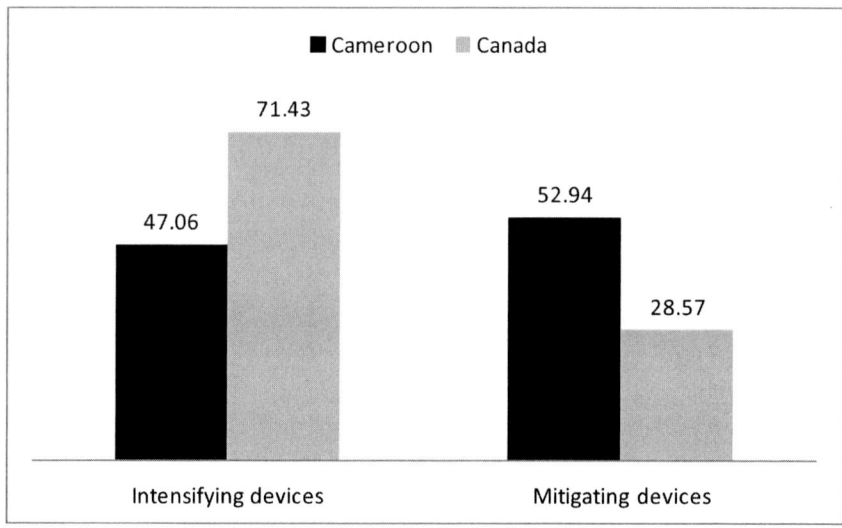

Figure 10: Distribution of syntactic devices in Cameroonian and Canadian compliments on skills

As shown in Table 10 and Figure 2, the participants of both groups adopt opposite choices in the use of stylistic/syntactic devices. The Cameroonians use devices to mitigate compliments slightly more than the intensifying ones, contrary to the Canadians, who by far prefer intensifying devices. Apart from these quantitative differences, it was found that the types of devices chosen by the Cameroonians are much more varied and complex than those appearing in the Canadian responses. The Cameroonian participants employ 16 intensifying devices and 18 mitigating devices, while the Canadian respondents make use of 10 intensifying syntactic devices and 4 mitigating devices. Nine sub-types of stylistic devices are identified in the Cameroonian responses, whereas the Canadian respondents employ only four sub-types. A look at the intensifying devices and, more specifically, the comparative devices reveals that, while the Cameroonian participants exclusively employ comparative structures, the Canadians make use of comparative as well as metaphorical structures. The intensifying devices found in both data sets are listed and explained below.

- *Comparative devices:* The respondents make use of these devices to indicate that the complimented topic is the best ever. Here are some examples from the data.

13) *Je n'ai jamais goutté d'aussi bon plat.* [M, CMF]
    'I have never had such an appetizing meal.'
14) *Tu as joué comme une reine.* [S, CF]
    'You played like a queen.'
15) *J'ai jamais vu quelqu'un patiner d'même.* [S, CF]
    'I have never seen someone skate like that.'
- *Hyperbolic expressions:* These structures are employed to reinforce the illocutionary force of the compliment. More precisely, the attested expressions serve to verbalize the following aspects:

Total success or engagement in achieving the complimented object as in (16), (17) and (18).

16) *Vous avez **assuré à fond**.* [S, CMF]
    'You gave it your best shot.'
17) *J'ai tout vu **ce que j'attendais de toi**.* [S, CMF]
    'I saw everything I expected from you.'
18) *Tu as capté mon attention **du début à la fin**.* [P, CF]
    'You captured my attention **from the beginning to the end**.'

(Total) satisfaction of the speaker with the situation as in (19), (20) and (21).

19) *J'ai pris du plaisir à vous observer.* [S, CMF]
    'I had pleasure in watching you.'
20) *J'ai savouré **chacune des secondes** de ta présentation.* [P, CMF]
    'I enjoyed **each second** of your presentation.'
21) *Il avait **le goût qu'il faut**.* [M, CF]
    'It had **the taste it had to have**.'
- *Devices expressing eagerness or sincerity.* These expressions are characterized by the use of verbs like *devoir* 'must'; *tenir à* + verb (infinitive) ('to (really) want to'), *vouloir* 'to want to' employed in the present/past tense or conditional and reinforced in some cases by *vraiment*. Some of these structures contain other verbs or verbal constructions employed to stress the sincerity of the compliment or to prepare the ground for an upcoming compliment, as shown in the examples below.

22) *Je tenais vraiment à vous féliciter.* [S, CMF]
    'I really wanted to congratulate you.'
23) *Salut, j'ai regardé le match et **je dois t'avouer que** ton jeu m'a impressionné.* [S, CMF]
    'Hi, I watched the match and **I must admit that** your play style impressed me.'
24) *Salut toi, on se connait pas, mais **je veux te dire que** ta présentation était vraiment bonne.* [P, CF]
    'Hi there, we don't know each other, but **I want to tell you that** your presentation was really good.'
25) *Je ne te connais pas beaucoup, mais **je vais prendre ce temps-ci pour te dire que** tu as fait un travail remarquable.* [P, CF]
    'I don't know you very well, but **I'll take this time to tell you that** you did a remarkable job.'

In order to soften their compliments the participants employ the following mitigating devices, such as *on dirait que / on peut dire que* 'one could/can say that', *je crois que* 'I think that', *je trouve (que)* 'I think/find that'. These devices aim at softening the content of the compliment, by making it appear as the point of view of the speaker or a general point of view. Here are some examples from the data.

26) ***On dirait que*** *c'est un prof qui parle.* [P, CF]
    '**One could say** you sound like a professor.'
27) ***On peut dire que*** *vous êtes l'homme du match.* [S, CMF]
    '**One can say** you are the man of the match.'

Aimer + conditional: This device is only used by the Cameroonian participants. An example from the data is (28).

28) ***J'aimerais te dire que*** *tu as été parfait tout au long de ton exposé.* [P, CMF]
    '**I would like to tell you that** you were perfect during your presentation.'

Consultative devices: The expression t *u sais* 'you know' is used by a Cameroonian to get the attention of the addressee, as can be seen in (29).

29) *Oh la la!tu sais j'ai bien aimé ta façon de jouer et tu as un grand talent.* [S, CMF]
'Oh lala! '**You know** I really liked your play style and you have a great talent.'

Cost minimizers: This group comprises compliment minimizing devices with *juste* 'just' used to minimize any threat to the addressee's face (time, privacy, etc.) (e.g. *C'est juste pour vous dire que.* 'It's just to tell you that.'), as in (30) and (31).

30) *Salut! je voudrais juste vous dire que votre travail était bien et m'a beaucoup plu.* [P, CMF]
'Hi, **I just wanted to tell you that** your work was good and really pleased me.'

31) *Yo, j'voulais juste te dire que j'ai VRAIMENT aimé ton exposé.* [P, CF]
'Yo, **I just wanted to tell you that** I REALLY loved your presentation.'

Expressions of embarrassment: By using this strategy, the speaker recognizes the face threat posed by the compliment to a stranger and hopes that by explicitly acknowledging the embarrassment the recipient would downplay it, as in the following example.

32) *Vous avez fait une excellente présentation, **mais je ne savais pas comment vous dire**.* [P, CMF]
'You gave an excellent presentation, **but I didn't know how to tell you that**.'

Preparators: These devices are employed to indicate the reason for the interaction, thus preparing the ground for an upcoming compliment. As can be seen in (33) such devices may be used as negative politeness strategies to reinforce the preceding apology.

33) *S'il te plait! excuse-moi, **mais c'est pour la présentation de tout à l'heure** tu as été excellent.* [P, CMF]
'Sorry, excuse me, **but it is about the presentation you just gave**, you were excellent.'

4.4. EXTERNAL MODIFICATION

4.4.1. TYPES AND FREQUENCY OF EXTERNAL MODIFICATION

Overall, the Cameroonian respondents use 162 and the Canadian participants 95 external modifications, which appear either before or after the head acts. Ten different types/groups of external modification devices are identified in the data: pre-compliments, thanks, wishes, comments, questions, advice, requests, promise, joy, and joke. These acts are used either to mitigate or to intensify the head acts, depending on situational variables such as topic (i.e. type of complimented skills), social distance, and power distance. Table 23 shows the types and frequencies of external modifications used by informants of the two groups.

Table 23: Distribution of external modification devices in Cameroonian and Canadian compliments on skills

External modification type		Cameroon	Canada
Pre-compliments		75 (46.30%)	36 (37.89%)
Post-compliments	Thanks	40 (24.69%)	29 (30.53%)
	Wishes	19 (11.73%)	10 (10.53%)
	Comments	11 (6.79%)	6 (6.32%)
	Questions	6 (3.70%)	4 (4.21%)
	Advice	5 (3.09%)	3 (3.16%)
	Requests	4 (2.47%)	3 (3.16%)
	Promise	1 (0.62%)	3 (3.16%)
	Joy	1 (0.62%)	0
	Joke	0	1 (1.05%)
Total		162 (100%)	95 (100%)

With regard to the general use of pre-posed and post-posed acts, Figure 11 shows similar choices by the respondents of both groups. As a matter of fact the Canadian and the Cameroonian speakers of French produce much more post-compliments than pre-compliments. However, the frequency of post-compliments in the Canadian data is much higher than that in the Cameroonian responses.

4.4. EXTERNAL MODIFICATION

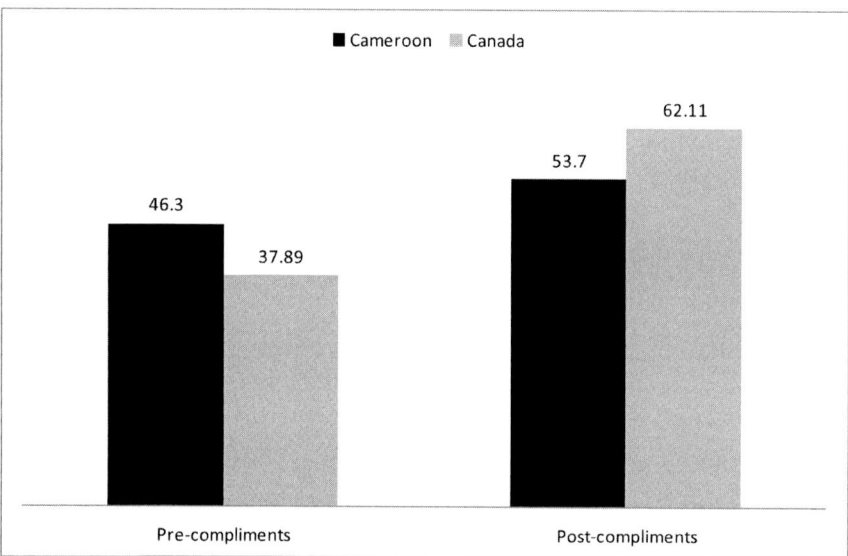

Figure 11: Distribution of pre-compliments and post-compliments in each variety of French

The distribution of the types of supportive moves in both corpora is summarized in Table 23 above and Figure 12 below.

Table 23 and Figure 12 show that the three most frequent external modification devices in both varieties of French are pre-compliments, thanks and wishes.

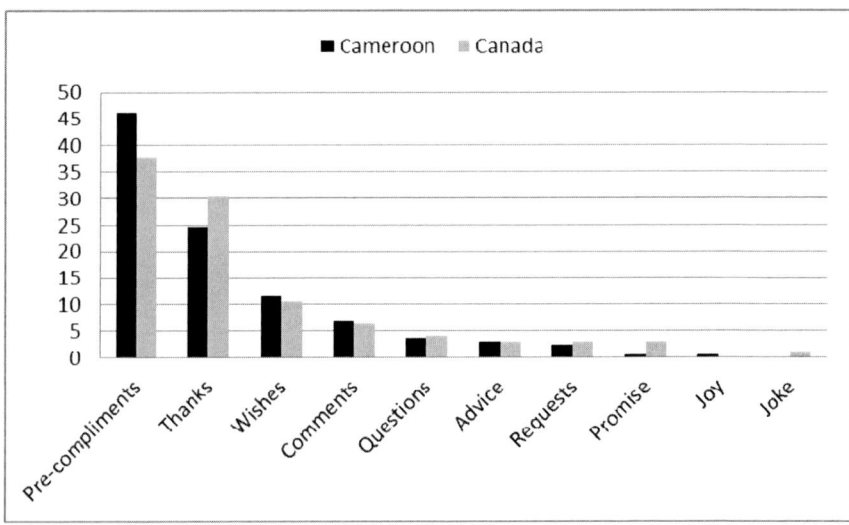

Figure 12: Distribution of external modification devices in both varieties of French

4.4.2. PRE-COMPLIMENTS

4.4.2.1. NOMINAL ADDRESS TERMS

Overall, the participants of both groups employ 41 address terms: 31 by the Cameroonians and 10 by the Canadians. The address terms in both varieties occur mostly in the meal situation (14 examples). The Cameroonian respondents show a more significant variety of address terms than the Canadian informants. The Cameroonians use terms of respect (6 instances) such as *madame/monsieur* 'madam/sir', kinship terms (7 tokens) such as (*chers / mes chers / les) parents* '(dear/my dear/the) parents'; *papa/maman* 'dad/mom' and terms of friendship, affection, closeness (18 occurrences) such as *(cher) camarade* '(dear) friend' , *ma chérie* 'my darling' , *mon pote* 'buddy' , *ce gars* 'this boy/man' , *garcon* 'boy'. The Canadian respondents choose terms of respect (5 instances) such as *monsieur/madame*, a first name *Josée* and friendship and solidarity terms (4 examples) such as *hey man, yo, hey toi* 'hey you' , *hey bravo*. It should be noted that the use of kinship terms with the parents of a friend by the Cameroonian informants is a means of flattering the positive face of (superior) addressees, since their seniority and biological status (status of parents) is explicitly recognized. In this case, such kinship terms reinforce the compliment offered. This feature does not occur in the Canadian data. This result seems to suggest a major difference in the perception of social rapports and asymmetrical relationships in both cultures. While the Cameroonian participants show explicit respect and deference to their friend's parents (the compliment recipients) and treat them as parents, the Canadian informants do not express, at least at the level of address forms, any deference.

4.4.2.2. INTERJECTIONS

Twenty-one interjections appear in the data. The Canadian respondents use more interjections (18 tokens) to express surprise or pleasure prior to the core compliments than their Cameroonian counterparts, who only produce three interjections. The interjections found in the Canadian compliments are *wow* (9 tokens), *Hum* (1 example), *Mhm* (1 instance), *Ah* (1 example), *hey* (3 tokens), *Ooohh* (1 example), *Oh my god* (1 occurrence), *Shit* (1 example). The Cameroonian informants use the following interjections: *Ummm* (1 instance), *Oh* (1 token) and *Oh la la* (1 example). Major differences appear in the situational distribution of these attention getters. While the Canadian participants employ several interjections in the presentation situation (9 instances), the Cameroonian respondents use none. The presentation situation also reveals noteworthy differences between the Cameroonian and Canadian responses. Here the Cameroonians show more creativity and variety in the use of greetings and apologies as compared to the other two situations.

4.4.2.3. GREETINGS

The use of greetings shows considerable differences between the Cameroonian and the Canadian participants: while the Cameroonian participants use greetings 27 times, only one Canadian informant employs a greeting formula. The Cameroonians used this strategy to introduce compliments in the sports (9 tokens) and presentation situations (18 examples), two situations where social distance prevails. The Cameroonian participants use the following greeting forms: *Salut* 'Hi' (9 examples); *Bonjour* 'Good morning' (2 tokens); *Bonjour monsieur/madame* 'Good morning sir/madam' (3 occurrences); *comment tu vas?* 'how are you doing?' (1 token); *Salut jeune fille/mademoiselle/chère(e) ami(e)/camarade* 'Hi young lady/miss dear friend / buddy' (6 occurrences) ; *Bonjour Salut* 'Good morning, hi' (2 examples); *Bonsoir toi / champion / compagnon / cher camarade* 'Good evening you / champion / buddy / dear friend' (4 instances); *Stenlai*[28] , *bonjour* 'Stenlai, good morning' (1 token). As the examples show, one or two greeting formulas appear alone before a single, double or triple head as in (34) and (35) or is accompanied by either address forms as in (36) and (37) or other supportive moves, such as *apologies* as in (38) and *self-Introductions* as in (37).

34) **Salut** *j'aimerais te dire que tu as fait un bon travail.* [P, CMF]
   '**Hi**, I would like to tell you that you did a great job.'
35) **Salut, comment tu vas?** *Tu as été magnifique tout à l'heure – sérieux, tu m'as presque*
   subjugué. [P, CMF]
   '**Hi, how are you?** You were magnificent, seriously, you almost charmed me.'
36) **Salut chère(e) ami(e).** *Ton exposé a été extraordinaire. J'ai savouré chacune des secondes de ta presentation. Bravo!* [P, CMF]
   '**Hi, dear friend.** Your presentation was extraordinary. I enjoyed every second of your presentation. Bravo!'
37) **Bonjour cher camarade** *, j'aimerais beaucoup te connaître et profiter de l'occasion pour te dire que tu es été superbe.* [P, CMF]
   '**Good morning, buddy**, I would really like to know you and use the opportunity to tell you that you were amazing.'
38) **Salut moi c'est malaica** *et j'ai vraiment apprécié ta présentation.* [P, CMF]
   '**Hi, my name's Malaica** and I really enjoyed your presentation.'
39) **Salut!** *C'est vrai qu'on n'a pas eu l'occasion de causer mais j'ai trouvé votre présentation excellente.* [P, CMF]
   '**Hi! It's true that we didn't have an opportunity to talk**, but I found your presentation excellent.'

4.4.2.4. SELF-INTRODUCTION

Self-introductions are exclusively used by the Cameroonian participants, and most of the examples (3 out of 4) are produced in the presentation

---
[28] The first name was used by the respondent to address the compliment recipient.

situation, where the speaker combines this strategy with greeting formulas, as in (40).

40) *Bonjour toi! je m'appelle Muriel au fait je voulais juste te dire que j'ai beaucoup aimé ta prestation en classe.* [P, CMF]
'Good morning you! **my name is Muriel**, in fact I just wanted to tell you that I liked your performance very much.'

4.4.2.5. APOLOGIES

The apologies in the Cameroonian data appear in the sports (n= 4) and presentation situations (n= 6), two situations where compliments are offered to strangers (i.e. to an unknown player, and to a classmate the compliment giver is not familiar with). This is an indication that some of the Cameroonians and Canadians consider compliments in these two situations to be face threatening acts that they mitigate, by means of appropriate external modifiers like apologies or greetings. The most frequently used forms to express apology in both varieties are *Excuse-moi* 'Excuse me' and *S'il te plait* 'Please'. However, some respondents in both groups use apologies in which they directly acknowledge the fact that they don't know the addressee that much and thus indirectly allude to the potential threat of the compliment as in (41) and (42).

41) *Je sais que je ne te connais pas beaucoup, mais j'ai trouvé que ta présentation était vraiment intéressante.* [P, CF]
'**I know that I don't know you that much,** but I found that your presentation was very interesting.'

42) *Salut! C'est vrai qu'on n'a pas eu l'occasion de causer, mais j'ai trouvé votre présentation excellente.* [P, CMF]
'Hi! **It's true that we haven't had the opportunity to talk**, but I found your presentation excellent.'

Of the seventeen apologies found, ten are employed before compliments by the Cameroonian respondents and seven by their Canadian counterparts. The Cameroonian apologies are realized as follows: *Excusez-moi* (4 tokens); *S'il te/vous plait!* (4 examples); *Pardon de te perturber* 'Excuse me for disturbing you' (1 instance); *C'est vrai qu'on n'a pas eu l'occasion de causer* 'It's true that we have not had the opportunity to talk' (1 token). The Canadian apology forms are: *Excuse moi* (2 occurrences); *Je sais que je ne te connais pas (beaucoup)* (2 tokens); *On se connait pas* 'We don't know each other' (1 example); *Scuse-moi si je t'ai pas beaucoup parlé* 'Excuse me if I haven't talked to you much' (1 token). Generally, the apology appears before a single head or a double head act, and could be intensified by a greeting or other supportive moves appearing after the direct compliments as in the following examples.

43) ***S'il vous plait**, juste pour vous dire que votre exposé était sans reproche.* [P, CMF]
'**Excuse me**, just to tell you that your presentation was without fault.'

44) *Bonjour compagnon.* ***Pardon de te perturber** mais j'aimerais te dire que tu as été parfait tout au long de ton exposé et je conte m'intégrer dans ton groupe la prochaine fois qu'il y aura encore exposé.* [P, CMF]
'Good morning, buddy. **I am sorry for bothering you**, but I would like to tell you that you were perfect during your presentation and I intend to join your group the next time we have another presentation.'

4.4.3. POST-COMPLIMENTS

4.4.3.1. THANKS

Table 11 above shows that thanks are the second most preferred means of external modification by the Cameroonian (40 instances) and the Canadian participants (29 tokens). Similarities are also found with regard to the positions and situational distributions of this supportive act. The Cameroonian and Canadian informants mostly make use of thanking in the meal situation, where the combination of a single head and the supportive move is the most frequent pattern. Generally, thanking occurs before a compliment (21 instances in the Cameroonian corpus vs. 23 tokens in the Canadian data). In the Cameroonian data, there are also instances in which thanking appears after a single head (3 examples) or is combined with two head acts, appearing either before (6 tokens) or after (2 examples) the double head. In very few cases are thanks combined with a compliment and another supportive move. In the Canadian data, thanking also occurs after a single head act (4 occurrences) or is associated with a single head and another supportive move (1 token). There is no instance where gratitude is combined with a double head. The following examples from both data sets are illustrative of the major positions of thanks with respect to the single or double head.

45) *C'était délicieux, **merci bien**.* [M, CMF]
'It was delicious. **Thanks very much.**'
46) *C'était vraiment bon, **merci**!* [M, CF]
'It was really delicious. **Thanks.**'

4.4.3.2. WISHES

In the Cameroonian data, the attested wishes are mostly used in the sports situation (9 instances of 19), where they occur after single or double head acts. In the Canadian data, this external modification device is mostly (4 examples of 10) employed in compliments on the addressee's oral presentation. The wishes expressed are either hearer-oriented or speaker-oriented. In other words, the compliment givers either express the wish to perform as well as the recipients or they express the wish/hope that the compliment receivers continue to perform well. Representative examples from both data sets are shown below.

47) *Bonjour moi c'est José, j'ai vraiment admiré votre manière de jouer, je vous donne tous mes encouragements **et j'espère que vous irez plus loin**.* [S, CMF]
'Good morning, I am José, I really admired your play style, you have all my encouragements **and I hope you'll go very far.**'

48) *C'était une très bonne présentation, **j'espère avoir une aussi bonne note que toi**.* [P, CF]
'That was a very good presentation, **I hope I'll have a good grade like you.**'

4.4.3.3. COMMENTS

They are mostly employed in the presentation situation by the Cameroonian participants (6 out of 11) and are evenly used in the three situations by the Canadian informants (2 examples in each situation). Common examples from Cameroonians' and Canadians' responses include (49) and (50).

49) *Tu étais très bon ce matin. **Je tenais à te le dire**.* [P, CF]
'You were very good this morning. **I wanted to let you know that.**'

50) *Vous avez fait une excellente présentation **mais je ne savais pas comment vous dire**.* [P, CMF]
'You did an excellent presentation **but I didn't know how to tell you that.**'

4.4.3.4. QUESTIONS

Questions are used differently by the participants of both groups. The Cameroonian informants employ questions six times, while the Canadian participants use questions in four instances. The results show that although most of the questions in the Cameroonian data appear after the head acts, there are occurrences of questions as pre-compliments by Cameroonians and mostly by the Canadians. Examples from both data sets include the following samples.

51) *Ton travail était parfait.* **Pendant combien de temps l'as-tu constitué**? [P, CMF]
'Your work was perfect. **How long did it take you to prepare for it?**'

52) *Monsieur,* **quel est le nom de votre mets**, *car votre repas est savoureux.* [M, CF]
'Sir, **what is the name of your meal**, the meal is delicious.'

53) **Comment tu as fait?** *J'ai vraiment apprécié ta façon de faire et surtout ton courage.* [P, CMF]
'**How did you do it?** I really loved the way you did it and your courage above all.'

4.4.3.5. ADVICE AND ENCOURAGEMENTS

The respondents of both groups employ advice/encouragement to modify their compliments. By using this supportive move, the speaker tells the addressee to keep up the good work. In other words, this supportive move serves as an intensifier, since it indicates that the respondents are also overtly encouraging the addressee. The respondents of both groups employ this supportive move to modify their compliments exclusively in the sports situation, with similar percentages. The advice/encouragement generally occur after a compliment. Common examples from the data are given below.

54) *T'as vraiment bien joué ce soir,* **continue comme ça**. [S, CF]
'You really played well this evening, **keep up the good work!**'

55) *J'admire votre façon de jouer au football et* **moi à ta place j'en ferais d'avantage pour** *évoluer dans un club en étranger.* [S, CMF]
'I admire your play style in soccer **and if I were you, I would train more in order to play in a club abroad.**'

4.4. EXTERNAL MODIFICATION

4.4.3.6. REQUESTS

This external modifier is used to ask for information, help, or anything that would help the speaker to stay in contact with the compliment receiver (e.g. phone number, autograph, etc.). The respondents of both French varieties do not show any statistically significant difference in the use of this strategy (4 examples in the Cameroonian corpus vs. 3 instances in the Canadian data), and this supportive move is most frequent in the sports situation in both data sets. Some of the requests are also intensified by another supportive move (e.g. *promise* or *advice*), as shown in the following examples.

56) *Comment tu fais pour être aussi bon?* **Il faut que tu m'apprennes.** *Je vais revenir à tous tes match.* [S, CF]
'What do you do to be so good? **You have to teach me.** I'll attend all your games.'

57) *Vous jouez très bien, continuez dans la même lancée,* **un orthographe SVP si possible votre numéro.**[S, CMF]
'You play very well, keep up the good work, **can I please have an autograph, your phone number if possible?**'

4.4.3.7. PROMISE

By using this external modification, the speaker makes a promise to the compliment receiver in connection with the compliment topic (e.g. to pay another visit, to come pick up the recipe, etc.). This strategy is used in one instance in the Cameroonian data and three times in the Canadian data. As the examples below show, the speech act of promising functions as an intensifying device, by which the speaker shows a very strong interest in the complimented object.

58) *Merci pour votre repas il était vraiment bien,* **je passerai pendre la recette pour moi.** [M, CMF]
'Thanks for the meal, it was really good, **I'll come pick up the recipe for myself.**'

59) **Je vais venir souvent.** *C'est très bon chez vous. C'est quoi la recette? C'est un des meilleurs plats que j'ai jamais mangés.* [M, CF]
'**I'll come by very often.** The food tastes very good here. What is the recipe? It is one of the best dishes I have ever had.'

4.4.3.8. OTHER EXTERNAL MODIFICATIONS

There is one example of *expressing joy* in the Cameroonian data and one instance of *joking* in the Canadian data. Both strategies function as positive politeness devices. In the Cameroonian example, the speaker expresses joy in having watched the match, thus reinforcing the preceding compliment. The Canadian speaker uses a jocular expression (intensified by laughter) to tease the compliment receiver.

60) *Merci pour le spectacle, vous avez merveilleusement joué* **et j'étais vraiment heureux d'avoir assisté à ce match.** [S, CMF]
'Thanks for the performance, you played very well and **I was very happy to have watched the game.**'

61) *Ton exposé était bon.* **Mais le mien était meilleur [rire].** [P, CF]
'Your presentation was good. **But mine was better (laughter).**'

4.4.4. SITUATIONAL DISTRIBUTION OF EXTERNAL MODIFICATION

As Table 24 below shows, there are differences in distribution of supportive moves across the three situations in both French varieties.

Table 24: Situational distribution of supportive moves in Cameroonian and Canadian compliments on skills

External modification		Meal		Sports		Presentation	
		CMF	CF	CMF	CF	CMF	CF
Pre-compliments		12	6	24	9	39	21
Post-compliments	Thanks	39	28	1	1	0	0
	Wishes	3	0	9	6	7	4
	Comments	3	2	2	2	6	2
	Questions	1	2	1	2	4	0
	Advice	0	0	5	3	0	0
	Requests	1	0	3	3	0	0
	Promise	1	2	0	1	0	0
	Joy	0	0	1	0	0	0
	Joke	0	0	0	0	0	1
Total		60	40	46	27	56	28

In both varieties of French, pre-compliments are mostly used with compliments on the oral presentation situation, while thanks occur much more in compliments on a meal and not at all in the oral presentation situation. This result suggests a strong tendency to accompany compliments on food with the expression of gratitude in both varieties of French.

4.5. SUMMARY OF THE FINDINGS

The results obtained in this chapter show similarities and differences in the ways Cameroonian and Canadian speakers of French offer compliments on skills.

Move structure and head acts

The Canadians employ the 'head act only' pattern much more frequently than their Cameroonian counterparts. The 'head act(s) + supportive move(s)' pattern is more common in the Cameroonian than in the Canadian data. The 'supportive only' pattern is attested only in the Cameroonian data set. The informants of both groups employ several head acts, albeit with some differences. While the Cameroonians prefer double head acts, the Canadian participants mostly choose single head acts. The results reveal that indirect realizations of head acts occur only in the Cameroonian data set. The analysis also reveals some differences with regard to situational distributions of the head act strategies.

Lexical and stylistic devices

It was found that the compliments in both data contain a very high number of adjectives. The Canadian participants use more adjectival compliments (95 adverbs in 116 compliments, or 81.89%) than the Cameroonian informants (98 adverbs in 162 compliments, i.e. 60.49%). Positively loaded verbs, more precisely verbs that express liking, admiration, surprise, know-how, etc., appear in the Cameroonian data much more than in the Canadian responses. This trend is also observed in the use of positively loaded nouns to reinforce compliments. With regard to stylistic/syntactic devices, the results show that the Cameroonian participants almost produce the same number of intensifying and mitigating devices, while the Canadian respondents make more use of intensifying devices. In all, the repertoire of positive evaluation markers in the Cameroonian data is larger and more varied.

External modification

The results here reveal that the participants of both groups make use of many types of preparatory acts and post-posed supportive moves. Overall, the most preferred external modification devices in both data sets are, in decreasing order of frequency, pre-compliments, thanking, wishing, and commenting. The analysis of pre-compliments shows that the Cameroonian informants mostly use greetings and self-introductions whereas only one Canadian response contains a greeting formula. This result may indicate differences in the perception of compliments to strangers. By employing so many greetings to open their compliments, the Cameroonian participants seem to consider compliments to unknown people as face threatening acts that need to be softened. To them, giving a direct compliment in such situations entails the risk of provoking negative responses. The greetings are therefore employed as a face-saving strategy. The Canadian informants also perceive this fact, but mostly prefer other types of pre-compliments, namely apologies and address terms, as mitigating devices for compliments to strangers. In general, the use of external modifiers shows that the participants of both groups consider complimenting as a complex activity that comprises other speech acts. The abundant use of external modifications may indicate that the compliments served as pretexts to reach other communication goals.

CHAPTER 5

COMPLIMENTS ON POSSESSIONS

This chapter describes patterns employed by the Cameroonian and Canadian French speakers to offer compliment possessions. The scenarios used to elicit examples from the informants of both groups focused on a) compliments on the (new) mobile phone of an unknown student, b) compliments on the (new) house / apartment of the speaker's friend / friend's parents, and c) compliments on the teacher's / professor's (new) car. In the mobile phone situation, the interlocutors have equal social status and they do not know each other [=P, +D]. The house situation is a case where the compliment giver and receiver have equal social status and know each other very well [=P, -D]. In the car situation, the addressee has a higher social status / power position and the interlocutors know each other as acquaintances [+P, =D].

The chapter treats the move structures (5.1) and head act strategies used in the realization of compliments (5.2). Lexical and stylistic devices found in the data are discussed in 5.3, while external modification patterns are described in 5.4. The summary of the findings is provided in 5.5.

5.1. MOVE-STRUCTURES IN THE REALIZATION OF COMPLIMENTS

The 94 participants provided 274 answers to the three questionnaire tasks. The Cameroonians produced 162[29] compliments: 53 compliments on the new mobile phone, 53 compliments on the friend's (parents') new house / apartment and 56 compliments on the teacher's new car. The Canadian

---
[29] Four responses were coded as wrong. The participants said what they would do in the indirect form (e.g. *je lui dirais que*. 'I would tell him/her that.'). We obtained 56 tokens (instead of 55) in the new car situation because one participant offered two examples.

5. Compliments On Possessions

informants provided 112[30] examples: 36 compliments on the new phone, 39 compliments on the friend's (parents') new house / apartment and 37 compliments on the teacher's new car. The compliments occur as head acts only, as combinations of head acts and supportive moves, or as supportive moves only. The distribution of the move structures is presented in Table 25 and Figure 13.

Table 25: Distribution of move structures in Cameroonian and Canadian compliments on possessions

	Cameroon	Canada
Head acts only	29 (17.90%)	38 (33.93%)
Head acts + supportive moves	129 (79.63%)	69 (61.61%)
Supportive moves only	4 (2.47%)	5 (4.46%)
Total	162 (100%)	112 (100%)

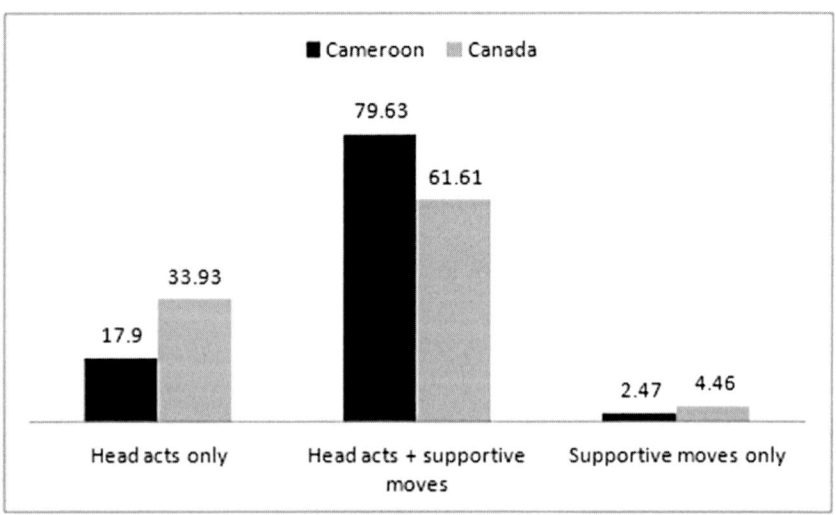

Figure 13: Distribution of move structures in Cameroonian and Canadian compliments on possessions

---

[30] Five examples were not included in the analysis because, as in the case of the Cameroonians, some informants used the descriptive mode in lieu of the direct responses.

Table 25 and Figure 13 indicate that the 'head acts + supportive moves' pattern is the most preferred in both data sets. This pattern appears much more in the Cameroonian (76.93%) than in the Canadian (61.61%) data. While 'head acts only' occurrences are the second most common patterns in Cameroon and Canadian French, the number of instances in the Cameroonian data is much lower (17.90%) than that in the Canadian (33.93%) corpus. The 'supportive moves only' examples are the least used in the both varieties of French.

5.2. HEAD ACTS

Of the 33 instances of head acts in the Cameroonian data set, 29 are direct head acts and 4 are indirect heads. The Canadian produce 43 occurrences of head acts of which 38 are direct and 5 are indirect.

The direct head acts in the Cameroonian data consist of 11 instances (33.33%) of single acts as in (1) and 18 examples (54.54%) of multiple heads. The category of compound compliments comprise 16 instances of double head acts as in (2) and 2 examples of triple head acts as in (3).

1) *Il est vraiment très beau ton téléphone.* [T[31], CMF]
   'Your phone is really very beautiful.'
2) *Quelle jolie maison, je n'ai jamais vu une aussi belle.* [H/A, CMF]
   'What a beautiful house, I have never seen such a beautiful one.'
3) *Bravo madame vous êtes une femme qui sait ce qu'elle veut. J'apprécie beaucoup votre véhicule.* [C, CMF]
   'Congratulations madam, you are a woman who knows what she wants. I like your car very much.'

The 38 direct head acts in the Canadian data set consist of 26 instances of single head acts as in (4) and 12 examples of multiple heads. The category of multiple heads comprise 10 instances of double head acts as in (5) and 2 occurrences of triple head acts as in (6).

4) *Nouveau char il est cool.* [C, CF]
   'Your / the new car is cool.'

---

[31] The following abbreviations will be used in the examples: T stands for examples from the 'Telephone' situation, H/A stands for examples from the *'House/Apartment'* situation and C stands for examples from the 'Car' situation.

5) *J'aime bien ton téléphone, il est cool avec toutes ces options.* [T, CMF]
   'I really love your phone, it is cool with all those options.'
6) *Quelle belle maison! Je suis vraiment impressionné, très bon achat.* [H/A, CF]
   'What a beautiful house! I am really impressed, very nice buy.'

The Canadians choose more single head acts than the Cameroonians. In the Cameroonian corpus, the single direct head acts are most common in the house situation, while the Canadian mostly use single direct heads in compliments on the teacher's new car. The double heads appear mostly in compliments on the house/apartment in the Cameroonian and the Canadian responses.

The Cameroonians produce 4 instances of indirect heads while the Canadians use 5 indirect heads. An instance of the indirect compliments in the Cameroonian data appears in the telephone situation and is realized in the form of a positively loaded question as in (7).

7) *Wow! qui t'a gâté avec cet option?* [T, CMF]
   'Wow, who spoiled you with that option?'

The example above functions as a conventional indirect compliment, since the interrogative structure contains a positively loaded verb *gâter* (*quelqu'un avec quelque chose)* 'to spoil somebody [with something]'. Thus, the question *qui t'a gâté comme ça?* has been conventionalized as an indirect form of admiration. Although some respondents may respond to the question by indicating the person who "spoiled them", the complimentary connotation of the question is generally understood. As the example shows, the positive connotation of the question is reinforced by the interjection *wow*. Generally, indirect compliments (on possessions) in the Cameroonian data contain positively loaded lexical devices such as *palais* 'palace' in (8) or are realized through the expression of the desire/wish to possess the complimented object as in (9).

8) *Dis-moi que tu habite maintenant le palais.* [H/A, CMF]
   'Tell me you now live in the palace.'
9) *Moi, j'aimerais avoir aussi une voiture identique à la votre.* [C, CMF]
   'I would also like to have a car identical to yours.'

In the Canadian corpus, the indirect compliments appear in various forms.

One pattern employed by a respondent in the car situation is to express the wish or the request to use/drive the car as in (10).

10) *J'espère que vous me laisserez conduire.* [C, CF]
'I hope you'll let me drive.'
11) *Combien elle a couté votre voiture, j'en veux une pareille.* [C, CF]
'How much did your car cost, I want to own one like that.'

Another way is to combine many speech acts as in (12) or the expression of desire with another speech act (e.g. a question) as in (13).

12) *Chanceux! Je désire ce téléphone depuis un ans! Je n'arrête jamais d'en parler à mes parents.* [T, CF]
'Lucky you, it's a year now that I want to have that phone. I can't stop talking to my parents about it.'
13) *Où tu l'as achetée? J'en veux un pareille!* [T, CF]
'Where did you buy it? I want to have one like that.'

In (13) the fact that the compliment giver desires the phone and has been talking about it is an indirect way of saying how worthy it is.

There are differences in the distribution of the direct and indirect heads across the three situations, as presented in Table 26.

Table 26: Situational distribution of head acts in compliments on possessions

Head act strategies	Telephone		House		Car	
	CMF	CF	CMF	CF	CMF	CF
Single heads	1	5	7	8	3	13
Double heads	2	1	8	5	6	4
Triple heads	0	0	0	1	2	1
Indirect heads	1	3	3	0	0	2
Total	4	9	18	14	11	20

5.3. LEXICAL AND STYLISTIC DEVICES IN HEAD ACTS

5.3.1. LEXICAL DEVICES

The Cameroonians use 336 lexical devices, consisting of 163 adjectives, 112 adverbs, 45 verbs and 16 nouns, while the Canadians employ 202 lexical devices, consisting of 99 adjectives, 68 adverbs, 34 verbs, and two nouns.

5.3.1.1. ADJECTIVES

5.3.1.1.1. TYPES AND FREQUENCY OF ADJECTIVES

The respondents of both groups use many different types of adjectives and there are differences with regard of the frequencies of these devices, as can be seen in Table 27.

Table 27: Frequency of adjectives in Cameroonian and Canadian compliments on possessions

	Cameroon	Canada
Beau / belle 'beautiful/nice'	77	52
Joli(e) 'beautiful/nice'	28	2
Optionné 'has many options'	2	0
Genial 'genius'	3	0
Puissant 'efficient/powerful'	1	0
Grand 'big'	3	4
Bon 'good'	3	5
Haute 'high'	1	0
Superbe 'superb'	2	1
Admirable	1	0
Cool	2	8
Mortel 'nice'	1	0
Blasant 'amazing'	1	0
Magnifique 'magnificent'	9	4
Cher 'expensive'	0	1
Original	0	1

5.3. LEXICAL AND STYLISTIC DEVICES IN HEAD ACTS

Nice	0	4
Chil	0	1
Remarquable 'remarkable'	0	1
Hot	0	1
Chanceux 'lucky'	0	5
Splendide 'splendid'	1	0
Sublime	1	0
Esthétique 'esthetical'	1	0
Ravissante 'charming'	1	1
Éblouissant 'stunning'	1	0
Chaleureuse 'warm'	1	0
Ouverte (à tous) 'open (to all)'	1	0
Impressionné 'impressed'	1	1
Confortable	1	0
Nianga 'pretty'	1	0
Immense	1	1
Spacieuse 'spacious'	1	2
Classe	3	0
Chic	1	0
Bien 'good'	3	0
Impressionnant 'impressive'	2	0
Super	2	0
Merveilleuse 'marvellous'	1	0
Grosse 'big/immense'	0	2
Vraie 'real'	0	1
Écoeurant 'nice'	0	1
Imposant 'impressive'	1	0
Discrète (couleur) 'unostentatious (colour)'	1	0
La meilleure 'the best'	1	0
Luxueuse 'luxurious'	1	0
Élégante 'elegant'	1	0
Luisante 'shining'	1	0

| Irréversible 'irreversible' | 1 | 0 |
| Total | 165 | 99 |

Table 27 shows that the most preferred adjective by the Cameroonians is *beau/belle* (77 examples of 165, i.e. 46.67%), the second most common is *joli(e)* (28 tokens of 165, i.e. 16.97%) and the third most frequent is *magnifique* 'magnificent' (9 instances or 5.45%). In the Canadian corpus *beau/belle* is by far the most common adjective. It is used in 52 examples (53.06%), the second most chosen is *cool* (8 examples or 8.16%), while *bon* and *chanceux* are, with five instances each (5.10%), the third most common adjectives in Canadian compliments on possessions. The Cameroonians demonstrate more expressivity and creativity in the use of adjectives. Their repertoire contains several adjectives with very strong positive connotations (e.g. *éblouissant, magnifique, sublime*) and some of the adjectives are neologisms formed by means of derivation (e.g. *optionné* 'has many options' derives from the noun *option* as in (14)), semantic shift (e.g. the adjective *blasant* 'amazing' is derived from the verb *blaser* 'to render insensitive' as in (15)), the negatively loaded adjective *mortel* is employed to qualify the complimented object as extraordinary/awesome as in (16)), or borrowing (e.g. the word *nianga* nice/beautiful' was borrowed from indigenous languages). Some of the Canadian adjectives are also results of semantic shift (e.g. *écoeurant* which literally means *disgusting* in international French is used in Canadian French as a positively loaded adjective meaning 'nice' as in (17)) or borrowing (the Canadians mostly borrow adjectives from English: e.g. *nice, hot* (as in (18)), *cool, chil*.

14) *Wow, quel beau téléphone! [...], il est très beau et **optionné**.* [T, CMF]
    'Wow, what a beautiful phone! [...], it's very beautiful and **has many options**.'
15) *Juste pour te dire que ton phone est vraiment **blasant**.* [T, CMF]
    'Just to tell you that your phone is really **amazing**.'
16) *C'est pas possible ton téléphone est **mortel**. Tu l'as depuis quand?* [T, CMF]
    'It's not possible your phone is **awesome**. Since when do you have it?

5.3. LEXICAL AND STYLISTIC DEVICES IN HEAD ACTS

17) *Wow, c't'écœurant! T'es chanceux d'habiter là.* [H/A, CF]
    'Wow, it's **beautiful**! You are lucky to live here.'
18) *C'est trop **hot** ton cell.* [T, CF]
    'Your cell phone is extremely **beautiful**.'

5.3.1.1.2. SITUATIONAL DISTRIBUTION OF ADJECTIVES

The distribution of the adjectives differs across the three situations in the two varieties of French, as presented in Table 28.

Table 28: Situational distribution of adjectives in compliments on possessions

Adjectives	Telephone		House		Car	
	CMF	CF	CMF	CF	CMF	CF
Beau/belle	22	5	24	26	31	21
Joli(e)	12	0	7	1	9	1
Optionné	2	0	0	0	0	0
Genial	2	0	1	0	0	0
Puissant	1	0	0	0	0	0
Grand	1	0	2	3	0	1
Bon	1	1	1	1	1	3
Haute	1	0	0	0	0	0
Superbe	1	1	0	0	1	0
Admirable	1	0	0	0	0	0
Cool	1	4	1	1	0	3
Mortel	1	0	0	0	0	0
Blasant	1	0	0	0	0	0
Magnifique	0	2	6	2	3	0
Cher	0	1	0	0	0	0
Original	0	1	0	0	0	0
Nice	0	1	0	0	0	3
Chil	0	1	0	0	0	0
Remarquable	0	1	0	0	0	0
Hot	0	1	0	0	0	0
Chanceux	0	1	0	4	0	0
Splendide	0	1	0	4	0	0

Sublime	0	0	1	0	0	0
Esthétique	0	0	1	0	0	0
Ravissante	0	0	1	0	0	0
Éblouissant	0	0	1	0	0	0
Chaleureuse	0	0	1	0	0	0
Ouverte (à tous)	0	0	1	0	0	0
Impressionné	0	0	1	1	0	0
Confortable	0	0	1	0	0	0
Nianga	0	0	1	0	0	0
Immense	0	0	1	1	0	0
Spacieuse	0	0	1	2	0	0
Classe	0	0	2	0	1	0
Chic	0	0	1	0	0	0
Bien	0	0	3	0	0	0
Impressionnant	0	0	2	0	0	0
Super	0	0	1	0	1	0
Merveilleuse	0	0	1	0	0	0
Grosse	0	0	1	0	0	0
Vraie	0	0	0	1	0	0
Écoeurant	0	0	0	1	0	0
Imposant	0	0	0	0	1	0
(couleur) discrète	0	0	0	0	1	0
La meilleure	0	0	0	0	1	0
Luxueuse	0	0	0	0	1	0
Élégante	0	0	0	0	1	0
Luisante	0	0	0	0	1	0
Irréversible	0	0	0	0	1	0
Total	47	20	64	47	54	32

Table 28 shows that the Cameroonians and the Canadians mostly use adjectives in compliments on the addressee's (parents') house. While the number of *beau/belle*, the most frequent adjective in both data sets, is very high across the three situations in the Cameroonian data, this adjective appears in a very low percentage in compliments on the mobile phone by the

5.3. LEXICAL AND STYLISTIC DEVICES IN HEAD ACTS

Canadian informants. Although the respondents of both groups use many adjectives, most of these devices are limited to one situation or compliment topic.

5.3.1.2. ADVERBS

5.3.1.2.1. TYPES AND FREQUENCY OF ADVERBS

The types and frequencies of the adverbs found in both data sets are presented in Table 29.

Table 29: Types and frequency of adverbs in compliments on possessions

Adverbs	Cameroon	Canada
Vraiment 'really'	21	43
Très 'very'	50	6
Bien 'very'	2	2
Beaucoup 'very (much)'	14	5
Trop 'very/a lot'	14	8
Particulièrement 'particularly'	1	1
Assez 'very'	0	1
Super	1	2
Si 'very/really'	1	0
Grave 'really/very'	3	0
Étrangement 'strangely'	1	0
Bien plus 'much more'	1	0
Plus 'more'	4	1
Aussi 'so'	1	0
Tellement 'so'	0	3
Beaucoup plus 'much more'	0	1
Donc ben 'very'	0	1
Donc bien 'very'	0	1
Full	0	1
100 x (fois) plus 'hundred times more'	0	1
Total	114	68

The number of adverbs in the Cameroonian data is higher than in the

Canadian corpus. While *très* (50 examples of 114 or 43.86%) is by far the most adopted adverb by the Cameroonians, the Canadians mostly choose *vraiment* (43 occurrences of 68 or 63.23%), which appears as the second most common adverb in the Cameroonian data (21 instances of 114 or 18.42%). *Trop* (8 examples of 68 or 11.76%) is the second most common item in the Canadian responses. As can be seen in Table 29, the other adverbs have a very low number in both data sets and most of them are used only in one of the varieties of French under investigation: for instance, *grave, étrangement, si* appear only in the Cameroonian data while *don ben, donc bien, tellement* are found only in the Canadian compliments. With regard to the types of adverbs, it is clear that the Cameroonians display a more varied repertoire than the Canadians and adverbs ending with *–ment* are less frequent than other types of adverbs in the Cameroonian corpus. Finally, one adverb in the Canadian data, namely *full*, results from two processes, namely borrowing and semantic shift. The English adjective *full* is employed in Canadian French with the purpose of intensifying the compliment. In this case *full* could be replaced by *très* or *vraiment* as in (19). Some Cameroonian participants employ the adjective *grave* to express intensity in their compliments. As can be seen in example (20) below, *grave* appears at the end of the utterance.

19) *Ta maison est **donc ben** grande. C'est full_ beau.* [H/A, CF]
 'Your house is **really** big. It's **very** beautiful.'
20) *Ton phone me blase **grave**.* [T, CMF]
 'Your phone **really** amazes me.'

5.3.1.2.2. SITUATIONAL DISTRIBUTION OF ADVERBS

Table 30 below shows that, apart from the most two common adverbs, namely *vraiment* and *très*, in both data sets, several adverbs are situation specific. For instance, *beaucoup* is used in compliments on the unknown student's telephone and the teacher's new car by the participants of both groups, while this adverb is not found in compliments on the friend's (parents') house in the Cameroonian and the Canadian data. Also, the Cameroonians use many more adverbs in compliments on the teacher's car than in the other two situations. In the Canadian corpus, adverbs are much more

5.3. LEXICAL AND STYLISTIC DEVICES IN HEAD ACTS

used in the new house situation and less frequently in compliments on the teacher's new car.

Table 30: Situational distribution of adverbs in compliments on possessions

Adverbs	Telephone		House		Car	
	CMF	CF	CMF	CF	CMF	CF
Vraiment	5	10	7	15	9	9
Très	15	2	11	2	24	2
Bien	0	2	2	0	0	0
Beaucoup	4	2	0	0	10	3
Trop	1	4	3	4	10	0
Particulièrement	0	1	1	0	0	0
Assez	0	1	0	0	0	0
Super	1	0	0	2	0	0
Si	1	0	0	0	0	0
Grave	2	0	0	0	1	0
Étrangement	0	0	1	0	0	0
Bien plus	0	0	1	0	0	0
Plus	0	0	4	1	0	0
Aussi	0	0	1	0	0	0
Tellement	0	0	0	2	0	1
Beaucoup plus	0	0	0	1	0	0
Donc ben	0	0	0	1	0	0
Donc bien	0	0	0	1	0	0
Full	0	0	0	1	0	0
100 x (fois) plus	0	0	0	1	0	0
Total	29	22	31	31	54	15

5.3.1.3. VERBS
5.3.1.3.1. TYPES AND FREQUENCY OF VERBS

The participants of both groups make use of some verbs of liking and verb phrases in their compliments on possessions. Table 31 presents a breakdown of the types and frequencies of the verbs found in both sub-corpora.

Table 31: Types and frequency of verbs in compliments on possessions

Verbs and verbal phrases	Cameroon	Canada
Plaire 'to please'	17	0
Aimer 'to like'	3	25
Apprécier 'to like'	5	0
Admirer 'to admire'	1	0
Adorer 'to adore/love'	2	4
Envier 'to envy'	1	1
Kiffer 'to like'	2	0
Avoir de la valeur 'to have value'	1	0
Attirer / être attire par 'to attract or be attracted by'	3	0
Tuer 'to amaze/stupefy'	2	0
Gâter 'to give/do something good to somebody'	1	0
Blaser 'to amaze/stupefy'	1	0
Valoir cher 'to cost a lot'	0	1
Refléter la beauté 'to reflect the beauty'	0	1
Sortir de l'ordinaire 'to be extraordinary'	1	0
Convenir à 'to suit/fit'	1	0
Être à sa juste valeur 'to be valued'	1	0
Tirer 'to attrack/charm'	1	0
Déchirer 'to be nice'	1	0
Incarner ta personnalité 'to reflect your personality'	1	0
Total	45	32

Table 31 shows that the Cameroonians mostly prefer *plaire*, whereas the Canadians mostly choose *aimer*. The other verbs have very low frequencies in both varieties of French. Some verbs are found only in one of the two varieties of French. It can be seen in Table 31 that some of the attested verbs

5.3. LEXICAL AND STYLISTIC DEVICES IN HEAD ACTS 117

(mostly in the Cameroonian data set) are products of semantic shift. For example, the verb *tuer* is used to intensify compliments on the addressee's cell phone and could be paraphrased with *impressionner/ être impressionné par* 'to impress / be impressed by' as in (21). Another example is the verb *blaser*, which is employed to indicate the high quality of a possession and its positive impact on the speaker as in (21).

21) *Salut Man ton téléphone me **tue**.* [T, CMF]
    'Hi man your phone impresses me / I am impressed by your phone.'
22) *Wow ! Ton phone me **blase** grave.* [T, CMF]
    'Wow! Your phone really baffles me.'

5.3.1.3.2. SITUATIONAL DISTRIBUTION OF VERBS

There are also differences in the situational distribution of verbs, as can be seen in Table 32. The Cameroonians mostly use *plaire* with compliments on the addressee's new car. The most frequent verb in the Canadian data, *aimer*, appears in a very high percentage with compliments on the addressee's new phone.

Table 32: Situational distribution of verbs in compliments on possessions

Verbs and verbal phrases	Telephone		House		Car	
	CMF	CF	CMF	CF	CMF	CF
Plaire	5	0	2	0	10	0
Aimer	0	15	1	5	2	5
Apprécier	2	0	1	0	2	0
Admirer	1	0	0	0	0	0
Adorer	1	1	0	1	1	2
Envier	1	0	0	1	0	0
Kiffer	1	0	1	0	0	0
Avoir de la valeur	1	0	0	0	0	0
Attirer / être attiré par	3	0	0	0	0	0
Tuer	1	0	0	0	1	0
Gâter	1	0	0	0	0	0
Blaser	1	0	0	0	1	0
Valoir (cher)	0	1	0	0	0	0
Refléter la beauté	0	1	0	0	0	0

Sortir de l'ordinaire	0	0	1	0	0	0
Convenir à	0	0	0	0	1	0
Tirer	0	0	0	0	1	0
Déchirer	0	0	0	0	1	0
Incarner la personnalité	0	0	0	0	1	0
Total	18	18	6	7	21	7

5.3.1.4. POSITIVELY LOADED NOUNS
5.3.1.4.1. TYPES AND FREQUENCY OF NOUNS

The use of positively loaded nouns in compliments on skills is summarized in Table 33.

Table 33: Types and frequency of positively loaded nouns in compliments on possessions

Positively loaded nouns	Cameroon	Canada
Technologie 'technology'	2	0
Splendeur 'splendor'	1	0
La mort du téléphone 'the best phone'	1	0
Option	0	1
Classe	1	1
Fantôme 'monster'	2	0
Merveille 'marvel'	1	0
Marque de mes rêves 'brand of my dreams'	1	0
Femme (qui sait ce qu'elle veut) 'woman who knows what she wants'	1	0
Château 'castle'	1	0
Palais 'palace'	1	0
Mini-paradis 'mini-paradise'	1	0
Maison blanche 'White House'	1	0
Hôtel 'hotel'	1	0
Luxe 'luxury'	1	0

5.3. LEXICAL AND STYLISTIC DEVICES IN HEAD ACTS 119

Beauté 'beauty'	1	0
Jackpot	1	0
Total	18	2

The Cameroonians employ more tokens than the Canadians. While some of the devices found in the Cameroonian data set occur in complex expressions, some of the participants use metaphorical nouns or noun groups with the purpose of intensifying their expression of admiration. For instance, in the example (23) below, the expression *la mort du téléphone* is a metaphoric structure that serves as an expression of superlative in Cameroon French by which the speaker acknowledges that an object has reached the peak of a given quality. In this example, the expression could be paraphrased with *the best brand of cell phone* or *the most beautiful cell phone*. In other words, the expression serves to highlight the awesomeness of the addressee's cell phone.

23) *Tu as **la mort du téléphone** tu l'as acheté à combien?* [T, CMF]
'You have **the best brand of cell** / the most beautiful cell phone. How much did you buy it?'

The majority of positively loaded nouns occur in compliments on a new house or apartment (e.g. *palais, mini-paradis, maison blanche*) and mostly in metaphors or comparisons. Some examples from the corpus are offered below:

24) *Ma chérie, votre résidence ressemble à **mini-paradis**.* [A/H, CMF]
'Darling, your residence looks like a **mini-paradise**.'

25) *Wow, votre maison est comparable à la **maison blanche**.* [A/H, CMF]
'Wow, your house is like the **White House**.'

5.3.1.4.2. SITUATIONAL DISTRIBUTION OF NOUNS

As Table 34 below shows, the nouns found in the data are limited to specific possessions.

5. COMPLIMENTS ON POSSESSIONS

Table 34: Situational distribution of nouns in compliments on possessions

Positively loaded nouns	Telephone		House		Car	
	CMF	CF	CMF	CF	CMF	CF
Technologie	2	0	0	0	0	0
Splendeur	1	0	0	0	0	0
La mort du téléphone	1	0	0	0	0	0
Option	0	1	0	0	0	0
Classe	0	0	1	0	0	1
Fantôme	0	0	0	0	2	0
Merveille	0	0	0	0	1	0
Marque de mes rêves	0	0	0	0	1	0
Femme qui sait ce qu'elle veut	0	0	0	0	1	0
Château	0	0	1	0	0	0
Palais	0	0	1	0	0	0
Mini-paradis	0	0	1	0	0	0
Maison blanche	0	0	1	0	0	0
Hôtel	0	0	1	0	0	0
Luxe	0	0	1	0	0	0
Beauté	0	0	0	0	1	0
Jackpot	0	0	0	0	1	0
Total	4	1	7	0	7	1

5.3.2. SYNTACTIC AND STYLISTIC DEVICES

The Cameroonian informants use 16 devices while the Canadians employ 5 tokens, as shown in Table 35.

Table 35: Distribution of syntactic devices in Cameroonian and Canadian compliments on possessions

	Cameroon	Canada
Intensifying devices	9 (56.25%)	3 (42.86%)
Mitigating devices	7 (43.75%)	4 (57.14%)
Total	16 (100%)	7 (100%)

5.3. LEXICAL AND STYLISTIC DEVICES IN HEAD ACTS 121

With regard to the general functions of the devices found, Table 35 and Figure 14 indicate that the Cameroonians use more intensifying devices than those with mitigating functions, while the Canadians do just the opposite.

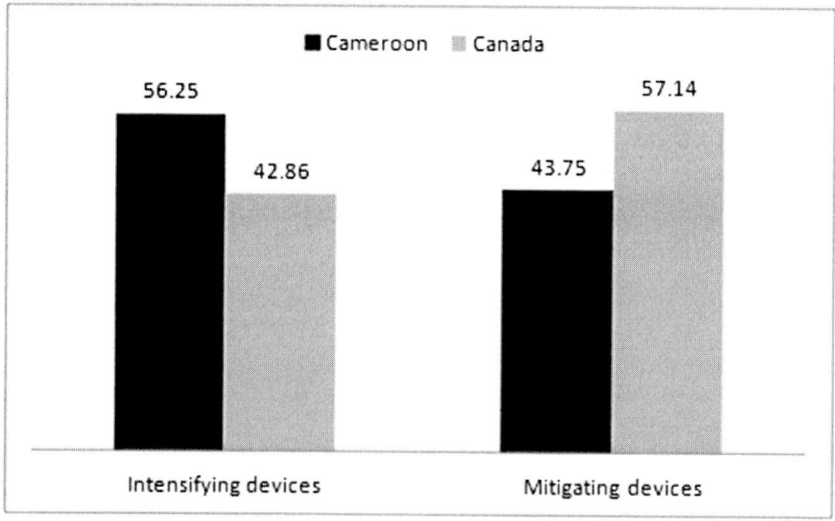

Figure 14: Distribution of syntactic devices in Cameroonian and Canadian compliments on possessions

Devices with intensifying functions found in the Cameroonian responses are as follows:

- *Devices expressing the irresistibility of the complimented object*

The compliment giver indicates that the complimented object (new phone) was irresistible or that its awesomeness is unspeakable and irresistible, as in shown in the following examples:

26) (...) ***mais je ne peux résister à** la splendeur de votre téléphone.* [T, CMF]
 '(...) **but I cannot resist** the splendor of your phone.'

27) *(...) mais il m'était impossible de vous traverser sans vous dire combien j'apprécie votre téléphone.* [T, CMF]
   '(...) **but it was impossible to pass you by without telling you** how much I like your phone.'
28) *(...) **Je ne saurais vous dire combien** est ce que j'admire ce téléphone.* [T, CMF]
   '(...) **I don't know how to tell you** how much I admire that phone.'
- *Comparative structures or expressions* used with the purpose of stressing the high quality of the complimented object: e.g. *ressemble à* 'to resemble', *semblable à* 'similar to', *est comparable à* 'is comparable to', *comparer à* 'compared to'. These expressions are usually combined with positively loaded nouns, as shown in the examples below.
29) *Quelle merveilleuse maison **semblable à** un hôtel!* [H/A, CMF]
   'What a marvelous house **similar to** a hotel.'
30) *Ma chérie, votre résidence **ressemble à** mini-paradis.* [H/A, CMF]
   'My darling, your residence **resembles** a mini-paradise.'
31) *Wow, votre maison est **comparable à** la maison blanche.* [H/A, CMF]
   'Wow, your house is **comparable to** the White House.'
32) ***Comparer à celle** où vous étiez avant, votre nouvelle maison est vraiment belle.* [H/A, CMF]
   '**Compared to the house** in which you lived before, your new house is really beautiful.'

The Canadian respondents employ comparative structures *(e.g. ressemble à)*, expressions acknowledging (positive) change (e.g. *ça fait changement* 'it makes a change') and emphatic structures introduced by *ça c'est*, as shown in the following examples.

33) *Wow! **Ça c'est** ce que j'appelle une vraie maison.* [H/A, CF]
   'Wow! **This is** what a call a beautiful house.'
34) *J'aime ta nouvelle maison, **sa fait changementde** ton 4 1/2.* [H/A, CF]
   'I like your new house, **it makes a change from** your (former) 4 room apartment.'

With respect to syntactic devices with mitigating functions, the Cameroonians employ markers of subjectivity such as *on dirait* 'one would say', *je trouve / pense que* 'I think that', to stress the subjective nature of their compliments. Some of the participants use devices such as *juste pour vous dire que* 'just to tell you that' *and je voulais vous dire que* 'I wanted to tell you that' to introduce their compliments and at the same time minimise any inconvenience they might create as in (35). This mitigating strategy is also attested in some of the Canadians compliments as in (36).

35) *(...) Au fait je voulais juste te dire que je trouve ton phone très beau.* [T, CMF]
'(...) **In fact I just wanted to tell you that** I find your cell phone very beautiful.'

36) *(...) mais je voulais juste te dire que j'aime trop ton cell.* [T, CF]
'(...) **but I wanted to tell you that** I like your cell phone very much.'

5.4. EXTERNAL MODIFICATION

5.4.1. TYPES AND FREQUENCY OF EXTERNAL MODIFICATION

In terms of pre-posed and posed supportive moves, the Cameroonians and the Canadian made different choices, as presented in Figure 15 below. The Cameroonians choose pre-compliments much more than post-posed supportive moves, while the Canadians use post-compliments more than pre-compliments.

Differences also emerge concerning the types and frequencies of supportive moves, as can be seen in Table 36 and Figure 16.

In all, the Cameroonians and the Canadians respectively use eight different types of external modification devices. As Table 36 and Figure 16 indicate, there is a significant statistical difference in the use of supportive moves. The Cameroonians employ a total of 247 tokens while their Canadian counterparts only make use of 48 occurrences. In both data sets, pre-compliments are by far the most favoured type of external modification. The other most common supportive moves are, in decreasing order, questions (15.79% in CMF: vs. 26.61% in the CF), wishes (6.48% in CMF vs. 11% in CF), and comments (6.07% in CMF vs. 12.84% in CF). The other supportive moves appear in very low percentages.

5. COMPLIMENTS ON POSSESSIONS

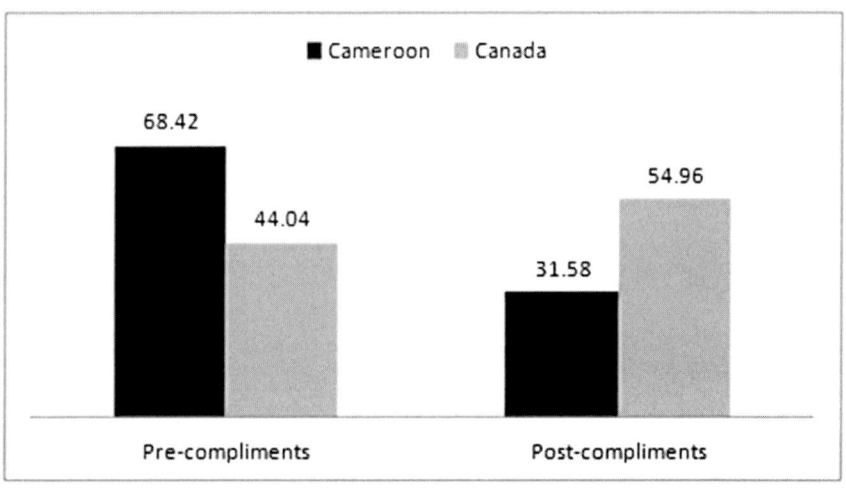

Figure 15: Distribution of pre-compliments and post-compliments in each variety of French

Table 36: Distribution of external modification in compliments on possessions

	External modification	Cameroon	Canada
	Pre-compliments	169 (68.42%)	48 (44.04%)
Post-compliments	Question	39 (15.79%)	29 (26.61%)
	Wish	16 (6.48%)	12 (11%)
	Comment	15 (6.07%)	14 (12.84%)
	Request	6 (2.43%)	3 (2.75%)
	Advice	1 (0.40%)	0
	Reminder	1 (0.40%)	0
	Regret	0	1 (0.92%)
	Suggestion	0	1 (0.92%)
	Promise	0	1 (0.92%)
	Total	247 (100%)	109 (100%)

5.4.2. PRE-COMPLIMENTS

As already mentioned, the Cameroonian participants strongly prefer pre-compliments. The 169 tokens of this external modification comprise 64

5.4. EXTERNAL MODIFICATION

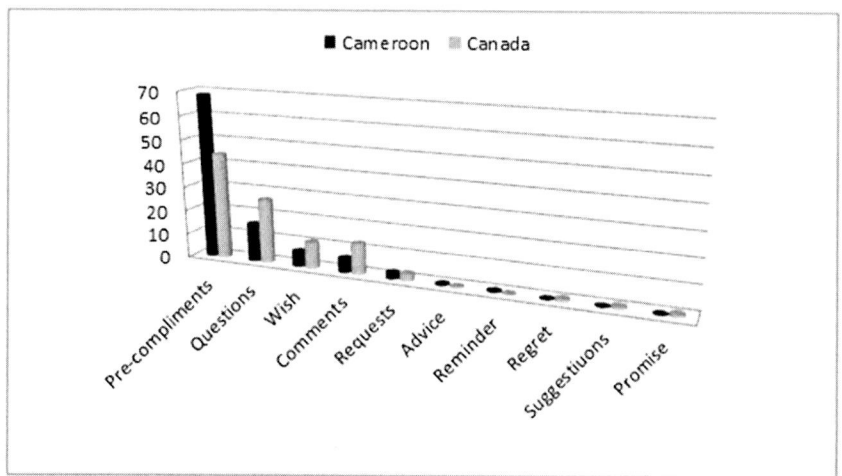

Figure 16: Distribution of external modification devices in both varieties of French [Note: the word "Suggestions" is misspelled in Figure 16.]

interjections, 50 nominal address terms, 43 greetings, 10 apologies and two instances of self-introductions. The Canadians also use pre-compliments to a great extent. The 48 instances found in their responses consist of 33 interjections, 10 nominal address terms, three apologies and two greetings.

5.4.2.1. INTERJECTIONS

The interjections found in the Cameroonian data are *ah!, c'est pas possible, mais alors, mais voilà, eh, mon dieu, oh*. The interjections appear alone, as in (37), or in combinations, as in (38).

37) ***C'est pas possible*** *ton téléphone est mortel.* [T, CMF]
    '**It's not possible** your phone is awesome.'
38) ***Oh! Mon dieu*** *quelle est magnifique ta maison.* [H/A, CMF]
    '**Oh! My god** your house is magnificent.'

The interjections used by the Canadians are *wow yé, haaa, oh mon dieu, shit, oh, putain d'merde, héhé, hein*. The interjections appear alone, as in (39) or in combination with other pre-compliments (e.g. terms of address), as in (40).

39) ***Oh mon dieu****. J'aime trop ton cellulaire!* [T, CF]
    '**Oh my god**. I really love your mobile phone!'

40) **Wow, professeur** , votre voiture est vraiment belle! [C, CF]
    '**Wow, teacher,** your car is really beautiful!'

5.4.2.2. NOMINAL ADDRESS TERMS

The nominal address terms attested in the Cameroonian data are terms of respects, endearment and familiarity / solidarity or in-group markers: *(cher) camarade, ma chérie, man, mademoiselle, grand frère, gars, Blandine, ma/la copine, monsieur* et *madame*. They are used either alone, as in (41), or in combination with other types of pre-compliments (e.g. greetings), as in (42).

41) **Madame** vous avez une jolie voiture! [C, CMF]
    '**Madam** you have a beautiful car!'
42) **Bonjour camarade** que ton téléphone est beau. [T, CMF]
    '**Good morning friend** your phone is nice.'

The nominal address terms employed by the Canadians are *hey, yo, chanceux, monsieur,* et *professeur*. They are used either alone, as in (43), or in combination with other supportive moves (e.g. questions), as in (44). Some participants placed the address forms after the compliments, as in (45).

43) **Monsieur/madame** , j'aime vraiment votre voiture. [C, CF]
    '**Sir/Madam**, I really like your car.'
44) **Hey**, où tu l'as eu ton cellulaire? Il est vraiment hot! [T, CF]
    '**Hey**, where did you get your mobile phone? It is really nice!'
45) Belle voiture **monsieur**, vous avez vraiment du goût. [C, CF]
    'Nice car **sir**, you really have taste.'

5.4.2.3. GREETINGS

Many Cameroonians use greetings as preparatory acts of their compliments. They mostly do so with compliments to unknown addressees (i.e. compliments on the phone of an unknown student) and with compliments to superiors (i.e. compliments on teacher's new car). The greetings appear in different patterns. Some greeting formulas occur alone or combined before the compliments proper, as in (46). In some cases, the greetings are immediately followed by other types of pre-compliments (e.g. an interjection or an address term), as in (47) and (48).

46) *Salut! Comment tu vas? C'est pas possible* ton téléphone est mortel. [T, CMF]
   '**Hi! How are you? It's not possible** your phone is awesome.'
47) *Salut monsieur* vous avez une très belle voiture! [C, CMF]
   '**Hi sir** you have a very nice car.'
48) *Bonjour cher camarade* votre téléphone est vraiment admirable puis-je le voir? [T, CMF]
   '**Good morning dear friend** your phone is really admirable can I see it?'

The two instances of greetings in the Canadian data set are realized indirectly, namely in form of questions about the addressee's name, as in (49).

49) *Hey, excuse-moi. C'est toi de ma classe de math, right? tu peux me rappeler ton nom?Mélanie?* [...], je voulais juste te dire que j'aime ton nouveau cell. [T, CF]
   '**Hey, excuse-me.You are in my maths class, right? Can you remind me your name? Mélanie?** [...] I just wanted to tell you that I like your new cell phone.'

5.4.2.4. APOLOGIES

Some Cameroonian respondents use apologies as pre-compliments, and these acts occur in different forms. Apologies generally appear in the form of *s'il vous plait* 'please', as in (50) or *excuse/excusez-moi* 'excuse me', as in (51). In some cases, the illocutionary force of apologies is intensified with other pre-compliments (e.g. greetings, terms of address, etc.) as in (50).

50) *S'il vous plait, j'ai aperçu votre téléphone de loin et je le trouve vraiment beau.* [T, CMF]
   '**Excuse me**, I saw your phone from far and I think it's really beautiful.'
51) *Bonjour! Camarade, comment-te-portes-tu? Excuse-moi de te déranger mais c'est juste que de loin j'ai aperçu ton téléphone qui est super beau et j'aimerais savoir comment est-ce que tu l'as eu.* [T, CMF]
   '**Good morning! Friend, how are you doing? Excuse-me for bothering you** but it's just that I saw your phone which is super beautiful and would like to know how you got it.'

Three Canadians combine their compliments on the addressee's possessions with apologies. As the examples show, the apologies occur in combination with other supportive moves (e.g. address forms, request).

52) *Yo, je sais que j't'ais jamais parlé,* mais je voulais juste te dire que j'aime trop ton cell. [T, CF]
'**Yo, I know I haven't spoken with you**, but I just wanted to tell you that I really love your cell phone.'

53) ***Excusez-moi*** , mais je voudrai savoir la marque de votre téléphone, car il est très beau. [T, CF]
'**Excuse me**, but I would to know the brand of your phone, because it is very beautiful.'

5.4.2.5. SELF-INTRODUCTIONS

Two participants introduce themselves prior to offering the compliments. This supportive move is associated with greetings, as in (54). This supportive does not appear in the Canadian data.

54) ***Salut, moi c'est Rodrigue*** , tu as un très joli téléphone portable. [T, CMF]
'**Hi, my name is Rodrigue**, you have a very nice mobile phone.'

5.4.3. POST-COMPLIMENTS

5.4.3.1. QUESTIONS

The respondents of both groups use questions to seek information about the brand, price or date of acquisition of the complimented item. As such, the interrogative structures employed mostly contain adverbials such as *où* 'where', *quand* 'when', *combien* 'how much', *comment* 'how', *quel/quelle* 'what (type/brand)', etc. While the Cameroonians mostly prefer structures beginning with the interrogative words, as in (55) and indirect questions, as in (56), the interrogatives in the Canadian corpus appear in different forms: some of them occur in form of declarative structures with rising intonation (with or without interrogative words) as in (57). Some participants use the interrogative words listed above at the beginning of their utterances as in (58), while another group of informants used combinations such as *c'est quand que* "when", *c'est combinen que* "how much", *c'est où que* "where", etc. to ask questions, as in (59).

5.4. EXTERNAL MODIFICATION

55) *Bonjour camarade que ton téléphone est beau.* **Comment as-tu fait pour l'avoir?** [T, CMF]
    'Good morning friend your phone is beautiful. **How did you get it?**'
56) *Salut, moi c'est Rodrigue, tu as un très joli téléphone portable.* **Puis-je savoir où tu l'as acheté?** [T, CMF]
    'Hi, I am Rodrigue, you have a very nice cell phone. **Can I know where you bought it?**'
57) *Wow yé bon ton cell shit* **tu la payé combien?** [T, CF]
    'Wow you cell phone is nice shit **how much did you pay for it?**'
58) *J'adore ton nouveau cell!* **Où est-ce que tu l'as acheté?** [T, CF]
    'I love your new cell phone! **Where did you buy it?**'
59) *C'est trop hot ton cell!* **C'est quand que tu l'as eu?** [T, CF]
    'Your cell phone is very nice. **When did you buy it?**'

5.4.3.2. WISHES

Some of the participants in both groups express the wish to possess the (same) complimented object or to use it. They mostly choose structures with the verb *aimer* (in the conditional) + *avoir* or *acheter*, as in (60) and (61). [Note: Reference numbers needed. Informed guess.]

60) *Quel beau téléphone, peux-tu me dire là où tu le acheté,* **j'aimerais avoir le meme.** [T, CMF]
    'What a nice phone, can you tell me where you bought it, **I would like to have the same (phone).**'
61) *J'aime vraiment ton téléphone! Combien t'a-t-il coûté? Et c'est quoi la marque de ton téléphone?* **J'aimerais l'acheter un jour.** [T, CF]
    'I really like your phone? How much did it cost you? And what is the brand of your phone? **I would like to buy it one day.**'
62) *Ta maison est vraiment belle!* **J'aimerais bien y habiter.** [H/A, CF]
    'Your house is really beautiful! **I would really like to live in it.**'

Some expressions of wish appear in hypothetical structures, as in (63).

63) *Mais alors, votre maison-ci est très jolie, j'aime bien son plan.* **Quand je serais grande je ferais une maison comme celle-ci.** [H/A, CMF]
    'Wow, your house is very beautiful, I really like its plan. **When I grow up I'll build a house like this one.**'

64) *Monsieur j'aime beaucoup votre nouvelle voiture. **J'aimerais avoir la même lorsque je serais plus grand.***[C, CMF]
'Sir, I like your new car a lot. **I would like to have the same car when I grow up.**'

Some wishes appear in the *si*-structure (if only), as in (65).

65) *J'adore votre voiture! **Si je pouvais en avoir une comme ça.*** [C, CF]
'I love your car! **If only I could have one like this.**'

5.4.3.3. COMMENTS

Some of the informants use comments as preparators, as shown in the following examples.

66) *Salut **en passent dans la cour j'ai aperçu ton téléphone**, il est très beau. Tu l'as acheter où?* [T, CMF]
'Hi, **I saw your phone passing by in the yard**, it is very beautiful. Where did you buy it?'

67) *Wow,**je pense que je vais venir habiter chez vous**. C'est vraiment beau mais c'est dommage que vous avez déménager.* [H/A, CF]
'Wow, **I think I will come and live with you**. It's really beautiful, it's sad that you moved.'

Some comments appear after the compliments and are used to reinforce the positive evaluation, as in (68) and (69).

68) *Elle est vraiment belle votre voiture monsieur **s'il m'arrive d'en acheter une un jour je n'hésiterai pas.*** [C, CMF]
'Sir your car is really beautiful, **if I happen to buy a car (like this) one day I will not hesitate.**'

69) *Votre maison est ravissante, **elle ressemble presque (à) la notre.*** [H/A, CF]
'Your house is beautiful, **it almost looks like ours.**'

5.4.3.4. REQUESTS

Some participants in both groups accompany their compliments with requests to see or to use the complimented object, as in (70) and (71). The requests in the Cameroonian data were indirect and they generally contained politeness markers such as *s'il vous plait* 'please', and *je peux / puis-je* 'can I.'

70) *Bonjour, je peux voir votre téléphone s'il vous plait? Il est tres joli.* [T, CMF]
'Good morning, **can I see your phone, please?** It is very beautiful.'
71) ***Vous me faites un lift**. Belle voiture!* [C, CF]
'**Can you give me a lift.** Nice car.'

5.4.3.5. OTHER EXTERNAL MODIFICATIONS

One Cameroonian combines an indirect advice and a reminder after the compliment on the addressee's new phone, as in (72). The two post-compliments may be interpreted here as strategies intended to consolidate the relationship between both partners.

72) *Wow, quel beau téléphone! où l'as-tu acheté?* ***Il n'est pas prudent de l'apporter à l'établissement, c'est interdit.*** [T, CMF].
'Wow, what a nice phone! Where did you get it? **It is not safe to bring it to school, it's not allowed.**'

There is respectively one occurrence for the following supportive moves in the Canadian data: Suggestion, as in (73), regret, as in (74), and promise, as in (75). These post-compliments are intended to pinpoint the value of the complimented object or the social value of the recipient.

73) *J'aime trop ta nouvelle maison.* ***On devrait venir ici plus souvent***[32]. [H/A, CF]
'I really love your new house. **One should be coming here very often.**'
74) *Wow, je pense que je vais venir habiter chez vous.* ***C'est vraiment beau mais c'est dommage que vous avez déménager.*** [H/A, CF]
'Wow, I think that I will come live with you. **It's really beautiful, but it's a pity that you moved.**'
75) *Hey, excuse-moi. C'est toi de ma classe de math, right? tu peux me rappeler ton nom ? Mélanie?* ***Je l'oublierai pas la prochaine fois*** *, je voulais juste te dire que j'aime ton nouveau cell.* [T, CF].
'Hey, excuse me. You are in my maths class, right? Can you remind me your name? Mélanie? **I will not forget it the next time.** I just wanted to tell you that I like your new cell phone.'

---

[32] The suggestion could be interpreted as an indirect form of self-invitation. And by so doing, the compliment giver expects the addressee to confirm his/her will to welcome the speaker anytime.

5.4.4. SITUATIONAL DISTRIBUTION OF EXTERNAL MODIFICATION

There are differences in the distribution of the various external modification devices across the three situations in both data sets, as shown in Table 37.

Table 37: Situational distribution of external modification in compliments on possessions

External modification		Telephone		House		Car	
		CMF	CF	CMF	CF	CMF	CF
Pre-compliments	Interjections	12	8	29	15	23	10
	Nominal address forms	10	8	5	0	35	2
	Greetings	32	2	3	0	8	0
	Apologies	7	3	0	0	3	0
	Self-introduction	2	0	0	0	0	0
Post-compliments	Question	35	26	1	0	3	3
	Comment	8	6	5	6	2	2
	Request	5	2	0	0	1	1
	Wish	1	5	7	3	8	4
	Advice	1	0	0	0	0	0
	Reminder	1	0	0	0	0	0
	Regret	0	0	0	1	0	0
	Suggestion	0	0	0	1	0	0
	Promise	0	1	0	0	0	0
Total		114	61	50	26	83	22

Table 37 shows that supportive moves are mostly used with compliments on the new phone in both data sets. This is due to the high number of pre-compliments (mostly greetings in the Cameroonian and nominal address terms in the Canadian responses), and this result reveals the tendency in both varieties of French to introduce compliments to strangers. These preparatory acts are used to establish contact prior to the compliments proper. Table 37 also indicates that pre-compliments (mostly address terms and interjections) are used to a great extent by the Cameroonians with compliments to superiors. In the Canadian data, by contrast, the number of pre-compliments in offering compliments to superiors is low. This difference may indicate that the Cameroonians consider it as (more) polite strategy to combine compliments to superiors with face-saving strategies such as terms of respects and greetings (negative politeness), while the Canadians seem to lay more emphasis on expressing their surprise (through interjections) when offering compliments to superiors (positive politeness). As can be seen in Table 37, questions, the second most preferred supportive move by the informants of both groups, are mostly used with compliments on the new phone in the two varieties of French. While wishes mostly accompany compliments on the addressee's (parent's) house or apartment in the Cameroonian corpus, this supportive move is almost equally distributed across the three situations in the Canadian data.

5.5. SUMMARY OF THE FINDINGS

Move structure and head acts
The participants of both groups prefer by far 'head acts + supportive moves' combinations. While 'head acts only' occurrences are the second most common patterns in Cameroon French and Canadian French, the number of instances of this pattern is much lower in the Cameroonian than in the Canadian corpus. The 'supportive moves only' examples are the least used to offer compliments on possessions in both varieties of French. Both groups employ more direct head acts than indirect head acts. The Cameroonians use more multiple direct head acts (double and triple heads) than single direct head acts. The Canadians, by contrast, choose single head acts much more frequently than multiple heads. There are some differences and similarities in the situational distribution of direct (single or multiple) head acts and indirect head acts in both data sets.

Lexical and stylistic devices
The results show that the Cameroonians use these devices much more frequently than the Canadians. Major differences also emerge concerning the types, frequency and situational distribution of adjectives, adverbs, verbs and positively loaded nouns. The Cameroonians demonstrate more expressivity and creativity in the use of lexical devices. For instance, their repertoire contains several adjectives with very strong positive connotations and

some of the adjectives are neologisms formed by means of derivation, semantic shift or borrowing. Some of the Canadian adjectives are also the result of a semantic shift or borrowing. In terms of syntactic devices, the Cameroonians use more intensifying syntactic modifiers than those with mitigating functions, while the Canadians did just the opposite.

External modification

The participants of both groups respectively use eight different types of external modification devices, which appeared either before (pre-compliments) or after (post-compliments) the compliments proper. In both data sets, pre-compliments (i.e. interjections, nominal address forms, greetings, apologies, self-introduction, etc.) are by far the most common supportive moves. The most frequent post-compliments in both corpora are questions, wishes and comments. With regard to pre-compliments, it was found that the Cameroonians adopt nominal address terms and greetings much more frequently than the Canadian respondents. The situational distribution of the external supportive moves in both data sets reveals a strong preference in both varieties of French to introduce compliments to strangers. It was also noticed that the Cameroonians use address terms and interjections much more frequently in compliments to superiors. The Canadians, by contrast, employ pre-compliments less frequently in offering compliments to superiors. Also, questions, the second most preferred supportive move by the informants of both groups, mostly occur with compliments on the new phone in both varieties of French.

CHAPTER 6

COMPLIMENT RESPONSES[33]

This chapter discusses the realization patterns of compliment responses employed by the Cameroonian and Canadian participants. It starts with an overview of the frequency and types of compliment responses and classifies the examples in terms of verbal vs. nonverbal responses and simple vs. complex responses (6.1). The compliment response patterns are described in 6.2, with a focus on the number of moves and speech acts used in the verbal responses (one-move responses vs. multiple move responses) and their politeness functions. The linguistic realization forms of major compliment responses in both language varieties are presented in 6.3, while the situational distribution of compliment responses in treated in 6.4.

6.1. OVERALL FREQUENCY AND COMPLIMENT RESPONSE TYPES

Table 38 and Figure 17 present the breakdown of responses in terms of the dichotomy verbal vs. non-verbal responses and the distinction between simple vs. complex responses.

Table 38 clearly shows differences and similarities between the two varieties of French. The fact that all the respondents use verbal responses seems to indicate that the speakers in both cultures consider verbal responses to compliments as the most appropriate ways of responding to verbal gifts. In other words, nonverbal responses may be interpreted in both cultural settings as a threat to the face of the compliment giver and that of the compliment receiver as well. Since a nonverbal reaction (e.g. silence)

---

[33] This chapter is based on our presentation at the 12th International Pragmatics Conference in Manchester (England) in July 2011. It is also an extended version of our article titled "Responding to compliments in Cameroon French and Canadian French" (2012).

6. COMPLIMENT RESPONSES

Table 38: Overall distribution of compliment response types

Types of responses		Cameroon	Canada
Non-verbal responses		0	0
Verbal reponses	Simple responses	109 (25.12%)	104 (33.66%)
	Complex responses	325 (74.88%)	205 (66.34%)
Total		434 (100%)	309 (100%)

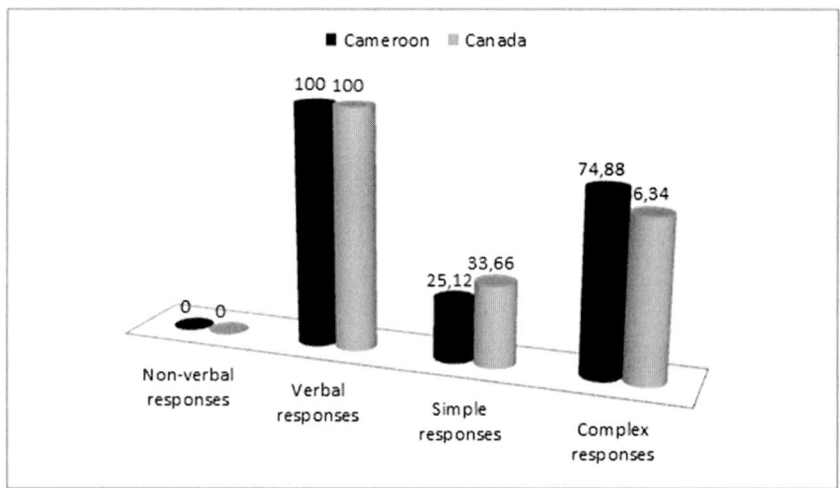

Figure 17: Overall distribution of compliment response types

may be seen as an uncooperative move, there is a strong tendency to react to a verbal gift by "saying something".

A second notable pattern concerns the frequency of simple and complex responses in both data sets. As can be seen in Table 38, the Cameroonian and Canadian respondents employ complex responses much more than simple responses. Complex responses occur in the Cameroonian data in 325 instances (74.89%), while the simple responses are identified in 109 examples (25.11%). The Canadian data also show the dominance of complex responses, found in 205 examples (66.35%), while the simple responses appeared in 104 occurrences (33.65%). The dominance of complex responses in both varieties of French may be interpreted as the preference of the participants of both groups to appear more expressive in their responses, as opposed to being too straightforward with simple responses.

6.2. COMPLIMENT RESPONSE PATTERNS

6.2.1. FUNCTIONS AND REALIZATION PATTERNS OF SIMPLE RESPONSES

Table 39 and Figure 18 below indicate the breakdown of simple responses in terms of the speech acts employed to respond to compliments.

Table 39: Distribution of one-move responses in both varieties of French

Simple responses	Cameroon	Canada
Thanks	71 (16.36%)	79 (25.57%)
Comment	2 (0.46%)	11 (3.60%)
Credit shift	9 (2.07%)	4 (1.29%)
Advice	10 (2.30%)	2 (0.65%)
Asking for confirmation	0	2 (0.65%)
Request	0	1 (0.32%)
Encouragement	0	1 (0.32%)
Offer	3 (0.69%)	1 (0.32%)
Question	0	1 (0.32%)
Downgrade	3 (0.69%)	1 (0.32%)
Agreement	2 (0.46%)	1 (0.32%)
Joy	5 (1.15%)	0
Praise upgrade	3 (0.69%)	0
Promise	1 (0.23%)	0
Total	109 (25.12%)	104 (33.66%)

Table 39 shows that the Cameroonian informants produce 109 simple responses to compliments, choosing the following ten speech acts / strategies: (a) thanks (71 tokens), (b) comment (2 examples), (c) credit shift (4 occurrences), (d) advice (2 examples), (e) offer (3 tokens), (f) downgrade (3 instances), (g) agreement (2 examples), (h) joy (5 tokens), (i) praise upgrade (3 instances), and (j) promise (1 example). The Canadian participants provide 104 simple responses to compliments, using of the following eleven

6. COMPLIMENT RESPONSES

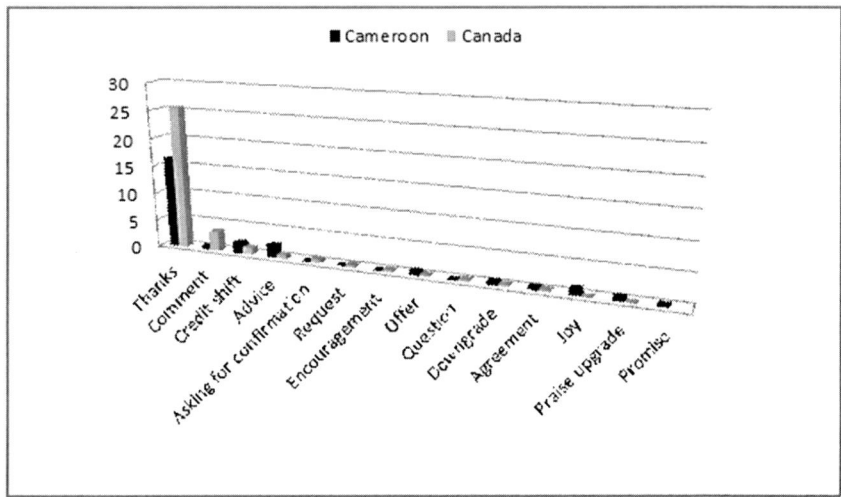

Figure 18: Distribution of one-move responses in both varieties of French

speech acts: (a) thanks (79 tokens), (b) comment (11 instances), (c) credit shift (9 occurrences), (d) advice (10 examples), (e) asking for confirmation (2 tokens), (f) request (1 occurrence), (g) encouragement (1 example), (h) offer (1 instance), (i) question (1 token), (j) downgrade (1 instance), and (k) agreement (1 example).

Overall, these results indicate that the speakers of both varieties of French display a strong preference for 'acceptance of the compliment' using thanks, with the Canadian respondents showing a much higher percentage. Contrary to the Canadian informants who exclusively use gratitude expressions to accept the compliments, five Cameroonians express joy as a way of accepting the compliments. The other speech acts used as simple responses show much lower percentages in both data sets. While strategies such as 'proffering advice', 'shifting credit', 'downgrading', 'offering', 'agreeing', and 'making comments' appear in both corpora, some speech acts were identified only in one variety. As a matter of fact, 'praise upgrade' is used only by the Cameroonian respondents, while 'promise', 'asking for confirmation', 'requests', 'encouragements' and 'questions' occur only in the Canadian data. 'Advice' and 'credit shifts' are the second and third most frequently used speech acts in Cameroonian simple responses, while 'comments' and 'credit shifts' are the second and third most preferred simple responses by the Canadians. The overwhelming use of gratitude expressions illustrates the perception of compliments as pleasant gifts by the participants of both groups. The other minor strategies may also indicate that the compliment recipient considered the exchange as an opportunity to strengthen interpersonal relationships, by, for instance, telling the compliment giver what s/he could do to have the same achievement or possess the compliment object (advice); alluding to the help of other people (credit shifts) or sharing some information in connection with the compliment topic with the compliment giver (comments), etc. The description below provides definitions and examples of the attested response types as well as their interpretation as politeness strategies.

6.2.1.1. THANKS

The compliment recipient uses this strategy to express gratitude for the verbal gift (i.e. the compliment) and to accept it. By so doing, the recipient realizes positive politeness, and more specifically, the "seek agreement' strategy, in Brown and Levinson's (1987: 112) terms. In other words, the person complimented claims "common ground with the complimenter stresses his/her agreement with the complimenter and satisfies the complimenter's desire to be right or to corroborated in his/her opinion" (Brown and Levinson 1987: 112). Typical examples from the data are provided below. [Note: with or when?]

1) *Merci professeur pour tout.* [CMF]
   'Thank you, professor for everything.'
2) *Merci beaucoup monsieur.* [CF]
   'Thanks very much sir'

6.2.1.2. ADVICE

By using this response type the recipient implicitly accepts the compliment and advises the compliment giver to undertake certain actions in order to achieve similar or the same results. From the politeness point of view, this strategy may be interpreted as indicative of the recipient's willingness to show solidarity with the compliment giver. Advice may be perceived here as a reciprocation/compensation of the verbal gift (compliment) and as a sign that the compliment recipient would not be jealous if the compliment-giver achieved the same results. In this light, advice enhances the face of both partners. Most of the examples in the Cameroonian data seem to confirm this analysis, since they were responses to compliments on the recipient's oral presentation where the compliment giver explicitly indicated that he/she would like to act like the recipient (*J'aimerais vraiment faire comme toi.* 'I would really like to do like you (did).'). In this case, it is safe to interpret proffering advice as a means to attend the other's needs, in the form of giving a gift in return or reciprocating. Contrary to compliment returns (verbal gifts), the speaker through his/her advice makes it clear that the actions he/she is encouraging the compliment giver to undertake are likely to lead his/her to the complimented object. This may also explain why the respondents mostly use direct forms in the realization of advice-giving. The Cameroonians mostly employ markers of deontic modality such as *il faut* 'you have to' as in (3) and devices alluding to the (minimal) condition to fulfill *il suffit de / tu n'as qu'à* 'you just have to' as in (4) and (5). This last pattern is also employed by the Canadians as in (6).

3) *Il faut beaucoup travailler et tu y arriveras.* [CMF]
   'You have to work a lot and you'll succeed.'
4) *Il suffit juste de mettre du sérieux dans ce qu'on entreprend.* [CMF]
   'You just have to be serious in what you are doing.'
5) *Tu n'as qu'a t'y mettre et tout sera très facile pour toi aussi.* [CMF]
   'You just have to do it and everything will be easy for you too.'
6) *Tu n'as qu'à t'appliquer et tu réussiras, je te garantis.* [CF]
   'You just have to be diligent and I guarantee you'll succeed.'

6.2.1.3. OFFER

Responses in this category are equivalent to the remark "I (implicitly) accept your compliment and offer to help you achieve what I did / I offer you the complimented object." In terms of politeness, offers have face-threatening and face-enhancing features (Barron 2005: 143). Offers threaten the hearer's face in that they exert pressure on the hearer to react and to accept what is being offered. On the other hand, offers enhance the hearer's positive face because they indicate the speaker's interest to the hearer, which may result in something beneficial to the hearer. Thus, when offers are used as responses to compliments they function as positive po-

6.2. COMPLIMENT RESPONSE PATTERNS 141

liteness strategies, since these speech acts indirectly express the recipient's appreciation of the verbal gift and the need to reciprocate. Offers are positive politeness strategies employed to assume or assert reciprocity (strategy 14 in Brown and Levinson's (1987: 129) theory) and to give tangible or symbolic gifts to the hearer (strategy 15 in Brown and Levinson's (ibid.) model). Contrary to attempts to return the same verbal gift (compliment), offers may focus either on the complimented items or on ways to get to the complimented objects. The only example in the Canadian data is a case where the recipient offers the complimented item, albeit in exchange for something else, as in (9). The Cameroonian respondents offer help, and they employ the conditional form *si tu veux* 'if you like' to mitigate their offers, as in (7). One participant uses the marker of deontic modality *il faut* 'you should' to encourage the compliment giver to accept the offer as in (8).

7) *Si tu veux je t'explique comment faire à la fin des cours.* [CMF]
   'If you like, I can explain how to do it at the end of class.'
8) *Alors, il faut souvent venir on travaille.* [CMF]
   'Then, you should come and work with me.'
9) *Vous me l'échangez contre votre ordinateur portable?* [CF]
   'Will you exchange it with your laptop?'

6.2.1.4. CREDIT SHIFT

By using this strategy, the compliment recipient indicates that "he/she is not (solely) responsible for the complimented object. Somebody else helped them out". This is a politeness strategy in that the compliment recipient demonstrates humility by shifting the credit to someone else. In other words, the recipient humbles himself/herself and raises somebody else. Some examples in both data sets show that credit can be shifted to the compliment giver, as in (10). In asymmetrical relationships, in teacher-student situations for instance, this type of credit shift is also a realization of deference (Brown and Levinson (1987: 178) by which the compliment recipient humbles herself/himself and enhances the compliment giver's positive face. Credit shifts may also be interpreted as indirect compliment returns or indirect expressions of gratitude. In the Cameroonian data, credit shifts contain expressions such as *tout le mérite revient à* 'all the credits go to', *sans votre aide* 'without your help', *c'est grâce à* 'it's thanks to', *c'est l'oeuvre de* 'it's the work of', *ce n'est pas moi qui* 'I am not the one who'. The Canadians employ the following expressions in their credit shifts: *sans l'aide de* 'without the help of', *c'est grâce à* 'its thanks to', *c'est vous qui* 'you are the one who', *sans votre* 'without your', *c'est X qui* 'it's X who'

10) *Tout le mérite revient à toi, car tu m'as bien encadré.* [E, CMF]
    'You deserve all the credit because you trained me well."
11) *Sans l'aide de mes coéquipiers, je n'aurai pas connu un fort match.* [S, CF]
    'I wouldn't have had a good performance without the help of my team mates.'

6.2.1.5. COMMENT

The compliment recipient comments on the complimented object. The remarks made include his/her feelings, attitude towards the action or object being complimented, etc. The comments could be interpreted as agreements. Representative examples from both corpora are listed below.

12) *C'est le travail qui paie papa.* [E, CMF]
    '[Hard] work pays, dad.'
13) *Voilà ce qui se passe quand je me force.* [CF]
    'That's what happens when I work hard.
14) *Disons que mes parents ne toléreraient un autre attitude de ma part.* [E, CF]
    'Let's say that my parents wouldn't tolerate any other attitude from me.'

6.2.1.6. DOWNGRADE

Examples belonging to this category can be paraphrased as: "the complimented objected is not as valuable as you say" or "I am not as good as you say/think". By using this strategy, the recipient agrees with the compliment giver to some extent and demonstrates humility, as shown in the examples below.

15) *J'ai juste fait mon devoir papa.* [E, CMF]
    'I just did what I had to do, dad.'
16) *Portant il ne coûte pas cher!* [T, CMF]
    'Nevertheless it [telephone] does not cost much.'

17) *Je fais de mon mieux c tout.* [CF]
   'I do my best, that's all.

6.2.1.7. AGREEMENT

The compliment recipient explicitly agrees with the positive evaluation: 'I see it the way you do'. Agreements are positive politeness strategies as they indicate common ground (in terms of taste), satisfy the compliment giver's desire to be right and thus construct solidarity. Common examples from the data are:

18) *Moi aussi je l'apprécie vraiment.* [CMF]
   'I really like it too.'
19) *C'est clair là!* [CF]
   'It is very obvious!'

6.2.1.8. JOY

Examples in this category can be paraphrased as follows: 'I am very happy to hear/know that you like the complimented object'. Besides showing agreement with the compliment giver and appreciation for the verbal gift, expressions of joy highlight the compliment giver's social competence of knowing how to make others feel good.

20) *Je suis content de le savoir.* [CMF]
   'I am happy to know that.'

6.2.1.9. PRAISE UPGRADE

With this strategy, the illocutionary force of the compliment is increased. The responses attested in this category are understood as 'I know that the complimented object is as good as you say'. or 'I did it / well as usual'. This strategy has an ambiguous status. On the one hand, the upgrading of a compliment in a compliment response may provoke a negative evaluation from the compliment giver and may also be interpreted as disregarding the modesty principle. In this case, the strategy threatens the face of the compliment recipient. On the other hand, we could argue that praise upgrade is a positive politeness strategy. As Baba (1999: 63) rightly indicates:

since compliments are considered to be verbal gifts, compliment responses may express one's appreciation of the gift. By upgrading a compliment in the [compliment response], the speaker can intensify the show of appreciation for the verbal gift. This upgrading of the compliment has the additional function of 'intensifying interest to [hearer]' by developing the topic of the compliment into an interesting explanation.

It should be noted that the positive politeness component of praise upgrade in compliment responses comes into play mostly in exchanges among acquaintances or between intimates (close friends or family members) and the praise upgrade is generally expressed in jocular forms. Praise upgrade could also serve as a strategy to test the sincerity of the compliment giver, i.e. to make him/her reiterate, reinforce or even mitigate his/her compliment.

21) *Je vous ai toujours dit que j'ai des talents culinaires rares.* [M, CMF]
'I have always told you that I have rare culinary skills.'
22) *Comme d'habitude.* [S, CMF]
'As usual.'
23) *Tu sais bien que je suis toujours stilé.* [H, CMF]
'You know well that I am always fashionably dressed.'

6.2.1.10. PROMISE

The compliment recipient promises to give/sell the complimented object to the compliment giver. This is another form of offering the complimented object, with the difference that in this case the compliment recipient expects something in return. Nevertheless, this type of response is a positive politeness strategy, since an offer or a promise "demonstrate [the recipient's] good intentions in satisfying [the compliment giver's] positive face wants" (Brown and Levinson 1987: 125), as shown in the following example.

24) *Quand vous avez l'argent si vous voulez je vous le [téléphone portable] vends à bon prix.* [T, CMF]
'When you have money, if you like I'll sell it [mobile phone] to you at a very reasonable price.'

6.2.1.11. ASKING FOR CONFIRMATION

Examples in this category can be understood as 'I have heard what you said but I would like you to reiterate your positive evaluation in order for me to believe you'. This is a strategy employed to indicate the compliment recipient's reluctance to accept the compliment. It could also be seen as a form of humility.

25) *Hein?! Pour vrai?* [CF]
'Hein, for real?'

6.2.1.12. REQUEST

The compliment receiver asks for a material gift (as an addition to the verbal). The only example attested in the corpus is used by a Canadian informant to request a financial reward from parents for academic excellence.

26) *Combien tu vas me donner?* [E, CF]
'How much will you give me?'

6.2.1.13. ENCOURAGEMENT

The hearer encourages the compliment giver by telling him/her that he/she can also achieve what is being complimented. This strategy has multiple positive politeness functions: it exerts reciprocity, expresses the compliment recipient's interest in the other and satisfies the compliment giver's desire to achieve what is being complimented.

27) *Ah lol tu peux aussi.* [CF]
'Ah, lol, you too can do it.'

6.2.1.14. QUESTION

The Canadian compliment recipient uses this speech act to ask for the identity of the interlocutor. It shows interest in the compliment giver.

28) *T'es qui?* [CF]
'Who are you?'

6.2.2. FUNCTIONS AND REALIZATION PATTERNS OF COMPLEX RESPONSES

When responding to compliments, the participants of both groups also use multiple-move strategies consisting of two-move, three-move as well as four-move responses. Table 40 and Figure 19, below, present the overall frequency of the complex responses in both data sets.

As can be seen in Table 40 and Figure 19, the most preferred pattern of complex responses is the combination of two-speech acts. This combination pattern is attested in 252 examples (77.54%) of the complex responses in

Table 40: Distribution of complex responses in both varieties of French

Types of complex responses	Cameroon	Canada
Two-move responses	252 (77.54%)	173 (84.39%)
Three-move responses	67 (20.62%)	31 (15.12%)
Four-move responses	6 (1.85%)	01 (0.49%)
Total	325 (100%)	205 (100%)

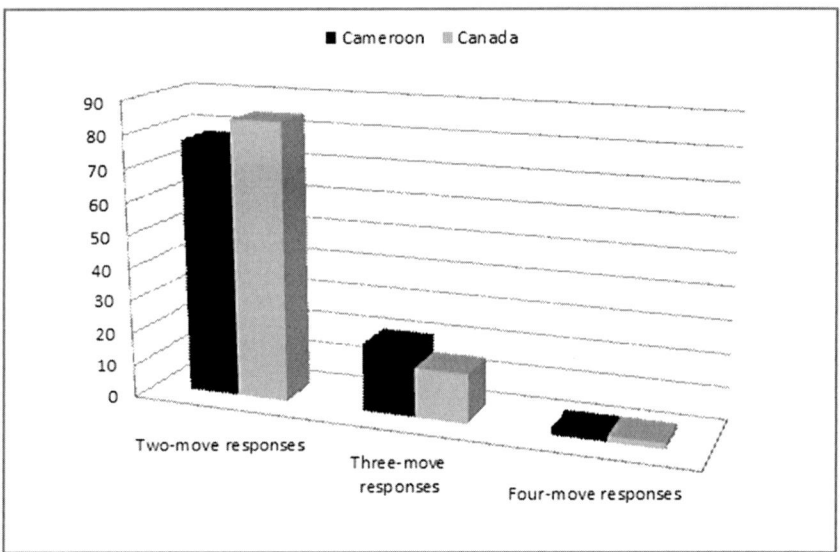

Figure 19: Distribution of complex responses in both varieties of French

the Cameroonian data set and in 173 instances (55.98%) of all the complex responses in the Canadian corpus. The combinations of three-speech acts appear with a much lower percentage in both data sets: the Cameroonians use this pattern namely in 67 examples (20.62%) of the attested complex responses, while the Canadians employ this pattern in 31 instances (15.12%) of their complex responses. The combinations of four speech acts are the least preferred patterns of the complex responses. Six examples (1.85%) appear in the Cameroonian data while one Canadian respondent employed this pattern. The next sections present a more detailed description of the types and number of speech acts involved in the complex compliment responses found in the data.

6.2.2.1. TWO-MOVE RESPONSES

Overall, the Cameroonian participants use 36 different combination patterns of two speech acts, whereas the Canadian informants employ 45 different combination patterns of two speech acts when responding to compliments. Some of these combinations are only found in one language variety. It can be observed that the Canadians display a greater level of variety and creativity in their combinations and that five combination patterns emerge as the most preferred by the participants of both groups. Table 41 and Figure 20 summarize the types and frequency of these five most frequently used combination patterns by the participants of both groups.

Table 41: Distribution of the five most preferred two-move responses

	Cameroon	Canada
Thanks + comment	65 (25.79%)	50 (28.90%)
Thanks + credit shift	64 (25.40%)	25 (14.45%)
Thanks + joy	20 (7.94%)	0
Thanks + thanks	19 (7.53%)	12 (6.94%)
Thanks + downgrade	10 (3.97%)	8 (4.62%)
Thanks + offers	0	7 (4.05%)
Total	178 (70.63%)	102 (58.96%)
Other two-move responses	74 (29.37%)	71 (41.04%)
Total (two-move responses)	252 (100%)	173 (100%)

As can be seen in Table 41, the frequency of the five most frequently used combinations of two speech acts in the Cameroonian data is significantly dominant (178 examples of 252 or 70.63%). The other 31 patterns of two-move responses show much lower percentages, ranging between one and eight examples (i.e. with a frequency below 2%). The five most common patterns in the Canadian informants also have a very significant dominance (102 occurrences of 173 or 58.95%). The remaining 40 patterns appear in examples ranging between one and five, i.e. with a frequency below 2%. The most frequently used speech act in both data sets is thanks, which

6. COMPLIMENT RESPONSES

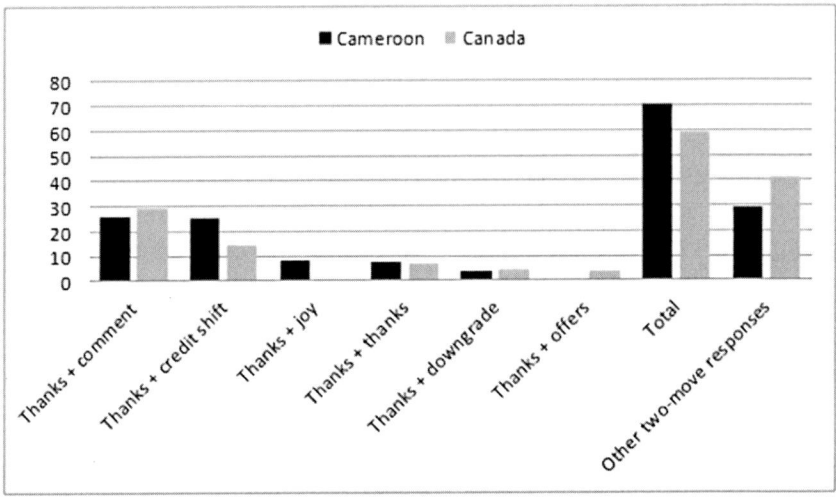

Figure 20: Distribution of the five most preferred two-move responses

appears in 20 of the 36 patterns by the Cameroonian informants and in 23 of the 45 patterns by the Canadian respondents. In both data sets thanks usually occupy the first position (18 examples of 20 in the Cameroonian responses and 18 instances out of 23 in the Canadian data). The five most frequently preferred patterns by the Canadian participants also have a very significant dominance (102 examples of 173 or 58.95%). The remaining 40 patterns in the Canadian data set appear in examples ranging between one and five, i.e. a frequency below 2%.

The participants of both groups show some similarities in terms of preference, although the percentage and types of the five most frequently used patterns reveals some minor divergences. One Canadian respondent uses the combination 'thanks + joy', while twenty examples of this pattern are found in the Cameroonian data. This difference should not be surprising, since there is no expression of joy strategy in the one-move responses. The five most favoured combinations in the Cameroonian corpus make up 70.63% of complex responses with two illocutions, while the five most common patterns in the Canadian data represent 58.95% of complex responses with two speech acts.

From the politeness perspective patterns such as 'thanks + comment', 'thanks + joy', 'thanks + thanks', 'thanks + offer' can be described as intensified positive politeness strategies, and patterns such as 'thanks + credit shift' and 'thanks + downgrade' function as mitigated positive politeness strategies. Below are definitions and examples of the five most common two-move compliment responses in Cameroonian and Canadian French.

Thanks + comment
Several participants in both groups express their gratitude for the compliment and make comments on the complimented object.

29) *Merci mère le travail est la porte du succès.* [E, CMF]
    'Thanks mom, work is the key to success.'
30) *Merci! J'ai travaillé vraiment fort pour avoir ce prix.* [E, CF]
    'Thanks! I really worked hard to have this prize.'

Thanks + credit shift
The compliment receiver expresses gratitude for the compliment and shift the credit to either the compliment giver or to another person.

31) *Merci, c'est grâce à vous que je travaille aussi bien à l'école.* [E, CMF]
    'Thanks, it is thanks to you that I work so well at school.'
32) *Merci, maman ceci est le résultat de votre bonne éducation.* [CF]
    'Thanks, mom, this is the result of your good training.'

Thanks + joy
Many Cameroonians express their gratitude for the verbal gift and indicate that they are (very) happy to receive the compliment or happy with the complimented object, as shown in the following example.

33) *Merci papa; je suis très contente d'avoir reçu ce prix.* [E, CMF]
    'Thanks dad, I am very happy to have been awarded this prize.'

Thanks + thanks
Some informants of both groups combine two expressions of gratitude when responding to compliments. In some examples, the first gratitude expression is followed by the expression of positive feelings about the compliment giver or about the positive evaluation, as shown in the following examples.

34) *Merci, c'est gentil (de ta/votre part).* [CMF]
'Thanks, that's kind (of you).'
35) *Merci, ça me touche beaucoup.* [CF]
'Thanks I am really moved by it (the compliment)'
36) *Merci, c'est très motivant de l'entendre.* [CF]
'Thanks, it is really motivating to hear that [the compliment].'

Thanks + downgrade

Some Cameroonians and Canadians respond with a combination of thanking the compliment giver and downgrading/scaling down the value of the complimented object. Common examples of this response type include (37) and (38).

37) *Merci pour le compliment. Même comme je sais que je n'ai pas été la meilleure joueuse.* [S, CMF]
'Thanks for the compliment. Although I know that I was not the best player.'
38) *Merci, mais je ne suis pas meilleur qu'un autre.* [CF]
'Thanks, but I am not better than anybody else.'

Thanks + offer

Some Canadian respondents express their appreciation for the compliment and offer help to enable the compliment giver to obtain the complimented object. A representative example is shown in (39).

39) *Merci! Si tu veux, nous pourrions collaborer ensemble pour le prochain exposé.* [P, CF]
'Thanks! If you like, we can work together for the next presentation.'

Overall, 248 occurrences (98.41%) of the 252 two-move responses in the Cameroonian data belong to the intensified complex responses and only 4 Cameroonians (1.59%) make use of ambiguous two-move responses. The bulk of two-move responses in the Canadian data (163 of 173, 94.22%) consist of intensified complex responses, while 10 instances of ambiguous complex responses (5.78%) are used by some of the Canadians. In the Cameroonian corpus, the ambiguous two-move responses occur in case where they respondents combine a gratitude expression and the act of upgrading praise, as shown in the following examples.

6.2. COMPLIMENT RESPONSE PATTERNS 151

40) *Merci, mon pote, quand on a de la classe dans le sang on ne peut pas faire autrement.* [CMF]
'Thanks, my friend, when you have class in your blood you cannot do otherwise.'

41) *Je le savais, monsieur que j'étais le meilleur mais merci de l'avoir remarquer.* [CMF]
'I already knew that, sir, that I was the best but thanks for having noticed it.'

The patterns of ambiguous two-move responses in the Canadian data are higher in number and much more varied than in the Cameroonian data. The ten responses produced by the Canadians are the result of the combination of thanks, praise upgrade, comment, agreement, and/or joke, as shown in the examples below.

42) *Normal qu'ils me vont bien, j'ai le sens de mode ! Merci.* [CF]
'It's normal that they fit me well, I have a great sense of fashion! Thanks.'

43) *Merci, j'ai toujours été un dieu en cuisine.* [CF]
'Thanks, I have always been a god in cooking.'

44) *Je sais, c'est moi qui l'ai fait.* [CF]
'I know, I am the one who baked it.'

Also, two Canadians repeat the negatively loaded response praise upgrade, thus producing an intensified two-move response, as shown in example (45).

45) *C'est normal, j'ai du style !* [CF]
'It's normal, I have class!'

6.2.2.2. THREE-MOVE RESPONSES

The 67 occurrences of three-move responses in the Cameroonian data appear in 38 different combinations, while the 31 three-move responses in the Canadian corpus occur in 25 different combinations. The results show that some patterns of these types of complex responses are only used in one data set. As a matter of fact, 30 of the 38 patterns identified in the Cameroonian examples appear only in this data set. Also, of the 25 patterns produced by the Canadians, 21 are not represented in the Cameroonian data. The speech act of thanking is mostly used by the participants of both groups in the responses involving three speech acts. The Cameroonians use thanks in 64 of the 67 occurrences (95.52%) and in 35 (92.10%) of the 38 combinations. Thanks occupy the first position in 27 instances (77.14%). In the Canadian data, thanks occur in 22 (88%) of the 25 combinations and in 27 (87.09%) of the 31 examples of responses involving three speech acts. Also, expressions of gratitude occupy the first position in 19 (86.36%) of the 22 combinations identified. Four patterns of three-move responses emerge as the most preferred by the Cameroonians. Each of them appear five times (7.46%). The 34 remaining patterns occur respectively between one to three times, thus showing a frequency below 1%. Below are examples of the four most common patterns

Thanks + credit shift + credit shift
The recipient expresses gratitude for the compliment and shifts the credit to the compliment giver or to someone else.

46) *Merci parce que c'est grâce à vous que j'ai reçu ce prix, c'est à vous que je le dois.* [CMF]
'Thanks because it is thanks to you that I received this prize, I owe you this.'

Thanks + comment + joy
Examples in this category can be paraphrased as 'I am grateful for the positive evaluation. I would like to let you know something else concerning the complimented object about which I very happy'.

47) *Merci bien, papa/maman. Il fallait véritablement que je me surpasse pour obtenir ce prix, mais aussi mon objectif a été de vous surprendre positivement. Alors, je suis fier de moi.* [CMF]
'Thanks a lot dad/mom. I really had to surpass myself in order to obtain this prize, but also my goal was to surprise you positively. So, I am proud of myself.'

Thanks + credit shift + comment
Some participants thank the speaker for the compliment, then indicate that the compliment giver or someone else contributed to the complimented object. Participants also made comments about the complimented object.

48) *Merci, c'est grâce à vous quelque part. Il faut bien que j'excelle quelque part.* [CMF]
'Thanks, it is somehow thanks to you. I have to excel somewhere.'

Thanks + downgrade + comment
The recipients express their appreciation for the compliment and then mitigate the force of the positive evaluation before making a comment.

49) *Je vous remercie, mais ce n'est pas vraiment grand-chose. En plus, j'ai pris du plaisir à le confectionner pour vous.* [CMF]
'I thank you, but it is not really a big thing. Moreover, I was pleased to do it for you.'

The four most preferred three-move responses in the Canadian data make up to 32.25% of complex responses featuring three speech acts. Each of the remaining 21 patterns appears only once (3.22%). While the first strategy occurs four times (12.90%), the other three combinations are respectively used in two instances (6.45%) in the data. Below are some examples of these types of responses.

Thanks + comment + joy

50) *Merci, effectivement j'ai travaillé très fort sur ce projet. Je suis fière de moi.* [CF]
'Thanks, indeed, I worked very hard on this project. I am proud of myself.'

Thanks + downgrade + comment

51) *Merci, ma présentation n'était pas la meilleure, mais j'ai beaucoup travaillé dessus.* [CF]
'Thanks, my presentation was not the best, but I worked a lot on it.'

Thanks + thanks + comment

52) *Merci ses gentil, mais j'ai travaillé fort pour avoir se prix.* [CF]
'Thanks, that's kind of you, but I worked hard to earn this prize.'

Thanks + thanks + downgrade

53) *Merci beaucoup, j'apprécie votre remarque, je fais de mon mieux.* [CF]
'Thanks so much, I appreciate your remark, I do my best.'

6.2.2.3. FOUR-MOVE RESPONSES

Six Cameroonians use the following combinations of four speech acts in response to compliments.

Thanks + thanks + comment + invitation

54) *Merci c'est gentil ! le prochain exposé c'est pour bientôt et je t'invite à prendre part.* [CMF]
'Thanks, that's kind of you. The next presentation is coming soon and I invite you to work with me.'

Thanks + comment + downgrade + advice

55) *Merci beaucoup mais ce n'était pas évident j'avais beaucoup de stress, mais c'est rien le secret c'est d'apprendre (étudier).* [CMF]
'Thanks very much, but it was not obvious, I have a lot of stress, but that's nothing, the secret is to learn.'

Thanks + downgrade + credit shift + credit shift

56) *Cher Monsieur/Madame, votre compliment me touche beaucoup car jamais je n'ai imaginé un seul instant que vous m'admiriez autant. Tout conte fait, c'est grâce à vous qui avez contribué à mon éducation scolaire et je dois aussi mon succès à mes parents qui m'ont toujours encouragé.* [CMF]
'Dear sir/madam, your compliment touches me a lot, for I have never imagined that you admired me that much. All the same, it's thanks to you who contributed to my education and I owed all my success to my parents who have always encouraged me.'

Thanks + surprise + comment + joy

57) *Merci beaucoup. Je ne pensais pas que cela vous plairait autant! Cela voudrait donc dire que je suis déjà un cordon bleu en pâtisserie, et je me réjouis de cet atout.* [CMF]
'Thanks very much. I didn't know that this could please you that much. It means that I am already a cordon bleu in baking and I am happy for this gift.'

Thanks + joy + comment + thanks

58) *Merci, et cela me va droit au cœur. Je ne savais pas que non seulement vous m'observiez tout au long du match, mais aussi que vous détectiez le/la meilleur joueur/joueuse! Merci encore, pour vos mots.* [CMF]
'Thank you and this goes directly to my heart. I didn't know that you not only watched me throughout the match, but you were also identifying the best player. Once more thanks for your words.'

Thanks + thanks + comment + credit shift

59) *Merci, c'est gentil de votre part. Mais vous savez, notre jeu dépend entièrement de vous spectateurs, et vous avez été très bons ce soir.* [CMF]
'Thanks, that's very kind of you. But you know, our game largely depends on you, spectators and you are very good this evening.'

Only one Canadian combines four speech acts to respond to a compliment as seen in the sample below.

Praise upgrade + comment + comment + thanks

60) *Je sais! J'arrête pas d'en manger, c'est trop bon. Merci!* [CF]
'I know! I can't stop eating it [cake], it's too delicious. Thanks!'

As can be seen from the examples above, thanks appear in all the four-move responses in both data sets. However, in the four examples from the Cameroonian data, gratitude expressions occupy the first position, while thanks appear in the final position in the Canadian response.

6.3. Linguistic features of compliment responses

This section presents realization patterns of the most frequently used speech acts in responding to compliments. The patterns are defined and/or illustrated below with representative examples from the data.

6.3.1. Expressions of thanks and/or joy

In both varieties of French under study, thanks are realized by the appreciation token *merci* 'thank you / thanks', employed alone or in combination with other elements. According to Jautz (2008: 150), "there are three optional elements often found along with expressions of gratitude: Speakers may name the benefactor of their gratitude, they may intensify their gratitude by adding particles [...] to the expression of gratitude they use, and they may give a reason why they are grateful". Kerbrat-Orecchioni (2005a: 129) also indicates that expressions of gratitude may focus on the speaker's feelings (gratitude, joy, pleasure), on the hearer, the benefactor, or the gift (the compliment in our study). In the following discussion, we will consider expressions of thanks and joy as strategies of compliment acceptance. The examples from the data show that when accepting compliments, some informants either express gratitude or joy. The results presented below take into account all the tokens employed to express gratitude and/or joy in simple and complex responses in both data sets. Overall, the Cameroonian participants 433 tokens (394 expressions of gratitude and 39 examples of joy expressions) and the Canadian informants employ 264 tokens (256 expressions of gratitude and eight joy expressions).

6.3.1.1. EXPRESSIONS OF GRATITUDE IN CANADIAN FRENCH

Let's look at the breakdown in Table 42 of gratitude and joy expressions employed by the Canadian respondents.

Table 42: Distribution gratitude and joy expressions in Canadian French

Expressions of gratitude and/or joy	Frequency
Merci 'thanks'	160 (60.60%)
(Mais) merci beaucoup '(But) thanks very much'	40 (15.15%)
Ah/haha/ben/bien/wow/oh/eh bien merci 'ah thanks very much'	22 (8.33%)
C'est gentil (de ta/votre part)//t'es gentil 'that's kind of you'	12 (4.55%)
(Bien) Merci monsieur/madame/professeur/tout le monde '(Good) Thank you, sir/madam/professor, everybody'	11 (4.17%)
(Bien) Merci beaucoup monsieur '(Good) Thanks very much sir'	5 (1.89%)
(Je suis) contente de/que '(I am) happy that'	4 (1.52%)

6.3. LINGUISTIC FEATURES OF COMPLIMENT RESPONSES 157

(Mais) Merci du compliment '(But) thanks for the compliment'	3 (1.14%)
Ça (me) fait plaisir/c'est un plaisir de l'entendre 'I am happy to hear that'	3 (1.14%)
Merci d'avoir Vé 'Thanks for having V-ed'	1 (0.38%)
Merci quand même 'Thanks all the same'	1 (0.38%)
J'en suis reconnaissant 'I am very grateful'	1 (0.38%)
Ça me touche beaucoup 'I am really touched'	1 (0.38%)
Total	264 (100%)

As indicated in Table 42, the Canadians overwhelmingly employ *merci* 'thanks / thank you'. The second most frequent pattern is the combination *merci beaucoup* 'thank you very much / thanks a lot' and the third pattern is the case where *merci* is preceded by interjections such as *ah, wow, bien* as in (61).

61) *Wow / Ah! merci !*
 'Wow / Ah thanks!'

Another form of gratitude in the Canadian data set is to name the compliment giver, by using nominal address forms such as *professeur* 'professor' , *madame* 'madam' , *monsieur* 'sir'. Some informants express their gratitude by combining elements of the categories mentioned before: e.g. *merci + adverb of intensity + address form* as in (62) and *interjection + merci + address form* as in (63)

62) *Merci beaucoup monsieur.* [CF]
 'Thanks a lot, sir.'
63) *Bien merci monsieur.* [CF]
 'Good thank you, sir.'

Naming reasons for gratitude also occurs in the Canadian responses. The participants employ structures such as *du + NP* as in (64) and *de + VP* as in (65) after the appreciation token *merci*.

64) *Merci du compliment.* [CF]
 'Thanks for the compliment.'
65) *Merci de ne pas t'avoir endormi avant la fin de mon exposé.* [CF]

'Thanks that you didn't fall asleep before the end of my presentation.'
The second example can be considered as an expanded form of the first structure, and serves as a reaction not to the compliment but to the attention paid to the presentation of the recipient. One Canadian informant combined several of intensifiers and indicated the reason for gratitude in the response, as in (66)

66) *Eh bien merci beaucoup pour cette remarque.* [CF]
'Well thanks a lot for that remark.'

6.3.1.2. EXPRESSIONS OF GRATITUDE AND JOY IN CAMEROON FRENCH

The Cameroonian participants use a wider range of linguistic forms to thank or express their joy to the compliment giver, as can be seen in Table 43, below.

Table 43: Distribution of gratitude and joy expressions in Cameroon French

Expressions of gratitude/joy	Frequency
Merci	136 (31.40%)
Merci papa/maman/professeur/camarade	115 (26.56%)
Merci pour/du NP (cela, le/ton/votre compliment/ l'appréciation, tout, ta présence, cette remarque)	45 (10.39%)
C'est gentil (de ta/votre part)	34 (7.85%)
Merci bien/beaucoup (monsieur/papa/camarade)	25 (5.77%)
Je te/vous remercie (beaucoup)	13 (3.00%)
Cela/ça/votre compliment / me touche vraiment / je suis très touché / c'est très touchant / encourageant	10 (2.30%)
J'en / je suis flatté / honoré / vous me flattez	8 (1.85%)
Merci de Ver / d'avoir Vé	8 (1.85%)
J'en / je suis ravi / vous m'envoyez ravi	6 (1.39%)
Ça/cela me va droit au cœur	6 (1.39%)
Je suis heureux / content de / que ...	5 (1.15%)
Oh merci	4 (0.92%)
Merci à vous	4 (0.92%)

6.3. LINGUISTIC FEATURES OF COMPLIMENT RESPONSES

Tout le plaisir est pour moi / le mien / ça me fait plaisir d'entendre	4(0.92%)
J'en suis reconnaissant	3(0.69%)
Je me réjouis / ça me donne une grande joie	2(0.46%)
Je suis vraiment émue / je suis fier	2(0.46%)
Merci de votre part	1(0.23%)
Dieu merci	1(0.23%)
Merci quand même	1(0.23%)
Total	433(100%)

The most common pattern is *merci* 'thanks / thank you', followed by structures in which the appreciation token *merci* is intensified by address terms such as *madame* 'madam' *monsieur* 'sir' *professeur* 'professor', *maman* 'mom', *papa* 'dad', *camarade* 'friend'. The other most preferred pattern is to give reasons for gratitude. This occurs in the form of *merci + pour/de/du + NP*. The *NP* consists of a word or group of words employed to indicate how the respondent's perception of the compliment. As the examples below show, some Cameroonians perceive compliments as *encouragement, appreciation, congratulation*, etc.

67) *Merci pour vos félicitations.* [CMF]
    'Thanks for your compliments.'
68) *Merci professeurs pour tout.* [CMF]
    'Thanks professor for everything.'
69) *Merci pour ton/votre appréciation/attention.* [CMF]
    'Thanks for your admiration/attention.'
70) *Merci monsieur de votre présence.* [CMF]
    'Thanks for your presence.'
71) *Merci de vos encouragements.* [CMF]
    'Thanks for your encouragements.'
72) *Merci pour le/du compliment!* [CMF]
    'Thanks for the compliment.'

Another pattern employed to express gratitude is *merci + de VP*. In the structures identified, the VP consist of verbs in the infinitive (*for V-ing*) form or in the *passé composé* (*for having V-ed*) as in (73), or verbs used to indicate the reasons for one's gratitude (*for having V-ed and for V-ing*) as in (74) – (76).

73) *Merci de l'apprécier à sa juste valeur.* [CMF]
'Thanks for appreciating it for its real value.' [Note: translation is problematic.]
74) *Merci d'avoir apprécié mon gâteau.* [CMF]
'Thanks for having liked my cake.'
75) *Merci d'avoir assisté au match.*
'Thanks for having watched the game.'
76) *Merci d'avoir assisté au match et de me faire cette remarque.* [CMF]
'Thanks for having watched the game and for making this remark to me.' [Note: translation is problematic.]

One Cameroonian expresses gratitude not for the compliment but for the compliment giver's contribution to the compliment recipient's education. This seems to explain the length of the response. In this context, this strategy may serve as an indirect response to the compliment on the speaker's success and a direct expression of gratitude for a non-verbal action that was beneficial to the compliment recipient.

77) *Merci M ou Mme pour tout ce que vous avez fait tout au long de l'année.* [CMF]
'Thanks Sir / Madam for everything you did during the (school) year.'

As Table 6 shows, the Cameroonians also use structures of the type *c'est gentil (de ta/votre part)* 'that's kind (of you). In addition to the forms already mentioned, some Cameroonians express their gratitude with performative structures such as *je vous remercie* 'I thank you' and *je te remercie pour ton compliment* 'I thank you for your compliment.'; *je vous suis reconnaissant.* 'I am grateful to you'. Expressions of joy are conveyed by structures containing the verb *se réjouir* "to rejoice / be glad', adjectives such *ému* 'touched', *fier* 'glad/proud/happy', or nouns such as *plaisir* 'pleasure', *(grande) joie* 'great joy'.

6.3.2. EXPRESSIONS OF CREDIT SHIFT

When responding to compliments, the addressee may shift credit to another person, a group of people or to the compliment giver. The choice of the target usually varies according to situations and the realization forms employed may also indicate if the compliment recipient totally or partially shifts the credit to someone else.

6.3.2.1. EXPRESSIONS OF CREDIT SHIFTS IN CAMEROON FRENCH

The most common way to shift credit is to use structures with *c'est grâce à* toi/vous 'thanks to you' or *c'est grâce à ton/votre* X 'it's due to your X' as can be seen in the following examples:

78) *C'est aussi grâce à votre soutient.* [CMF]
    'It's due to your support.'
79) *C'est grâce à toi que j'ai réussi.* [CMF]
    'I succeeded thanks to you.'

In other variants of this pattern, the informants combine the *c'est grâce à* with an *if-clause* in order to indicate the cause-effect relationship between the complimented object and the contribution of a different source as in (80).

80) *Si je suis arrivé à ce bon résultat c'est grâce à vous.* [CMF]
    'If I have achieved this result it's thanks to you.'

The second most preferred form is to explicitly indicate that without the contribution of a third person or the compliment giver the recipient would not have achieved the complimented object. This form is characterized by the use of the conjunction *sans* 'without', as shown in the following example.

81) *Sans vous je n'y serai pas arrivé.* [CMF]
    'Without you I wouldn't have achieved this (result).'

In some of the examples of this category, the participants employ conditional or causal structures as in (82) and (83)

82) *Je ne l'aurais pas eu si vous ne nous aviez pas dispensé des cours.* [CMF]
    'I wouldn't have passed my exam if you had not taught us.'
83) *J'ai réussi à mon examen parce que j'avais suivi vos conseils et je les avais respectés.* [CMF]
    'I succeeded in my exam because I followed and respected your advice.'

In some cases the informants either express emphatic credit shifts, i.e. those containing adverbs or adverbial clauses that maximize the sincerity of the compliment recipient as in (84) – (86), or express mitigated credit shifts, i.e. those containing adverbs or adverbial phrases with mitigating function as in (87) – (88).

84) *Tout cela grâce à vous et vos consignes.* [CMF]
   '(I did) **all this** thanks to your advice.'
85) *C'est **en grande partie** grâce à votre rigueur et votre discipline.* [CMF]
   'It's **mostly** due to your rigor and discipline.'
86) *C'est **en particulier** grâce à vous, **vous y êtes pour beaucoup**.* [CMF]
   'It's **particularly** thanks to you, you contributed a lot.'
87) *C'est **un peu** grâce à vous car vous m'avez bien tenu pendant toute mon année académique.* [CMF]
   'It's **a bit** thanks to your since you taught well during the academic year.'
88) *Tu y es pour **quelque chose**.* [CMF]
   'You **somehow** contributed to it.'

In some examples credit shifts are expressed by structures containing the expression *(tout) le mérite revient à / (tout) le merit vous revient* 'X deserves (all) the credit / you get (all) the credit.' Common examples from the data are (89) – (91).

89) *Tout le mérite revient à toi.* [CMF]
   'All the credit goes to you.'
90) *Le mérite vous revient d'une part pour nous avoir encadrés.* [CMF]
   'You deserve the credit on the one hand for having taught us.'
91) *Le mérite vous revient pour vos efforts à notre égard.* [CMF]
   'You deserve the credit for your efforts towards us.'

Some Cameroonian respondents explicitly express indebtedness using the verb *devoir* 'to owe.', as can be seen in (92) and (93).

92) *C'est à vous que je le dois.* [CMF]
   'I owe this to you.'
93) *Je dois aussi mon succès à mes parents qui m'ont toujours encouragé.* [CMF]
   'I also owe my success to my parents who always encouraged me.'

6.3. LINGUISTIC FEATURES OF COMPLIMENT RESPONSES

Credit shifts are also expressed by describing the contribution of the addressee or of someone else to the complimented objected. In this case, the compliment recipient generally chooses structures containing verbs such as *encourager* 'to encourage' and *aider* 'to help' and nouns like *aide* 'help' and *soutien* "support', as shown in samples (94) and (95).

94) *Vous m'avez beaucoup aidé et encouragé, votre soutien m'a été d'une grande aide.* [CMF]
 'You helped and encouraged me a lot, your support was of great help to me.'
95) *Vous m'avez vraiment encouragé.* [CMF]
 'You really encouraged me.'

Other structures are used to indicate the contribution of a third party. The expressions employed are generally introduced by *c'est*, as shown in the examples (96) and (97).

96) *C'est ma mère qui l'a appris.* [CMF]
 'My mother taught me (how to do it.'
97) *C'est ma mère qui me l'a offert pour mon bon résultat.* [CMF]
 'My mother offered it to me for my good results (at school).'

6.3.2.2. EXPRESSIONS OF CREDIT SHIFTS IN CANADIAN FRENCH

The expressions used to realize credit shift in the Canadian data follow the patterns presented below.

 Forms with *c'est grâce à*. They may be intensified or mitigated, as shown in (98) and (99).

98) *C'est gentil de faire la remarque, mais c'est aussi grâce à vous.* [CF]
 'It's kind to make the observation, but it is also thanks to you.'
99) *C'est **un peu** grâce à vous.* [CF]
 'It is a bit thanks to you.'

Some Canadian French speakers chose the strategy of describing the compliment giver's contribution as in (100) and (101)

100) *Mais c'est vous qui m'ont pousser à étudier.* [CF]
 'But you are the one who encouraged me to study.'
101) *Vous m'avez beaucoup aidé.* [CF]
 'You helped me a lot.'

Another strategy is to compliment the compliment giver as shown in (102) and (103).

102) *Non, c'est vous qui est un bon prof.* [CF]
 'No, you are a good teacher.'
103) *Mais faut dire que j'avais des bon profs.* [CF]
 'But I should say that I had good teachers.'

Also attested are forms with which the compliment recipient indicates that the complimented object/action would not have been acquired / taken place without the contribution of the compliment giver. Typical examples from the corpus are (104) and (105).

104) *Mais j'aurais pas réussi sans vous.* [CF]
 'But I would have succeeded without you.'
105) *Sans votre enseignement, peut-être que je n'aurai pas réussi.* [CF]
 'Without your teachings, perhaps I wouldn't have succeeded.'

Also appearing in the data set are forms indicating the contribution of someone other than the compliment giver. The third party may be an individual as in (106) and (107) or a group of people (e.g. a team) as in (108) – (114).

106) *C'est ma chère qui m'a donner la recette!* [CF]
 'My mother gave me the recipe.'
107) *Mais ce n'est pas moi qui l'a faite.* [CF]
 'But I am not the one who did it.'
108) *Mais sans l'équipe je n'aurai pas aussi bien joué.* [CF]
 'But without the team I wouldn't have played well.'
109) *Mais faut dire qu'on a une bonne équipe.* [CF]
 'But I should say that we have a good team.'
110) *Sans l'aide de mes coéquipiers, je n'aurai pas connu un fort match.* [CF]
 'Without the help of my team-mates I wouldn't have had a good match.'
111) *C'est grâce à toute l'équipe si nous avons remporté!* [CF]
 'It's thanks to the entire team that we won.'
112) *Mais ce n'est pas grâce à moi, l'équipe y était présente aussi.* [CF]
 'But it's not thanks to me, the team was also present.'
113) *Mais le reste de l'équipe a très bien joué.* [CF]
 'But the rest of the team played very well.'

114) *Je le dois à mes coéquipiers!* [CF]
'I owe it (the success) to my team mates.'

In some cases the recipients combine credit shift and compliments as in (115).

115) *C'est aussi grâce à vous qui êtes un si bon prof.* [CF]
'It is thanks to you who are a very good teacher.'

The Canadians seem to express credit shift in much the same manner as the Cameroonians

6.3.3. EXPRESSIONS OF ADVICE

6.3.3.1. EXPRESSIONS OF ADVICE IN CAMEROON FRENCH

The realization patterns of advice in the Cameroonian data are illustrated below with examples from the corpus.

Allusion to the action the compliment giver has to take

The compliment giver is informed of the (minimum) condition to be fulfilled. The vast majority of examples belonging to this category are structures with *il suffit de* 'you just need to'. In some cases the advice is mitigated with the downtoner *juste* 'just'.

116) *Il suffit d'être concentré et de savoir pourquoi tu es devant tes camarades.* [CMF]
'You need to be concentrated and to know why you are in front of your friends.'

117) *Il suffit juste de beaucoup travailler.* [CMF]
'You just need to work hard.'

Another variant of these forms contains the structure *tu n'as qu'à* + V. 'you just have to V.'

118) *Tu n'as qu'à t'y mettre et tout sera très facile pour toi aussi.* [CMF]
'You just have to start and everything will be very easy for you too.'

Allusion to the action the compliment giver should take

The compliment recipient employs structures with *il faut/faudrait* 'you have to/should' that express deontic modality. Common examples from the data are listed below.

119) *Il faut beaucoup travailler et tu y arriveras.* [CMF]
   'You have to work hard and you'll make it.'
120) *Il faut te donner à fond.* [CMF]
   'You have to give your best.'
121) *Cher(e) Camarade il faut persévérer dans le travail.* [CMF]
   'Dear friend you have to persevere in your work.'
122) *Mais il faudrait juste travailler pour y parvenir.* [CMF]
   'But you just have to work toreach your goal.'

Indication that it is up to the compliment giver to do what he/she is advised to do

123) *Mais c'est à toi d'être sérieux et attentif et puis tout ira mieux.* [CMF]
   'But it's up to you to be serious and attentive and then everything will be better.'
124) *C'est très facile si tu le veux et si tu a confiance en toi et en tes recherches.* [CMF]
   'It is very simple if you want it and if you have confidence in yourself and in your research.' [Note: translation problematic.]

Direct advice with imperative structures

125) *Travaille et tu deviendras comme moi.* [CMF]
   'Work and you'll be like me.'
126) *Fais tes recherches à fond; là tu feras une belle présentation.* [CMF]
   'Do your research thoroughly; then you will do a great presentation.'

Indirect advice

127) *Mais ce travail suscite et exige un maximum de temps.* [CMF]
   'But this work demands a great deal of time.'
128) *Le secret c'est d'apprendre (étudier).* [CMF]
   'The secret is to study.'

6.3.3.2. EXPRESSIONS OF ADVICE IN CANADIAN FRENCH

The Canadians also use most of the patterns found in the Cameroonian corpus when offering advice as compliment responses.

Direct advice with imperative structures

In some cases, the imperative structures containing the advice are combined with the allusion to the positive consequences of the recommended action.

129) *Fais de gros efforts.* [CF]
   'Make great efforts.'
130) *Bon travail fort pi tu vas l'avoir.* [CF]
   'Then work hard and then you'll have it.'
131) *Étudie comme moi et force toi et tu verras que t'aura les mêmes résultats que moi.* [CF]
   'Study like me and do your best and you'll see that you'll have the same results like me.'

When giving advice, some respondents allude to the conditions to be fulfilled by using constructions with *si* '*if*', as shown in the following examples.

132) *Si tu travaille fort en oubliant le stress et en restant à l'aise tu aura d'excellent scores.* [CF]
   'If you work hard, don't think about stress and stay relaxed you'll have excellent grades.'
133) *Si tu veux faire comme moi, force toi.* [CF]
   'If you want to do like me do your best.'

The Canadian participants also employ structures alluding to what the compliment giver has to / get to or should do. They use structures with either *il suffit* 'you have to', *il faut/faudrait* 'you should', or *tu n'as qu'à V* 'you just have to V', as can be seen in the following examples.

134) *Il suffit d'avoir la bonne information.* [CF]
   'You have to get the right information.'
135) *Il faut persévérer et travailler fort et se pratiquer.* [CF]
   'You have to persist and work hard and practice.'
136) *Il faut juste que tu apprend bien le texte et que tu sois naturel.* [CF]
   'You just have to learn the text well and be natural.'
137) *Tu n'as qu'à t'appliquer et tu réussiras, je te garantis.* [CF]
   'You just have to apply yourself more and you'll succeed, I guarantee you.'

Apart from some minor differences, the Cameroonians and the Canadians employ the same patterns when giving advice as compliment responses.

6.3.4. Expressions of downgrading

6.3.4.1. Expressions of downgrading in Cameroon French

The speakers of Cameroon French minimize the value of the complimented object in many different ways. Some participants describe the complimented object as literally 'nothing (valuable / miraculous / worthy of praise)' as in (138), (1390, and (140), as 'something everybody can do' as in (141). Other respondents prefer structures that are normally used to respond to gratitude expressions, as in (142).

138) *C'est rien.* [CMF]
  'It's nothing.'
139) *Non ce n'est pas un miracle.* [CMF]
  'No it's not a miracle.'
140) *Mais ce n'est pas vraiment pas grand-chose.* [CMF]
  'But it's not really a big deal.'
141) *Tu sais, c'est n'est que du travail; tout le monde peut faire une bonne prestation.* [CMF]
  'You know it's just work, everybody can give a good presentation.'
142) *De rien / Il y a pas de quoi.* [CMF]
  'Don't mention.'

The compliment recipient may indicate that the complimented object/action is *(very) easy/simple/natural* or is *not difficult to achieve*. Common examples are

143) *C'est très facile.* [CMF]
  'It's very easy.'
144) *Ce n'est pas du tout difficile.* [CMF]
  'It's not difficult at all.'
145) *Mais ce n'était pas difficile!* [CMF]
  'But it was not difficult.'

When responding to compliments on (new) possessions, some respondents scale down the (monetary) value of the object, as shown in the following examples.

146) *Il n'est pas cher.* [CMF]
  'It was not expensive.'

6.3. LINGUISTIC FEATURES OF COMPLIMENT RESPONSES

147) *C'est pas si cher.* [CMF]
'It's not that expensive.'
148) *Ce n'est peut-être pas le meilleur sur le marché.* [CMF]
'It's perhaps not the best on the market.'

In some examples, the respondents indicate that the action of the recipient is not a big deal compared to what the manufacturer did.

149) *J'ai juste eu le privilège de faire un bon choix.* [CMF]
'I just had the privilege to make the right choice.'

Some participants indicate that the admired performance is not the result of an individual effort. This pattern could also be interpreted as an act of shifting credit.

150) *Mais je n'ai pas joué seule.* [CMF]
'But I did not play alone.'

Downgrading a compliment is also realized by hoping that the compliment giver is not wrong in their judgement. This pattern may also functions as a demand for confirmation/reiteration of the compliment.

151) *Mais, j'espère que vous ne vous tromper pas.* [CMF]
'But I hope you are not wrong.'

Another strategy to downgrade is to present the admired action as something that happened by chance.

152) *Mais je me suis débrouillé, tu sais.* [CMF]
'But I just managed to do it, you know.'

Some participants either indicate that the compliment is exaggerated or ask the compliment giver not to exaggerate.

153) *Vous en faites trop.* [CMF]
'You are exaggerating.'
154) *Vous me gêner, vous en faites trop.* [CMF]
'You annoy me, you are exaggerating.'
155) *N'exagérez pas tout de même.* [CMF]
'Don't exaggerate, however.'

In some instances, the recipient minimizes the value of the action by indicating that it was motivated by a quite different cause.

156) *J'ai juste fait mon devoir papa.* [CMF]
 'I just did what I had to do dad.'

Also attested are examples in which the respondent indicates that the recipient is not great / the best.

157) *Même comme je sais que je n'ai pas été la meilleure joueuse.* [CMF]
 'Even as I know that I was not the best player.'
158) *Je ne suis pas un grand cuisinier.* [CMF]
 'I am not a great cook.'

Explicit surprise could also be interpreted as a sign of humility, as shown in the following example.

159) *Je n'ai imaginé un seul instant que vous m'admiriez autant.* [CMF]
 'I never imagined that you admired me that much.'

Some informants reinforce the strategy of downgrading with the expression of encouragement as in (160)

160) *Ce n'est pas un miracle car toi aussi tu peux le faire.* [CMF]
 'It's not a miracle since you can also do it.'

6.3.4.2. EXPRESSIONS OF DOWNGRADING IN CANADIAN FRENCH

The patterns used to scale down the compliment / the complimented object in Canadian French parallel those of the Cameroonian participants. Some Canadians describe the complimented object as literally 'nothing (valuable/miraculous) worthy of praise', as in (161) or as something natural / not as difficult as it seems as in (162) and (163). Others prefer patterns used to respond to gratitude expressions, as in (165).

161) *C'est rien.* [CF]
 'It's nothing.'
162) *C'est tout naturelle.* [CF]
 'It's natural.'
163) *C'est pas aussi dure que ça en a l'air tu sais.* [CF]
 'It's not as hard as it seems you know.'
164) *Bah. C'est pas si difficile.* [CF]
 'Well, it was not that difficult.'
165) *De rien Ma et Pa!* [CF]
 'Don't mention Mom and Dad!'

Some Canadian informants indicate that they are not the best or that their performance is not the best.

166) *Ma présentation n'était pas la meilleure.* [CF]
'My presentation was not the best.'
167) *C'était pas si bon que ça.* [CF]
'It was not as good as you think.'

When responding to compliments on (new) possessions, some Canadians scale down the (monetary) value of the object, as shown in the following examples.

168) *Je les ai eu pas cher.* [CF]
'I bought them at a moderate price.'
169) *Mais le téléphone est a bon marché.* [CF]
'But the phone is very cheap.'

Some Canadians indicate that they just did/do their best or managed to do their best.

170) *Je fais de mon mieux.* [CF]
'I am doing my best.'
171) *J'essaye de faire de mon mieux.* [CF]
'I try to do my best.'

Some examples in the Canadian data set allude to circumstances that helped the compliment recipient to perform well.

172) *Mais le gardien de l'autre équipe ne portait pas ses lunettes.* [S, CF]
'But the goalkeeper of the other team was not wearing his glasses.'

There is also an instance of self-denigration as strategy to scale down the compliment, as shown in (173).

173) *Je trouvais que j'étais moche.* [CF]
'I found that I was ugly.'

Some Canadian participants indicate that they would accept the compliment only because the compliment giver said so, thus presenting in the verbal gift as subjective.

174) *Si vous le dites.* [CF]
'If you say so.'

6.4. SITUATIONAL DISTRIBUTION OF COMPLIMENT RESPONSES

This section will discuss each of the eight questionnaire situations. The analysis will help to answer the question whether the compliment responses vary as the situation changes. By situation, we understand the combination of social distance (friend, stranger, and acquaintance), power distance (equal, superior) and topic (possession, appearance, and skills). The first part of the section will focus on the situational distribution of the most frequently used types of compliment responses in both corpora and the second part will deal with the description of the individual situations.

6.4.1. MOST FREQUENT COMPLIMENT RESPONSE STRATEGIES

Situational variation can be observed with regard to the three major / most frequent compliment response strategies in both language varieties. It should be reminded that, when responding to compliments the Cameroonian and Canadian French speakers mostly prefer the following types of responses as presented in Table 44 and Figure 21.

Table 44: Distribution of the three most favoured response types

	Cameroon	Canada
Thanks	71 of 434 (16.36%)	79 of 309 (25.57%)
Thanks + comment	65 of 434 (14.97%)	50 309 (16.18%)
Thanks + credit shift:	64 of 434 (14.74%)	25 of 309 (8.09%)

Apart from the statistical differences in the distribution of the three major response types in both data sets, the results also reveal differences with regard to the distribution of the major compliment responses across the eight situations for both varieties of French, as can be seen in Table 45.

6.4. SITUATIONAL DISTRIBUTION OF COMPLIMENT RESPONSES

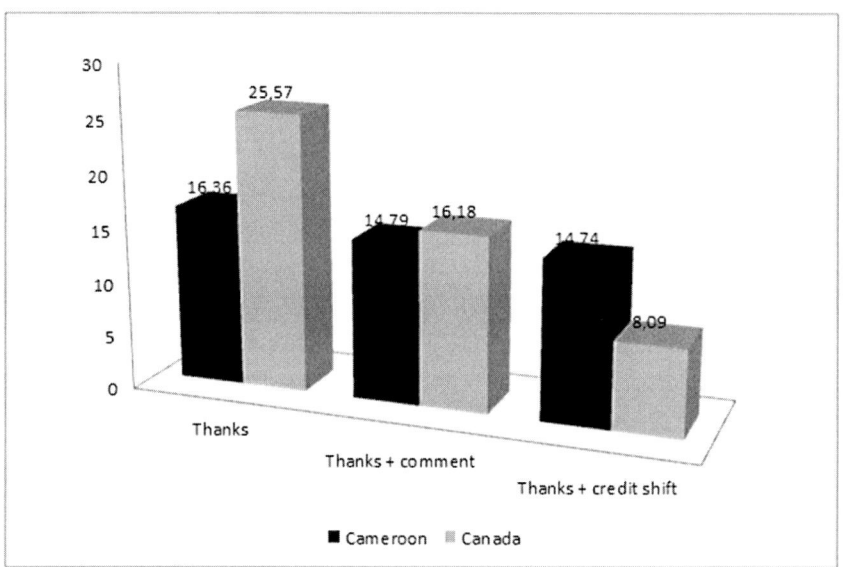

Figure 21: Distribution of the three most favoured response types

Table 45: Situational distribution of the major compliment response types

Situations	Thanks		Thanks + Comment		Thanks + Credit shift	
	CMF	CF	CMF	CF	CMF	CF
1	5 (7.04%)	9 (11.39%)	9 (13.85%)	7 (14%)	13 (20.31%)	3 (12%)
2	1 (1.40%)	5 (6.32%)	5 (7.69%)	3 (6%)	0	0
3	8 (11.26%)	7 (8.86%)	3 (4.62%)	3 (6%)	25 (39.06%)	11 (44%)
4	14 (19.71%)	5 (6.32%)	11 (16.92%)	9 (18%)	3 (4.69%)	2 (8%)
5	10 (14.08%)	10 (12.65%)	8 (12.31%)	3 (6%)	6 (9.38%)	5 (20%)
6	10 (14.08%)	9 (11.39%)	6 (9.23%)	10 (20%)	15 (23.43%)	1 (4%)
7	14 (19.71%)	10 (12.65%)	11 (16.92%)	13 (26%)	2 (3.12%)	0

8	9	24	12	2	1	3
	(12.67%)	(30.37%)	(18.46%)	(4%)	(1.56%)	(12%)
Total	71 (100%)	79 (100%)	65 (100%)	50 (100%)	64 (100%)	25 (100%)

Situation 1 [Academic award]; Situation 2 [Class presentation]; Situation 3 [Exam]; Situation 4 [Baking skills]; Situation 5 [Sports skills]; Situation 6 [New cell pone]; Situation 7 [New shoes]; Situaton 8 [Sports skills].

While Thanks, the most common compliment response type in both language varieties, is by far most favoured in situation 8 (sport skills) (30.37%) by the Canadian participants, it is used with equal distribution in situations 4 (baking skills) and 7 (new shoes) (19.71% each) by the Cameroonians. The second major strategy, thanks + comment, is employed with fairly equal distribution in situations 4 (baking skills, 16.92%), 7 (new shoes, 16.92%) and 8 (sports skills, 18.465%) by the Cameroonians, whereas it is clearly favoured in situation 7 (new shoes, 26%) by the Canadians. The third strategy, thanks + credit shift, is by far most frequent in situation 3 (exam, 39.06%) and used with fairly equal distribution in situations 6 (new mobile phone, 23.43%), and 1 (academic award, 20.31%) in the Cameroonian data set. By contrast, thanks + credit shift is by far most favoured in situation 3 (exam, 44%) by the Canadian informants and appears with very low frequency in most of the other situations.

6.4.2. Description of the individual situations

6.4.2.1. Situation 1: Academic award

Situation 1 scenario: *Tu viens de recevoir un prix d'excellence / une bourse pour ton travail scolaire / académique et ta mère / ton père te dit: "Bravo, mon fils / ma fille! Tu as fait du bon travail!" Tu réponds:*

'You just received an award or scholarship for your academic work and your mother or father says: "Bravo, my son/daughter! You did a good job!" You answer:'

This situation is a case where the recipient has a lower power position and the interlocutors know each other very well [-P, -D]. The task here was to respond to the compliments of recipient's parents on his/her academic

6.4. SITUATIONAL DISTRIBUTION OF COMPLIMENT RESPONSES

award. Table 46 and Figure 22, below, summarize the choices of participants of both groups.

Table 46: Distribution of compliment responses in situation 1

Types of responses	Cameroon	Canada
One-move responses	11 (20.37%)	12 (30.77%)
Two-move responses	30 (55.56%)	23 (58.97%)
Three-move responses	13 (24.07%)	4 (10.26%)
Total	54 (100%)	39 (100%)

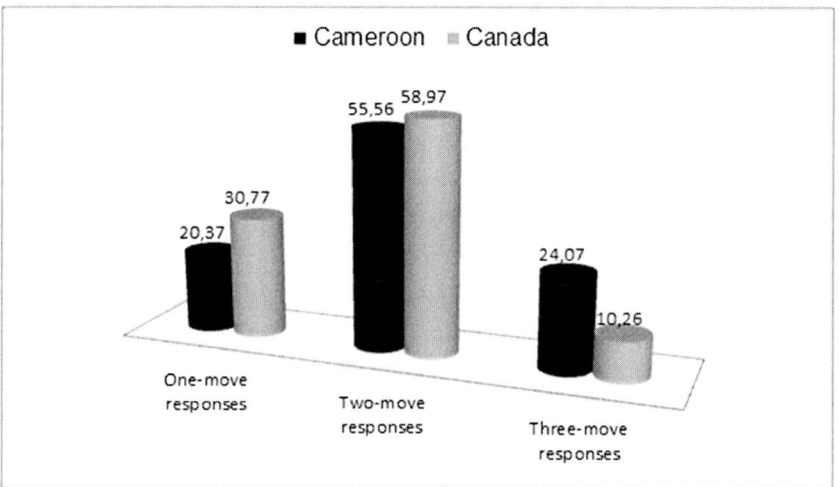

Figure 22: Distribution of compliment responses in situation 1

The respondents of both groups mostly favour complex responses, with the Canadian participants using much more simple responses than the Cameroonians. While the speech acts of thanking and shifting credit are fairly equally distributed in the realization of simple responses by the Cameroonian respondents, the Canadians overwhelmingly choose thanks as simple responses. When responding to compliments from parents, the Cameroonians mostly favour complex and more precisely two-move responses (355.56%) and the most popular pattern of two-move response in this situation is thanks + credit shift (24.07%). The Canadians mostly use complex and more precisely two-move responses. The most common pattern of two-move response in the Canadian data set is thanks + comment (17.94%). While three-move responses are clearly more favoured (24.07%) than one-move responses (20.37%) in this situation by the Cameroonians, the Canadian participants use one-move responses (30.77%) more than three-move responses. In terms of combination patterns of the two-move responses, the Canadians seem to be more creative than the Cameroonians. As a matter of fact, the Canadians use 11 different combinations of two-move responses, while their Cameroonian counterparts employ six different patterns. By contrast, the Cameroonians are more creative than the Canadians in the production of three-move responses: the former use 10 different patterns, whereas the latter provide only 3 patterns of three move-responses. Overall, expressions of gratitude are employed at least once in most of the complex responses in both data sets. Generally, the speech act of thanking occupies the first position of the complex responses where it is associated with the following speech acts: comment, downgrade, credit shift, agreement, wish, promise, joy, request compliment return, etc.

6.4.2.2. SITUATION 2: ORAL PRESENTATION

Situation 2 scenario: *Tu viens de faire une présentation / –un exposé en classe. A la fin du cours, l'un(e) de tes camarades vient te voir et te dit: "Wow, Tu as fait un excellent travail. J'ai vraiment aimé ta présentation. J'aimerais vraiment faire comme toi." Tu réponds:*

'You have just made a presentation or a talk to your class. At the end of the lesson, one of your friends comes up to you and says: "Wow, you did an excellent job. I really liked your presentation. I would like to do as well as you." You reply:'

This situation is a case where the interlocutors have equal power and know each other as acquaintances [=P, -/+D]. The recipient is responding to the compliment of a classmate on recipient's oral presentation (skills). Table 47 and Figure 23 give a picture of the types of responses found in situation 2.

In this situation, the informants of both groups use more complex responses than simple responses to compliments. Complex responses in the Cameroonian data set consist of two moves, whereas there was no instance

6.4. SITUATIONAL DISTRIBUTION OF COMPLIMENT RESPONSES

Table 47: Distribution of compliment responses in situation 2

Types of responses	Cameroon	Canada
One-move responses	16 (29.09%)	8 (20.51%)
Two-move responses	25 (45.45%)	26 (66.67%)
Three-move responses	12 (21.82%)	5 (9.09%)
Four-move responses	2 (3.64%)	0
Total	55 (100%)	39 (100%)

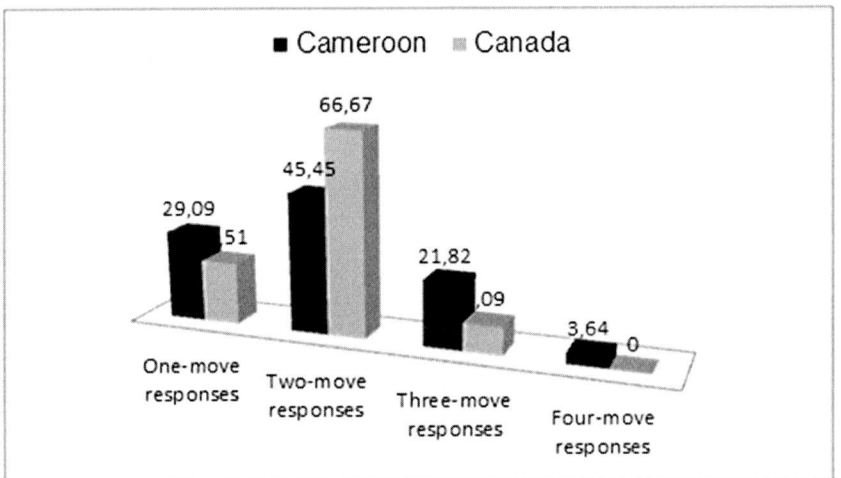

Figure 23: Distribution of compliment responses in situation 2

of four-move response in the Canadian data set. Within the category of complex responses, two-move responses are the most favoured response types by the Cameroonians and the Canadians, although the Canadians appear to employ two-move-responses much more than the Cameroonians (Canadians 66.67% and Cameroonians 45.45%). The dominant combination patterns found in the Cameroonian corpus, namely thanks + advice (10.91%), downgrade + advice (9.09%) and thanks + comment (9.09%), are used with fairly equal distribution. In the Canadian data set, by contrast, there is one combination pattern, namely, thanks + offer (15.38%). Overall, there are 14 different combinations found in the 26 Canadian examples of two-move responses, and 9 different combinations found in the 25 Cameroonians occurrences. Differences also appear with regard to three-move responses. The Cameroonians employ three-move responses (21.82%) much more than the Canadians (9.09%). There are 12 different combinations found in the 12 Cameroonian tokens, while the Canadians employ only 5 different combinations to produce three-move responses. Two Cameroonians employed four-move responses. The Cameroonians also use much more one-move responses than the Canadians. *Advice* is the most common one-move response in the Cameroonian corpus, while *thanks* is the most preferred one-move response by the Canadians.

6.4.2.3. SITUATION 3: EXAM SUCCESS

Situation 3 scenario:

Tu as réussi à ton examen de fin d'année. Tu rencontres ton ancien(ne) professeur(e) qui est content(e) d'apprendre la bonne nouvelle. Il/elle te dit: "Félicitations. Tu as fait du bon travail. Tu as toujours été un(e) élève/étudiant(e) travailleur/travailleuse et discipliné(e)." Tu réponds:

'You passed your final exam. You meet your former professor who is happy to learn of the good news. He or she says: "Congratulations. You did good work. You were always a hardworking and disciplined student." You reply:'

This situation is a case where the recipient of the compliment, i.e. the person who realizes the compliment response, has a lower power position, and the interlocutors know each other as acquaintances [-P, -/+D]. The task of the informants was to respond to the compliment of a former teacher on recipient's success in his/her exam. The results are summarized in Table 48 and Figure 24.

Table 48: Distribution of compliment responses in situation 3

Types of responses	Cameroon	Canada
One-move responses	10 (18.52%)	12 (30.77%)
Two-move responses	36 (66.67%)	24 (61.54%)
Three-move responses	7 (12.96%)	3 (7.69%)
Four-move responses	1 (1.85%)	0
Total	54 (100%)	39 (100%)

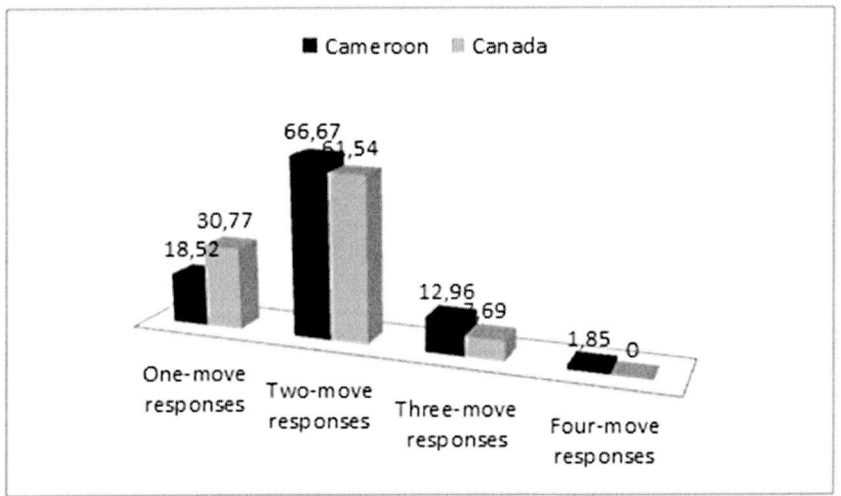

Figure 24: Distribution of compliment responses in situation 3

The respondents of both groups mostly employ complex responses. However, the frequency of the Cameroonian complex responses is much higher. By contrast, the frequency of the one-move responses is higher in the Canadian data. Both the Canadians and the Cameroonians mostly favour two-move responses. There are seven combinations found in the 36 Cameroonian two-move responses and the dominant pattern is thanks + credit shift (46.30%). The Canadians use 11 different combinations to produce 24 examples and thanks + credit shift (30.77%) is by far the most preferred pattern. Although the participants of both groups employed three-move responses, each group chooses combinations of three speech acts, which only occur in their respective data sets. One Cameroonian uses a combination of four speech acts as a compliment response strategy. Overall, two speech acts, namely thanks and credit shifts, are present in the vast majority of complex responses. With regard to one-move responses, the expression of gratitude was the dominant speech act in both data sets.

6.4.2.4. SITUATION 4: BAKING SKILLS

Situation 4 scenario:

Pour fêter ton anniversaire tu as apporté un gros gâteau en classe que tu as fait toi-même. Tes amis aiment ton gâteau et disent: "Ummm, ton gâteau est vraiment délicieux!" Tu réponds:

'To celebrate your birthday you brought a big cake to class that you made yourself. Your friends like your cake and say: "Yum, your cake is really delicious!" You reply:'

This is a case where the compliment giver and recipient have equal power position and know each other as classmates. The task of the informants was to respond to the compliment of classmates on the recipient's baking skills. The summary of the frequency and types of responses is provided in Table 49 and Figure 25, below.

Table 49: Distribution of compliment responses in situation 4

Types of responses	Cameroon	Canada
One-move responses	17 (31.48%)	8 (20.51%)
Two-move responses	28 (51.85%)	24 (61.54%)
Three-move responses	8 (14.81%)	5 (12.82%)
Four-move responses	1 (1.85%)	1 (2.56%)
Total	54 (100%)	39 (100%)

The informants of both groups use more complex responses than simple responses, with the Canadian showing a higher frequency. With regard to one-move responses, the Cameroonians and the Canadians mostly use thanks (14 instances in each group), while the other speech acts, namely credit shift (2 examples) and praise upgrade (one occurrence) in the Cameroonian data set and comment (2 examples) and credit shift (one instance) in the Canadian corpus, appear significantly less frequently. In both corpora the dominant complex responses are those involving two speech acts. There are 12 different combinations found in the 28 Cameroonian examples and 11 combinations in the 24 Canadian responses with two speech acts. The most preferred pattern by the respondents of both groups is thanks + comment and the other combinations appear significantly less frequently. There is only one instance of four-move response in each language variety.

6.4. SITUATIONAL DISTRIBUTION OF COMPLIMENT RESPONSES

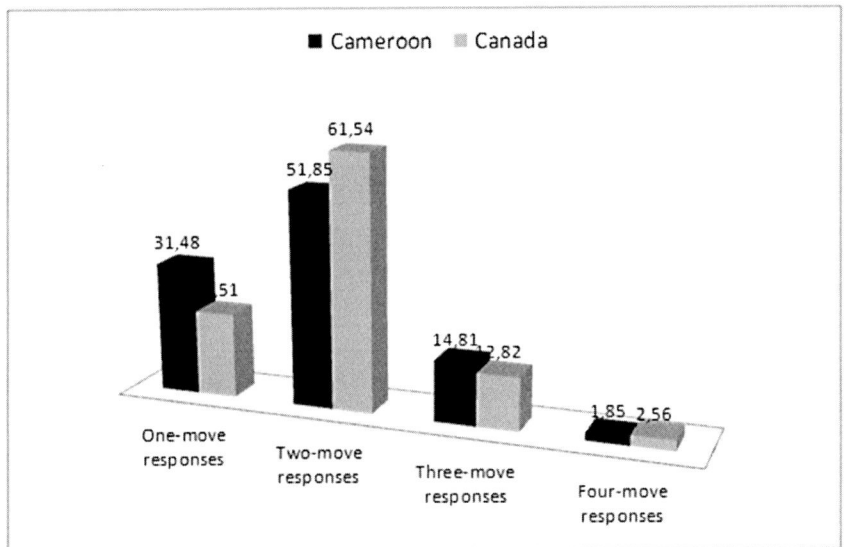

Figure 25: Distribution of compliment responses in situation 4

The Cameroonian use five different combinations to produce eight three-move responses and their most favoured pattern is thanks + downgrade + comment (4 instances). There are five different combinations found in the three-move responses of the Canadian corpus. In both data sets, expressions of gratitude are much more used than other speech acts in the construction of complex responses and in most of the examples the gratitude expressions are combined with the following speech acts: agreement, credit shift, encouragement, joy, wish offer, downgrade, surprise, etc.

6.4.2.5. SITUATION 5: SPORTS SKILLS

Situation 5 scenario :

Tu as très bien joué au cours d'un match de soccer/hockey opposant ton école/collège/département à un(e) autre école/collège/département. Après le match, ton professeur vient te voir et te dit: "Tu as très bien joué. En fait, tu étais le meilleur joueur." Tu réponds:

'You played well during a soccer/hockey game where your school was competing against another school. After the game your teacher comes to see you and says: "You played very well. In fact, you were the best player." You respond:'

Table 50 and Figure 26 give a breakdown of the types and frequency of the responses in both varieties of French.

Table 50: Distribution of compliment responses in situation 5

Types of responses	Cameroon	Canada
One-move responses	12 (22.22%)	14 (35.90%)
Two-move responses	37 (68.52%)	19 (48.72%)
Three-move responses	4 (7.41%)	6 (15.38%)
Four-move responses	1 (1.85%)	0
Total	54 (100%)	39 (100%)

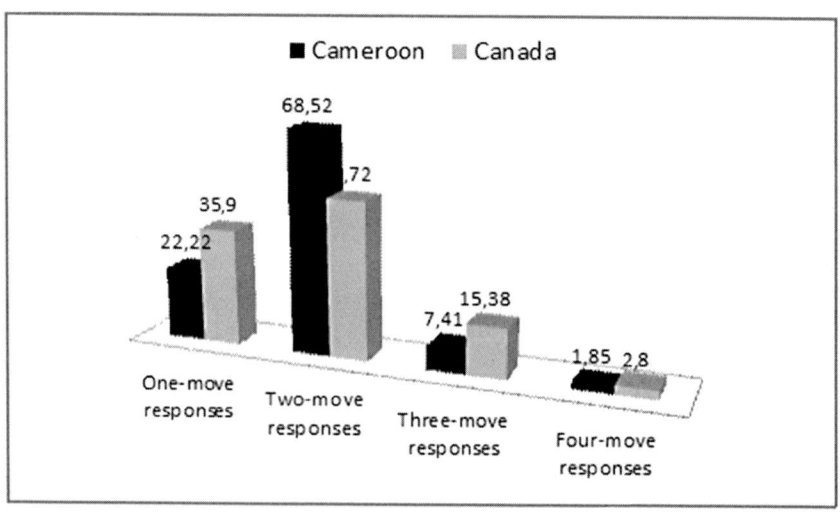

Figure 26: Distribution of compliment responses in situation 5

The participants of both groups use more complex responses than simple responses, with the Canadians employing significantly more simple responses than the Cameroonians. Gratitude expressions occur most often as simple responses in both corpora. With regard to complex responses, the Cameroonians use two, three and four combinations, whereas there is no instance of four-move responses in the Canadian corpus. There are 12 different combinations in the 37 two-move responses of the Cameroonian corpus and the dominant patterns are thanks + comment (8 examples), thanks + thanks (7 instances), thanks + credit shift (6 occurrences), thanks + joy (6 instances). There are nine different combinations found in the 19 responses provided by the Canadians and the dominant pattern thanks + credit shift (5 occurrences), thanks + thanks (3 examples), and thanks + comment (3 occurrences). With regard to the combination patterns used by the participants, the results show that each group produces patterns that do not appear in the other group. As a matter of fact, the Cameroonians use the following patterns: thanks + credit shift + credit shift, thanks + comment + joy, thanks + credit shift + comment, thanks + comment + wish. The Canadians produce the following patterns: thanks + comment + praise upgrade, thanks + downgrade + comment, thanks + thanks + downgrade, thanks + comment + thanks, downgrade + credit shift + thanks, thanks + downgrade + credit shift. Overall, gratitude expressions are used in the first position of the combinations much more in the Cameroonian data.

6.4.2.6. SITUATION 6: NEW MOBILE PHONE

Situation 6 scenario:

Tu viens d'acheter une nouvelle marque de téléphone portable. Ton professeur en est vraiment impressionné(e) et te dit: "Ton téléphone est vraiment beau! La forme me plait vraiment." Tu responds:

'You just bought a new cell phone model. Your professor is really impressed by it and says to you "Your phone is really nice! I really like the style." You reply:'

The results are summarized in Table 51 and Figure 27, below.

Table 51: Distribution of compliment responses in situation 6

Types of responses	Cameroon	Canada
One-move responses	16 (29.63%)	13 (34.21%)
Two-move responses	28 (51.85%)	23 (60.53%)
Three-move responses	10 (18.52%)	2 (5.26%)
Total	54 (100%)	38 (100%)

Table 51 and Figure 27 show that the Cameroonians and the Canadians

6. COMPLIMENT RESPONSES

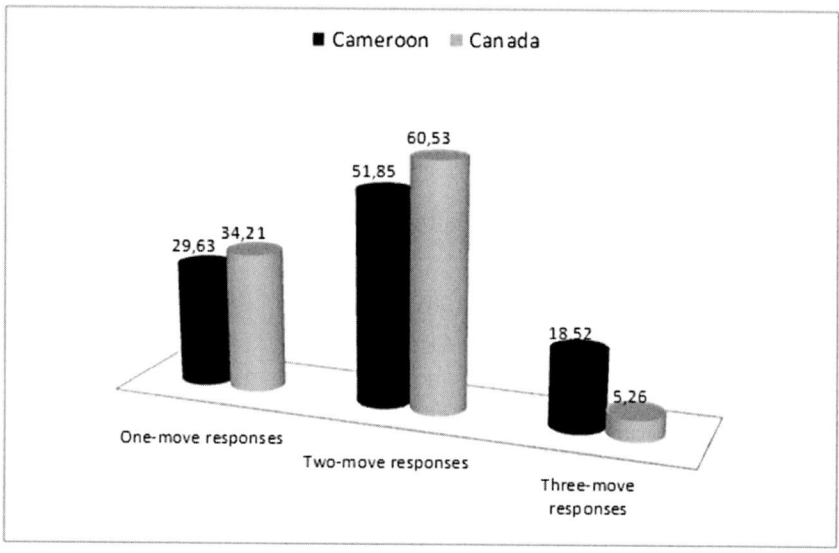

Figure 27: Distribution of compliment responses in situation 6

use more complex responses than simple responses, with the Canadians employing simple responses much more than the Cameroonians. The results show that the Cameroonian participants employ five different speech acts (thanks/joy, credit shift, agreement, promise) to generate simple responses, while their Canadian counterparts make use of three different speech acts (thanks, comment, offer) to realize simple responses to compliments. In both corpora, simple responses overwhelmingly appear in form of gratitude expressions. While the respondents of both groups employ two-move responses much more than three-move responses, Table 51 also indicates that the Canadians employ two-move responses much more than the Cameroonians. There are eight combinations of two speech acts in the 28 responses provided by the Cameroonians and thanks + credit shift (15 out of 28 instances) is by far the most preferred pattern. The picture is quite different in the Canadian corpus: there are 12 combinations in the 23 responses provided by the Canadians and the dominant pattern is thanks + comment (10 out 23 examples), with the other patterns appearing with significantly very low frequency. Overall, most of the combination patterns of two-move responses found in the Cameroonian data do not appear in the Canadian corpus. The Cameroonians use three-move responses much more than the Canadians. With regard to the type of speech acts used to generate complex responses, the findings show that gratitude expressions are much more often combined with other speech acts in the Cameroonian data set than in the Canadian one. Moreover, the Canadians combine speech acts such as agreement, comment, asking for confirmation, downgrade, etc., much more than the Cameroonians.

6.4.2.7. Situation 7: New shoes

Situation 7 scenario

Tu as mis une nouvelle paire de chaussures et un de tes camarades de classe te regarde longuement et dit: "Tes nouvelles chaussures te vont très bien. J'aime la couleur. Elle va très bien avec ton pantalon jeans!" Tu responds:

'You are wearing a new pair of shoes; one of your classmates looks at them for a long time and says: "Your new shoes really suit you. I like the colour. They look really good with your jeans!" You respond:'

This is a case where the compliment giver and receiver have an equal power position and know each other as classmates. The task of the participants was to respond to the compliment of a classmate on recipient's new shoes. Table 52 and Figure 28 give a breakdown of the findings in this situation.

Table 52: Distribution of compliment responses in situation 7

Types of responses	Cameroon	Canada
One-move responses	16 (29.63%)	11 (29.73%)
Two-move responses	31 (54.41%)	21 (56.76%)
Three-move responses	7 (12.96%)	5 (13.52%)
Total	54 (100%)	37 (100%)

The simple and complex responses in both data sets are fairly equally distributed in situation 7, as can be seen in Table 52 and Figure 28. In both corpora, simple responses overwhelmingly occur in form of gratitude expressions. The respondents of both groups adopt the same behaviour with regard to complex compliment responses: they use two-move and three-

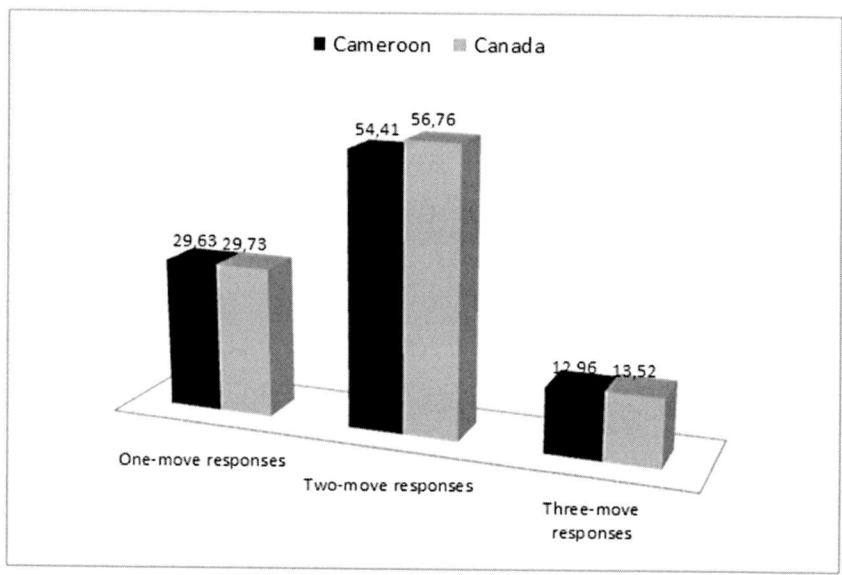

Figure 28: Distribution of compliment responses in situation 7

move responses. There are, however, differences regarding choice of combination patterns, with the Cameroonians demonstrating more creativity and variety. There are 15 combinations in the 31 two-move responses and seven different combinations in the three-move responses produced by the Cameroonians. The most preferred pattern by the Cameroonians is thanks + comment and the other patterns occur with significantly less frequency. There are seven combinations in the 21 two-move responses and five different combinations in the three-move responses of the Canadian data. The most common pattern of complex response in the Canadian corpus is thanks + comment. The results also show that the participants of both groups generally combine thanks with other positively loaded speech acts in the complex responses. However, some the responses found in the Cameroonian and the Canadian corpora may be considered as ambiguous since they combine gratitude expressions and expressions of self-praise. Given the high degree of familiarity between the interlocutors, it is safe to say that expressions of self-praise have a jocular connotation and may not necessarily be interpreted as face threatening.

6.4.2.8. SITUATION 8: SPORTS SKILLS

Situation 8 scenario

Après ton match de soccer/hockey/basketball, un spectateur que tu ne connais pas vient te voir et te dit: "Je voulais te dire que tu as très bien joué! Bravo!"Tu réponds:

'After your soccer/hockey/basketball game, a spectator that you do not know comes up to you and says: "I wanted to tell you that you played very well! Bravo!" You answer:'

This is a case where compliment giver and receiver have an equal power position and don't know each other. The task of the informants was to respond to the compliment of a stranger on recipient's sport skills. Table 53 and Figure 29 present the summary of the patterns employed by respondents of both groups.

Table 53: Distribution of compliment responses in situation 8

Types of responses	Cameroon	Canada
One-move responses	10 (18.18%)	25 (64.10%)
Two-move responses	37 (67.27%)	14 (35.90%)
Three-move responses	7 (12.73%)	0
Four-move responses	1 (1.82%)	0
Total	55 (100%)	39 (100%)

While the Cameroonians use responses consisting of up to four moves, the Canadians employ only one-move and two-move responses. The single responses in both data sets are overwhelmingly gratitude expressions. The Canadians employ more simple responses than multiple move (i.e. two-move) responses, whereas complex responses and, more precisely, two-move responses are the most preferred patterns by the Cameroonians. There are 11 different combinations found in the 37 two-move responses and six combinations in the seven three-move responses provided by the Cameroonians. The dominant two-combination patterns in the Cameroonian corpus are thanks + comment (21.82%) and thanks + thanks/joy (21.82%). The Canadians use seven combinations in 14 two-move responses and most of the patterns produced appear with fairly equal distribution. It should be noted that the speech acts of thanking is used a least once in all the

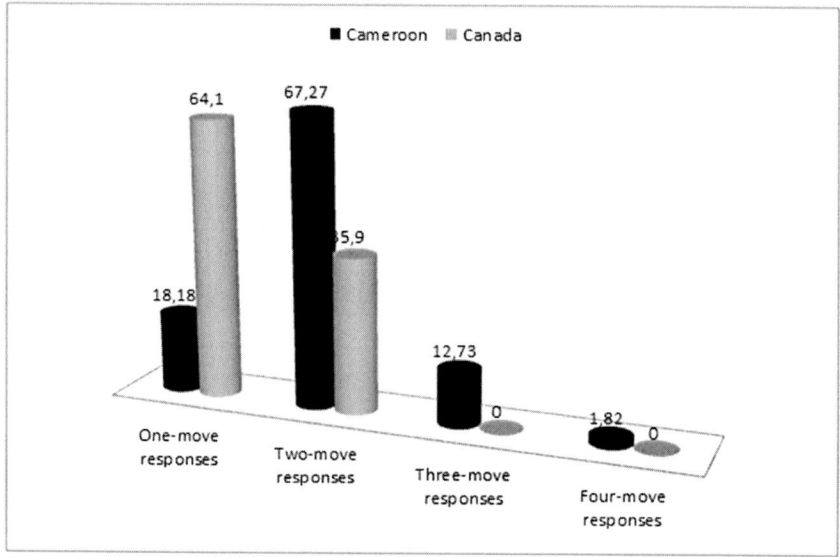

Figure 29: Distribution of compliment responses in situation 8

complex responses in both data sets. These features reflect the fact that the informants of both groups generally opt for gratitude, respect, harmony and the construction of solidarity in responding to compliments from strangers. These results also suggest that the Canadians are more straightforward when responding to compliments from strangers. The Cameroonians, by contrast, display a more verbose, complex and expressive response behaviour, as they tend to combine gratitude expressions with other positively affective speech acts (wish, credit shift, invitation, etc.). In short, the participants of both groups demonstrate politeness to unknown compliment givers in different ways.

CONCLUSION

The purpose of this book was to present results of the comparative study of two speech acts, namely compliments and compliment responses, in Cameroon French and Canadian French. The findings reveal quantitative and qualitative similarities and differences related to the research questions of the study.

The first research question concerned the strategies employed by Canadian and Cameroonian French speakers to offer compliments in eight different situations. The compliments collected by means of a written questionnaire were analyzed with regard to interactional structures, i.e. the move structure and realization patterns of head acts, the use of lexical and stylistic devices in compliment utterance and the use of external modification devices or supportive moves.

Interactional structures
In the examples obtained from the participants of both groups, the compliments occur either as unsupported head acts ('head acts only'), as combinations of head acts and supportive moves ('head acts + supportive moves'), or as supportive moves. Table 54 and Figure 30 below give a picture of the distribution of these three strategies.

Table 54: Overall distribution of move structures in both varieties of French

	Cameroon	Canada
Heads only	129 (30%)	132 (43.14%)
Heads + supportive moves	292 (67.91%)	169 (55.23%)
Supportive moves only	9 (2.09%)	5 (1.63%)
Total	430 (100%)	306 (100%)

As can be seen in Table 54, the Cameroonian respondents produced 430 and the Canadians 306 compliments. While the 'supportive moves only' strategy is the least used in the two data sets, 'head acts + supportive moves'

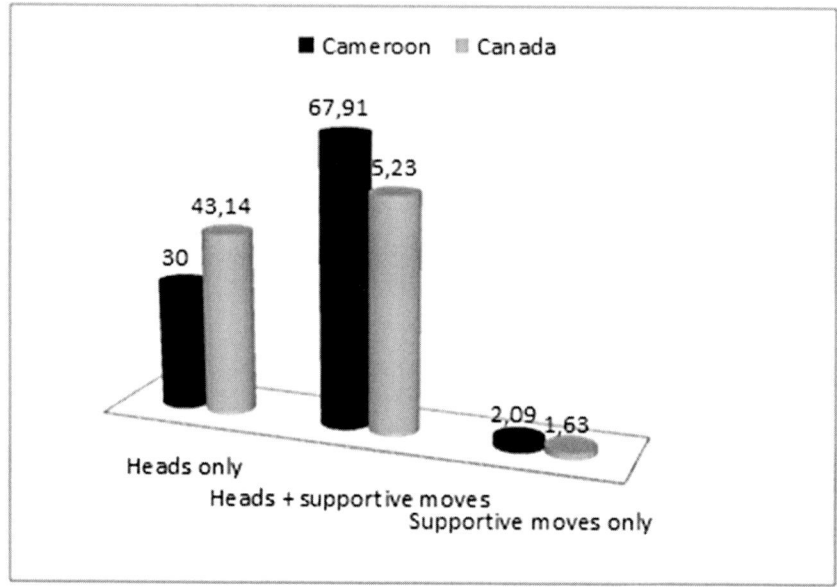

Figure 30: Overall distribution of move structures in both varieties of French

combinations are the most preferred by the respondents of both groups. The Cameroonians, however, employ this strategy much more than their Canadian counterparts (67:91% in CMF vs. 55.23% in CF). By contrast, the Canadians use 'head acts only' strategies much more than the Cameroonian participants (43.14% in CF vs. 30% in CMF). Overall, the speakers of the two varieties of French show a strong preference for 'head acts + supportive' combinations: more than half of the compliments in both corpora appear with this interactional structure.

Head act patterns

The findings reveal differences regarding the frequency of direct and indirect compliments in both varieties of French, as can be seen in Table 55 and Figure 31.

CONCLUSION

Table 55: Distribution of direct and indirect head acts in both varieties of French

	Cameroon	Canada
Direct head acts	129 (93.48%)	132 (96.35%)
Indirect head acts	9 (6.52%)	5 (3.65%)
Total	138 (100%)	137 (100%)

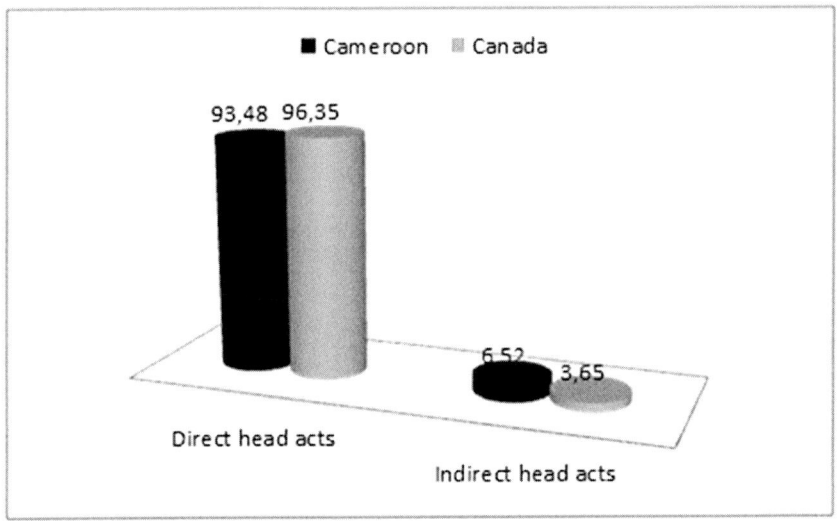

Figure 31: Distribution of direct and indirect head acts in both varieties of French

Table 55 indicates that direct compliments are clearly the dominant strategy in the two varieties of French, and this type of compliments accounts for 93.48% and 96.35% of the Cameroonian and Canadian compliments respectively. Although indirect compliments occur in both data sets with a much lesser frequency, the Cameroonians employ this strategy much more than their Canadian counterparts. These findings suggest that the Cameroonian and Canadian French speakers consider compliments as makers of positive politeness, i.e. as acts to enhance the positive face of the addressee. From this viewpoint, straightforwardness in offering compliments is deemed the most appropriate strategy.

Lexical and stylistic devices
The distribution of lexical devices in both varieties of French is summarized in Table 56 and Figure 32.

Table 56: Overall distribution of lexical devices in Cameroonian and Canadian compliments

Lexical devices	Cameroon	Canada
Adjectives	414 (43.26%)	260 (42.76%)
Adverbs	335 (35 %)	237 (38.98%)
Verbs	160 (16.72%)	101 (16.62%)
Positively loaded nouns	48 (5.02%)	10 (1.64%)
Total	957 (100%)	608 (100%)

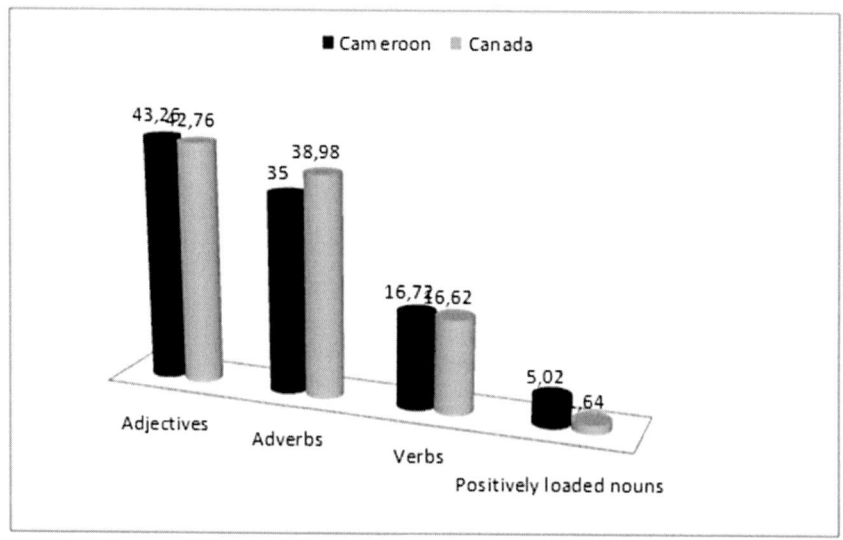

Figure 32: Overall distribution of lexical devices in Cameroonian and Canadian compliments

Overall, adjectives are the most frequently used lexical devices in both varieties of French. The three most favoured adjectives by Cameroonians are *beau/belle* (131 tokens of 414 or 31.64%), *joli(e)* (42 examples of 414 or 10.14%) and *délicieux* (33 instances of 414 or 7.97%). The three most

CONCLUSION 193

preferred adjectives by the Canadians are *beau/belle* (88 tokens of 260 or 33.85%), *bon* (63 instances of 269 or 24.23%) and *magnifique* (10 examples of 260 or 3.85%). The compliments in both data sets are often intensified by using adverbs. Adverbial intensifiers are the second most favoured lexical tokens. The four most common adverbs in the Cameroonian data sets are *très* (114 tokens of 335 or 34.02%), *vraiment* (60 examples of 335 or 17.91%), *bien* (39 instances of 335 or 11.64%) and *beaucoup* (30 tokens of 335 or 8.96%). The four most preferred adverbs by the Canadian participants are *vraiment* (87 examples 237 or 36.70%), *très* (44 tokens of 237 or 18.57%), *bien* (44 instances of 237 or 18.57%), *trop* (n = 12 or 5.06%). Verbs appear as the third most frequent lexical elements in both varieties of French. The Cameroonians mostly employ the following tokens: *aller à / convenir* à (43 examples of 160 or 26.87%), *apprécier* (29 instances of 160 or 18.12%), *aimer* (19 tokens of 160 or 11.87%) and *plaire* (18 occurrences of 160 or 11.25%). The most favoured verbs in the Canadian corpus are *aimer* (52 examples of 101 or 51.49%), *aller à* (20 occurrences of 101 or 19.80%) and *adorer* (5 examples of 101 or 4.95%). The use of positively loaded nouns is a marginal phenomenon in the Canadian data set.

Concerning stylistic devices, it was found that the respondents of both groups use intensifying devices much more than mitigating devices, as can be seen in Table 57 and Figure 33.

Table 57: Overall distribution of stylistic/syntactic devices in Cameroonian and Canadian compliments

	Cameroon	Canada
Intensifying devices	34 (50.75%)	14 (58.33%)
Mitigating devices	33 (49.25%)	10 (41.67%)
Total	67 (100%)	24 (100%)

In the light of the findings regarding lexical and stylistic devices, it could be said that the participants of both groups mostly maximize the force of compliments by using adjectives, adverbs, verbs, nouns and intensifying stylistic devices. The participants of both groups can be said to observe, to a great extent, the second positive politeness strategy, that is, 'Exaggerate interest, approval, sympathy with the other'.

Conclusion

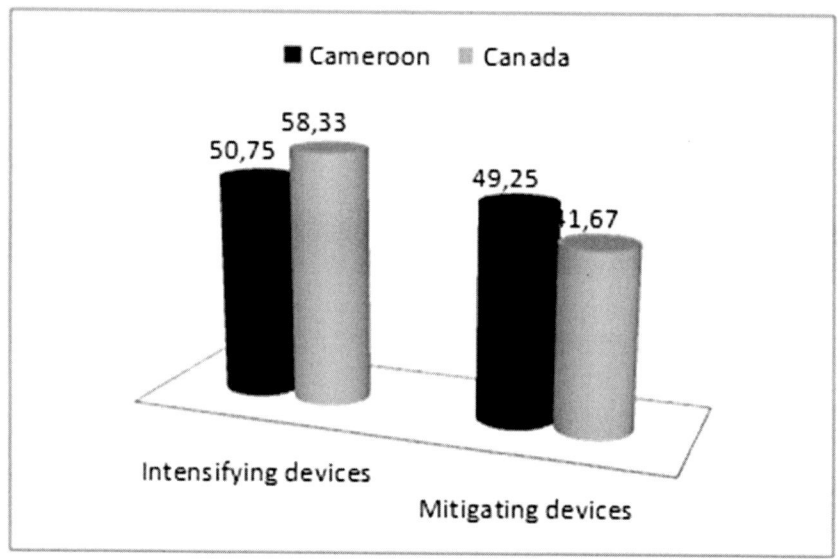

Figure 33: Overall distribution of stylistic/syntactic devices in Cameroonian and Canadian compliments

Situational variation can also be observed in the use of lexical devices in both varieties of French, as can be seen in Tables 58 and 59.

Table 58: Situational distribution of lexical devices in Cameroonian compliments

Situations	Adjectives	Adverbs	Verbs	Nouns	Total
Hairstyle	47	68	30	0	145
Outfit	52	56	28	4	140
Meal	60	28	10	9	107
Sports	40	47	26	10	123
Presentation	50	22	21	7	100
Phone	47	29	18	4	98
House	64	31	6	7	108
Car	54	54	21	7	136
Total	414	335	160	48	957

Table 58 shows that adjectives in the Cameroonian corpus most frequently appear in compliments on house and meal. The adverbs occur in most cases in compliments on appearance (hairstyle and outfit), while the verbs are also mostly employed in compliments on appearance.

Table 59: Situational distribution of lexical devices in Canadian compliments

Situations	Adjectives	Adverbs	Verbs	Nouns	Total
Hairstyle	28	41	29	3	101
Outfit	27	32	22	0	81
Meal	38	32	5	0	75
Sports	38	42	7	4	91
Presentation	30	22	6	1	59
Phone	20	22	18	1	61
House	47	31	7	0	85
Car	32	15	7	1	55
Total	260	237	101	10	608

Table 59 indicates that adjectives in the Canadian data are mostly employed in compliments on house, meal and sports skills. The adverbs are most preferred in compliments on sports skills and hairstyle, while verbs mostly appear in compliments on hairstyle.

External modification

The Cameroonians are found to employ significantly more pre-compliments (almost 64% of all external modification devices) than the Canadians who use pre-posed supportive moves in 48.64% of their total supportive moves. On the other hand, the Canadians appear to use more post-compliments (almost 52% of all external modification devices) than the Cameroonian participants who employ post-posed supportive moves in only 36% of all their total supportive moves. Table 60 and Figure 34 summarize the frequencies and distribution of the pre-posed and post-posed supportive moves in the two corpora.

Table 60: Overall distribution of external modifications in both varieties of French

	Cameroon	Canada
Pre-compliments	325 (63.98%)	125 (48.64%)
Post-compliments	183 (36.02%)	132 (51.36%)
Total	508 (100%)	257 (100%)

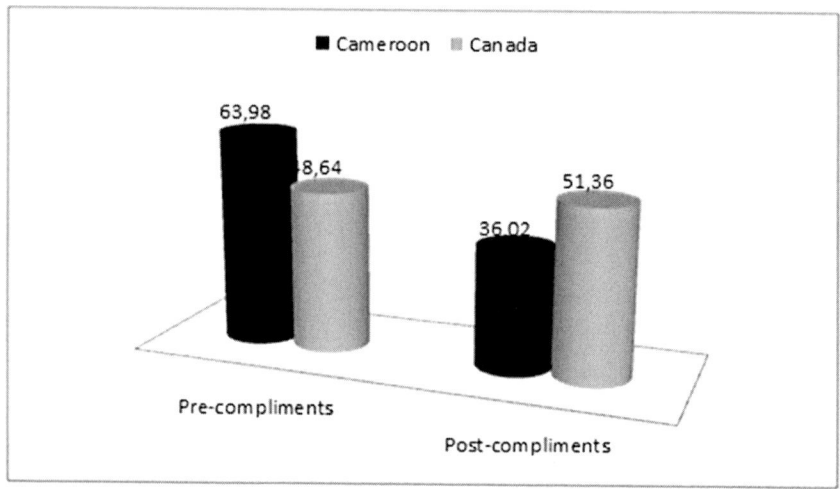

Figure 34: Overall distribution of external modifications in both varieties of French

Pre-posed supportive moves

The three major pre-posed supportive moves found in both varieties of French are presented in Table 61.

Table 61: Distribution of most common pre-compliments

	Cameroon		Canada	
	No.	%	No.	%
Address terms	133	40.92	41	32.80
Interjections	76	23.38	67	53.60
Greetings	74	22.77	-	-
Apologies	-	-	10	8

Table 61 shows that the most preferred pre-compliments in the Cameroonian data are: terms of address (133 tokens of 325), interjections (76 occurrences of 325) and greetings (74 instances of 325). The three most common pre-compliments in the Canadian corpus are: interjections (67 examples of 125), address terms (41 tokens of 125) and apologies (10 occurrences of 125).

On the level of the situational distribution of the pre-compliments, some differences emerge between the two varieties of French, as can be seen in Table 62.

Table 62: Situational distribution of pre-compliments in each variety

	Hair	Outfit	Meal	Sports	Presentation	Phone	House	Car	Total
Cameroon	22	59	12	24	39	63	37	69	325
Canada	20	21	6	9	21	21	15	12	125

Table 62 shows that the Cameroonians mostly use pre-posed supportive moves with compliments on possessions, namely a new car and mobile phone. In the Canadian data, by contrast, the pre-compliments are equally distributed in four situations.

Post-posed supportive moves
Overall, the Cameroonians employ 11 different speech acts as post-posed supportive moves, while the Canadians use 10 different types of post-compliments. In both data sets, four types emerge as the most frequently employed, as can be seen in Table 63 and Figure 35.

Table 63: Distribution of the four major post-compliments in both varieties of French

Post-compliments	Cameroon	Canada
Thanks	40 (21.85%)	29 (21.97%)
Wishes	36 (19.67%)	22 (16.67%)
Comments	28 (15.30%)	27 (20.45%)
Questions	49 (26.78%)	35 (26.51%)
Advice/Suggestions/ Encouragements	15 (8.20%)	7 (5.30%)
Total	128 (69.95%)	120 (96%)

The major post-posed supportive moves account for almost 70% and 96% of all Cameroonian and Canadian post-compliments respectively. Questions (26.78%) and thanks (21.85%) are the two most preferred post-compliments in both varieties of French. Situational variation also occurs

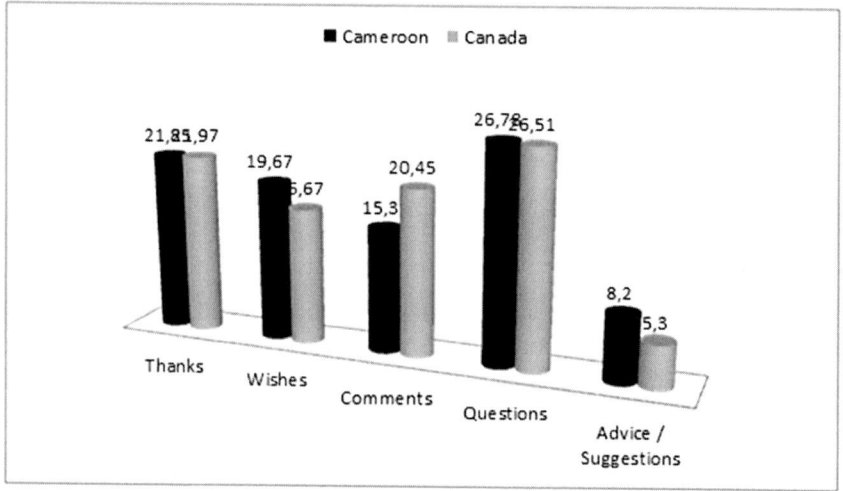

Figure 35: Distribution of the four major post-compliments in both varieties of French

with the major post-posed supportive moves across the two varieties of French, as shown in Tables 64 and 65.

Table 64: Situational distribution of the major post-posed supportive moves in the Cameroonian corpus

	Hair	Outfit	Meal	Sports	Presentation	Phone	House	Car	Total
Thanks	0	0	39	1	0	0	0	0	40
Wishes	0	1	3	9	7	1	7	8	36
Comments	1	1	3	2	6	8	5	2	28
Questions	3	1	1	1	4	35	1	3	49
Suggestions Advice Encouragements	8	1	0	5	0	1	0	0	15

Table 64 shows that thanks are exclusively used by the Cameroonians with compliments on food, wishes are most commonly employed with compliments on skills and possessions, giving advice is mostly frequent with compliments on hairstyle and questions mostly accompany compliments on phone.

Table 65: Situational distribution of the major post-posed supportive moves in the Canadian data

	Hair	Outfit	Meal	Sports	Presentation	Phone	House	Car	Total
Thanks	0	0	28	1	0	0	0	0	29
Wishes	0	0	0	6	4	5	3	4	22
Comments	5	2	2	2	2	6	6	2	27
Questions	1	1	2	2	0	26	0	3	35
Suggestions Advice Encouragements	2	1	0	3	0	0	1	0	7

Table 65 shows that thanks in the Canadian corpus appear with compliments on meals, questions most frequently occur with compliments on a new mobile phone, while wishes mostly appear in the post-sequence of compliments skills and possessions.

The second research question concerned the way Cameroonian and Canadian French speakers respond to compliments and how politeness functions in the compliment responses generated by the participants.

In terms of the choice between verbal and non-verbal responses, the findings show that the informants of both groups exclusively opt for verbal responses. This choice may suggest that there is a tendency to 'say something' when responding to compliments in both French-speaking regions. However, the method of data collection used for this study could have played a major role in the way the participants responded. Therefore, it is necessary to carry out further research based on data collected in spontaneous face-to-face situations, interviews and even role-plays. This may help to reach a better understanding of the importance, frequency and the meaning of non-verbal responses and the combination with verbal responses in Canadian and Cameroon French.

Also, the study clearly reveals the predominant use of complex responses in the two varieties of French. This result may suggest that the respondents of both groups consider simple responses to compliments as less appropriate and less relevant for rapport management than complex responses. Their choice may be also due to the multifunctional character of compliments. As previous studies have established, compliments are used to offer, negotiate or affirm solidarity, seek for information, open/sustain a conversation, encourage desired behaviour, strengthen or replace other face flattering acts or soften face threatening acts, etc., in a nutshell, compliments do more than just express admiration (Jarwoski 1995). Consequently, the participants in this study appear to do more than just responding to the expression of admiration. Although some Cameroonian and Canadian respondents clearly choose to react mainly to the primary function of compliments, most of the participants tend to take into account two or more other functions of compliments in their responses. Therefore, the attested simple and complex verbal responses in both data sets may be considered as indications that the recipients interpret the compliments as a gift, search for information, offering of solidarity, opening of conversation, request for something (verbal or non-verbal) etc.).

The description of simple responses reveals the dominance of appreciation tokens in both data sets. In fact, thanks represent 16.35% of the Cameroonian responses and 25.57% of the Canadian examples. This finding could be interpreted as a tendency to accept compliments in Cameroon and Canadian French. However, the analysis of complex responses suggests that gratitude expressions appear in most of the cases (more than 50% of all the responses in both varieties of French), in combination with one or more speech acts, in which the gratitude expressions are either intensified or mitigated by the other speech acts. Although compliment acceptance is the most common strategy within the category of simple responses, the analysis of complex responses highlights the tendency to combine gratitude expressions with other (positive) speech acts in both sub-cultures. The question regarding the rationale for this speech act behaviour (i.e. the combination of gratitude expressions with other speech acts in responding to compliments) in Cameroon and Canadian French cannot be addressed in this study. It is worth noting that a similar behaviour seems to prevail in France. According to Traverso (1996) and Kerbrat-Orecchioni (1998), appreciation tokens are rarely employed in response to compliments in France because this response type may tend to round up/close the compliment turn. Hence, combining gratitude expressions with other speech acts may serve as a means to indicate readiness to continue/expand the conversation. This explanation may also apply to Cameroonian and Canadian speakers of French. However, further research based on face-to-face conversations and interviews may shed more light on this issue.

Following the difference between positive and negative responses to compliments (Kerbrat-Orecchioni 1998), the results show that the vast majority of the participants in both groups employ positive (simple and complex) responses, i.e. responses that enhance the positive face of the compliment giver and/or the compliment recipient. Negative responses, i.e. those that verbalize negative affect to others such as disagreements, rejections, denying, doubting, etc., do not appear in the data. Although this does suggest that Cameroonians and Canadians do not reject compliments, a claim could be made that the Canadian and Cameroonian French speakers live in a culture in which responding positively to compliments is more valued that rejecting them.

It was found that praise upgrade or the expression of self-praise, which could be considered as a negative response, because it does not comply with the modesty principle, is employed by some Cameroonian respondents. There are three instances of this speech act (0.69%) in the simple responses, two of which are responses to compliments from classmates. In the complex responses praise upgrade is used in both data sets in combination with the following strategies thanks (2 tokens or 0.92% in CMF vs. 4 examples, or 1.29% in CF), comment (4 examples, i.e. 1.29% in CF), praise upgrade (2 occurrences, i.e. 0.65% in CF), joke (1 instance, i.e. 0.32% in CF), thanks + joy (1 token, i.e. 0.23% in CMF), thanks + request (1 example, i.e. 0.32% in CF), thanks + praise upgrade (1 example, 0.23% in CMF). Overall, the frequency of this 'negative' response strategy is very low in comparison with the other response strategies. Moreover, when the respondents choose praise upgrade to respond to compliments, they generally mitigate it with other speech acts. In addition to that, praise upgrade mostly appears in jocular forms in situations with acquaintances or close friends and the compliment.

As already mentioned, the goal of this book was to contribute to a growing body of research in regional pragmatic variation. The study focused on the complimenting behaviour of a small group of participants, namely secondary / high school students in Cameroon and Canada. As such, it is too early to draw conclusions with regards to students' choices in both French-speaking regions with regard to compliment and compliment response strategies. Also, the results obtained may not apply to all French-speaking Canadians and Cameroonians. It would therefore be necessary to deepen the present approach by examining a larger corpus of written data, other types of data, such as naturally-occurring conversations, role-plays, interviews involving students and other groups of French speakers in Canada and Cameroon. Also, it would be interesting to extend the scope of this research not only to other speech acts, pragmatic phenomena, but also to other regional varieties of French.

Needless to point out, that in order to account for the complexities of verbal communication in French-speaking regions, the forthcoming studies should address the issues under investigation on various levels of pragmatics research, namely the *formal level*, the *actional level*, the *interactive level*, the *topic level,* and the *organizational level*. Such an approach will definitely help to better understand the patterns of regional language use in the French-speaking world.

REFERENCES

Al Falasi, H. (2007). 'Just say Thank you': A study of compliment responses. *The Linguistics Journal*, 2(1), 28–42.
Anchimbe, E. (2011). 'Take a beer' – 'Thanks, Sorry, I prefer another day': A Postcolonial Pragmatic perspective on Offers and Offer Refusals. In Joachim, Frank & Lena, Steveker (eds.), *Anglistentag 2010 Saarbrücken Proceedings* (pp. 421-431). Trier: Wissenschaftlicher Verlag Trier.
Anchimbe, E. A., & Janney, R. W. (2011). Postcolonial pragmatics: An introduction. *Journal of Pragmatics*, 43(6), 1451-1459.
Barnlund, D. C., & Shoko, A. (1985). Intercultural encounters: The management of compliments by Japanese and Americans. *Journal of cross-cultural psychology*, 16(1), 9–26.
Barron, A. (2005). Variational pragmatics in the foreign language classroom. *System*, 33(3), 519–536.
Barron, A. (2008). The structure of requests in Irish English and English. In K.P. Schneider & A. Barron (eds.), *Variational Pragmatics. A Focus on Regional Varieties in pluricentric Languages* (pp. 35-67). Amsterdam/Philadelphia: John Benjamins.
Barron, A., & Schneider, K. P. (2009). Variational pragmatics: Studying the impact of social factors on language use in interaction. *Intercultural Pragmatics*, 6(4), 425-442.
Bernicot J., Comeau, J., & Feider H. (1994). Dialogues between French-speaking mothers and daughters in two cultures: France and Quebec. *Discourse Processes*, 18, 19-34.
Biloa, E. (2003). *La langue française au Cameroun*. Bern: Peter Lang.
Bilodeau, C. (2001). *Des moyens d'expression de l'intensité dans le langage des jeunes Québécois*. Mémoire de maîtrise. Université du Québec à Chicoutimi.
Brown, P., & Levinson, S. C. (1987). *Politeness: Some universals in language usage*. Cambridge: Cambridge University Press.
Blum-Kulka, S., House, J., & Kasper, G. (eds.) (1989). *Cross-cultural pragmatics: Requests and apologies*. Norwood: Ablex Publishing.
Cedar, P. (2006). Thai and American responses to compliments in English. *The Linguistics Journal*, 1(2), 6-28.
Chen, R. (1993). Responding to compliments: A contrastive study of politeness

strategies between American English and Chinese speakers. *Journal of pragmatics,* 20, 49–75.

Chen, S. E. (2003). Compliment response strategies in Mandarin Chinese: Politeness phenomenon revisited. *Concentric: Studies in English literature and linguistics,* 29(2), 157–84.

Clyne, M. (ed.) (1992). *Pluricentric languages. Different norms in different nations.* Berlin/New York: Mouton de Gruyter.

Daikuhara, M. (1986). A study of compliments from a cross-cultural perspective: Japanese vs. American English. *Working papers in educational linguistics,* 2(2), 103–34.

Downes, W. (1998). *Language and society.* Cambridge: Cambridge University Press.

Drescher, M. (2009). Sacres québécois et jurons français: Vers une pragmaticalisation des fonctions communicatives ? In B. Bagola (éd.), *Français du Canada – Français de France. Actes du huitième colloque international de Trèves, du 12 au 15 avril 2007* (pp. 177- 185). Tübingen: Niemeyer.

Dubois, C. (2000). *La grammaire de l'exclamation: aspects théoriques, français de référence et français québécois.* Mémoire de Maîtrise, Université de Sherbrooke.

Dumont, P. (1983). *Le français et les langues africaines au Sénégal.* Paris: Karthala.

Félix-Brasdefer, C. J. (2009). Pragmatic variation across Spanish(es): Requesting in Mexican, Costa Rican and Dominican Spanish. *Intercultural Pragmatics,* 6(4), 473–515.

Feussi, V. (2008). *Parles-tu français? Ça dépend ... Penser – Agir – Construire son français en contexte plurilingue. Le cas de Douala au Cameroun.* Paris: L'Harmattan.

Gajaseni, C. (1994). *A contrastive study of compliment responses in American English and Thai including the effect of gender and social status.* PhD diss., University of Illinois at Urbana-Champaign.

Golato, A. (2005). *Compliments and compliment responses: Grammatical structure and sequential organization.* Amsterdam: John Benjamins.

Herbert, R. K. (1989). The ethnography of English compliments and compliment responses: A contrastive sketch. In W. Oleksy (ed.), *Contrastive pragmatics* (pp. 3-35). Amsterdam: John Benjamins.

Holmes, J. (1986). Compliments and compliment responses in New Zealand English. *Anthropological Linguistics,* 28(4), 485-508.

Holmes, J. (1988). Paying compliments: A sex-preferential politeness strategies . *Journal of Pragmatics,* 12, 445-465.

Janney, R. W. (2009). Pragmatics in postcolonial contexts. *Annals of the Faculty of Arts and Social Sciences, University of Yaoundé I. Special edition in Honour of Professor Paul N. Mbangwana* (pp. 101-108). Yaoundé.

Jaworski, A. (1995). 'This is not an empty compliment!' - Polish compliments and the expression of solidarity. *International journal of Applied Linguistics,* 5(1), 63-94.

Kerbrat-Orecchioni, C. (1998). *Les interactions verbales. Vol. 3.* Paris: Armand Colin.

Kerbrat-Orecchioni, C. (2005). *Les actes de langage dans le discours.* Paris: Armand Colin.

Leech, N. G. (1983). *Principles of pragmatics.* London: Longman.

Macaulay, R. K.S (2009). Adolescents and identity. *Intercultural pragmatics,* 6(4), 597-612.

Manessy, G. (1994). *Le français en Afrique noire. Mythes, stratégies, pratiques.* Paris: L'harmattan.

Martineau, F., Mougeon, R., Nadasdi, T., & Tremblay, M. (2009). *Le français d'ici: études linguistiques et sociolinguistiques sur la variation du français au Québec et en Ontario.* Toronto: Éditions du GREF.

Mendo Ze, G. (1999). *Le français, langue africaine: enjeux et atouts pour la francophonie; éléments de stratégies.* Paris: PubliSud.

Mironovschi, L. (2009). *Komplimente und Komplimenterwiderungen im Russischen und im Deutschen.* Frankfurt am Main: Peter Lang.

Mougeon, R., & Beniak, E. (1989). *Le français canadien parlé hors Québec. Aperçu sociolinguistique.* Québec: Les Presses de l'Université Laval.

Mulo Farenkia, B. (2012a). Compliment strategies and regional variation in French: Evidence from Cameroon and Canadian French. *Pragmatics,* 22(3), 447-476.

Mulo Farenkia, B. (2012b). Expressing admiration Québec French and Cameroon French: A study in variational pragmatics. *PhiN* 60, 48-66. [On-line], [http://web.fu-berlin.de/phin/phin60/p60t3.htm]

Mulo Farenkia, B. (2012c). Actes de langage et variation en français périphériques: étude comparée du compliment chez les jeunes au Québec et au Cameroun. *Alternative francophone* 1(5), 1-25.

Mulo Farenkia, B. (2012d). Responding to compliments in Cameroon French and Canadian French. *US-China Foreign Language,* 10(5), 1135-1153.

Mulo Farenkia, B. (2006). *Beziehungskommunikation mit Komplimenten. Ethngraphische und gesprächsanalytische Untersuchungen im deutschen und kamerunischen Sprach- und Kulturraum.* Frankfurt am Main: Peter Lang.

Mulo Farenkia, B. (2005). Kreativität und Formelhaftigkeit in der Realisierung von Komplimenten: Ein deutsch-kamerunischer Vergleich. *Linguistik Online, 22*(1), 33-45.

Mulo Farenkia, B. (2004). *Kontrastive Pragmatik der Komplimente und Komplimenterwiderungen. Kamerunisch—Deutsch).* Aachen: Schaeker.

Nelson, G., El-Bakary, W., & Al-Batal, M. (1993). Egyptian and American compliments: A cross cultural study. *International Journal of Intercultural Relations,* 17, 293-313.

Placencia, M. E. (2012). Regional pragmatic variation. In G. Andersen & K. Aijmer (Eds.), *Pragmatics of Society* (pp. 79-113). Berlin/Boston: Walter De Gruyter.

Pöll, B. (2001). *Francophonies périphériques. Histoire, statut et profil des principales variétés du français hors de France.* Paris: L'Harmattan.

Pöll, B. (2005). *Le français langue pluricentrique? Étude sur la variation diatopique d'une langue standard.* Frankfurt am Main: Peter Lang.

Pomerantz, A. (1978). Compliment responses. Notes on the co-operation of multiple constraints. In J. Schenkein (Ed.), *Studies in the organization of conversational interaction* (pp. 79-112). New York: Academic Press.

Pu, Z. (2003). *La politesse en situation de communication sino-française. Malentendu et compréhension.* Paris: L'Harmattan.

Ravetto M. (2012). Compliment Responses in Italian and German. *International Journal of Innovative Interdisciplinary Research 2,* 77-100.

Rohrbacher, A. (2010). *Der Sprechakt der Bitte in Frankreich un Quebec. Ein interkultureller Vergleich aus dem Breich der Variational Prgamtics.* Saarbrücken: VDM.

Ruhi, Ş. (2006). Politeness in compliment responses: A perspective from naturally occurring exchanges in Turkish. *Pragmatics* 16(1), 43–101.

Ruhi, Ş., & Gürkan D. (2001). Relevance theory and compliments as phatic communication: The case of Turkish. In A. Bayraktaroglu & M. Sifianou(eds.), *Linguistic politeness across boundaries: The case of Greek and Turkish* (pp. 341–90). Amsterdam: John Benjamins.

Schneider, K. P. (1999). Compliment responses across cultures. In: M. Wysocka, (ed.), *On language theory and practice, vol. 1* (pp. 162-72). Katowice: Wydawnictwo Universytetu Slaskiego.

Schneider, K. P. (2005). *No problem, you're welcome, anytime.* Responding to thanks in Ireland, England, and the USA. In A. Barron & K. P. Schneider (eds.), *The pragmatics of Irish English* (pp. 101-139). Berlin/New York: Mouton de Gruyter.

Schneider, K. P. (2010). Variational Pragmatics. In M Fried., J.-O., Östmann, &

J. Verschueren (eds.), *Variation and change. Pragmatic Perspectives* (pp. 239-267). Amsterdam/Philadelphia: John Benjamins.

Schneider, K. P., & Barron, A. (2008b). Where pragmatics and dialectology meet: Introducing variational pragmatics. In K. P., Schneider & A., Barron (eds.), *Variational Pragmatics. A Focus on Regional Varieties in Pluricentric Languages* (pp. 1-32). Amsterdam/Philadelphia: John Benjamins.

Schneider, K. P., & Barron, A. (eds.) (2008b). *Variational Pragmatics. A Focus on Regional Varieties in Pluricentric Languages.* Amsterdam/Philadelphia: John Benjamins.

Schölmberger, U. (2008). Apologizing in French French and Canadian French. In K. P. Schneider, & A. Barron (eds.), *Variational Pragmatics. A Focus on Regional Varieties in Pluricentric Languages* (pp. 329-350). Amsterdam/Philadelphia: John Benjamins.

Sharifian, F. (2008). Cultural schemas in L1 and L2 compliment responses: A study of Persian-speaking learners of English. *Journal of Politeness Research,* 4(1), 55-80.

Sifianou, M. (2001). 'Oh! How appropriate!' - Compliments and politeness. In A. Bayraktaroglu & M. Sifianou (Eds.), *Linguistic politeness across boundaries: The case of Greek and Turkish* (pp. 391–430). Amsterdam: John Benjamins.

Tang, C. H., & Zhang, Q. G. (2009). A contrastive study of compliment responses among Australian English and Mandarin Chinese speakers. *Journal of Pragmatics,* 41(2), 325-345.

Thibault, A. (dir.) (2008). *Richesses du français et géographie linguistique.* Vol 2. Bruxelles: De Boeck.

Traverso, V. (1996). *La conversation familière. Analyse pragmatique des interactions.* Lyon: Presses Universitaires de Lyon.

Weil, S. (1983). *Trésors de la politesse française.* Paris: Belin.

Wieland, M. (1995). Complimenting behavior in French/American cross-cultural dinner conversations. *The French review,* 68(1), 796–812.

Wierzbicka, A. (2003[2]). *Cross-Cultural Pragmatics: The Semantics of Human Interaction.* Berlin/New York: Mouton de Gruyter.

Wiesmath, R. (2006). *Le français acadien. Analyse syntaxique d'un corpus oral recueilli au Nouveau-Brunswick/Canada.* Paris: L'Harmattan.

Yu, M.-C. (2005). Sociolinguistic competence in the complimenting act of native Chinese and American English speakers: A mirror of cultural value. *Language and speech,* 48(1), 91-119.

Zang Zang, P. (1998). *Le français en Afrique.* Munchen: Lincom Europa.

Romanistische Linguistik
hrsg. von Klaus Hölker

Astrid Gruschow
Die satzförmige Realisierung des präpositionalen Objekts im Spanischen
Untersuchungen auf der Basis einer empirischen Analyse
Präpositionale Objekte wurden im Spanischen bisher kaum systematisch untersucht. Der vorliegende Band analysiert und beschreibt Satz- und Infinitivkonstruktionen in dieser Funktion erstmals detailliert. Als theoretische Grundlagen wurden einerseits die Dependenzgrammatik und die Valenztheorie, andererseits die generative Grammatik herangezogen. Ein umfangreiches Korpus mit diversen Textsorten der aktuellen Schriftsprache bildet die empirische Basis. Für jeden Leser, der die spanische Sprache aus linguistischer Perspektive erkunden möchte, ein interessanter Band.
Bd. 8, 2009, 360 S., 39,90 €, br., ISBN 978-3-8258-1969-9

Christiane Maaß; Angela Schrott (Hg.)
Wenn Deiktika nicht zeigen: zeigende und nichtzeigende Funktionen deiktischer Formen in den romanischen Sprachen
Die im vorliegenden Band versammelten Beiträge analysieren zeigende und nichtzeigende Funktionen deiktischer Formen in den romanischen Sprachen. Das besondere Augenmerk gilt dabei zum einen der Entwicklung nichtdeiktischer Verwendungen aus ursprünglich deiktischen, zum anderen dem Phänomen, dass zahlreiche Deiktika in ihrem Verwendungsspektrum zeigende und nichtzeigende Funktionen vereinen. Die Beiträge untersuchen neben den Dimensionen deiktischer Verwendungen (lokal, temporal, personal und objektal) auch die Funktion des Verweisens in Texten sowie die von Deiktika geleisteten Fingerzeige in der sozialen Deixis. Einen weiteren Schwerpunkt bilden Prozesse des Funktionswandels, die zum Verlust der Deiktizität führen. Diese Übergänge werden in Synchronie und Diachronie analysiert, so dass sich ein für die romanischen Sprachen repräsentatives Bild zeigender und nichtzeigender Funktionen ergibt.
Bd. 9, 2010, 392 S., 44,90 €, br., ISBN 978-3-643-10551-6

LIT Verlag Berlin – Münster – Wien – Zürich – London
Auslieferung Deutschland / Österreich / Schweiz: siehe Impressumsseite